Breakfast
with
Beatrice

Also by Beatrice Ojakangas

Published by the University of Minnesota Press

Breakfast with Beatrice

250 RECIPES FROM SWEET CREAM WAFFLES TO SWEDISH FARMER'S OMELETS

BEATRICE OJAKANGAS

University of Minnesota Press
Minneapolis
London

The recipes in this book were originally published in the following cookbooks by Beatrice Ojakangas: *Gourmet Cooking for Two, The Great Holiday Baking Book, The Great Scandinavian Baking Book, Great Old-Fashioned American Desserts, Great Old-Fashioned American Recipes, Great Whole Grain Breads, Light and Easy Baking, Light Muffins, New Ideas for Casseroles, Pot Pies, Quick Breads, Scandinavian Cooking,* and *Scandinavian Feasts.*

Published by the University of Minnesota Press
111 Third Avenue South, Suite 290
Minneapolis, MN 55401–2520
http://www.upress.umn.edu

LIBRARY OF CONGRESS CATALOGING-IN-PUBLICATION DATA
Ojakangas, Beatrice, author.
Breakfast with Beatrice : 250 recipes from sweet cream waffles to Swedish farmer's omelets / Beatrice Ojakangas.
Minneapolis : University of Minnesota Press, 2018. | Includes index.
Identifiers: LCCN 017059960 | ISBN 978-1-5179-0495-1 (pb)
Subjects: LCSH: Breakfasts. | BISAC: COOKING / Courses & Dishes / Breakfast. | COOKING / Regional & Ethnic / Scandinavian. | LCGFT: Cookbooks.
Classification: LCC TX733 .O39 2018 | DDC 642—dc23
LC record available at https://lccn.loc.gov/2017059960

Printed in the United States of America on acid-free paper

The University of Minnesota is an equal-opportunity educator and employer.

24   10 9 8 7 6 5 4 3

Contents

3 Pastries and Coffee Cakes

4 Breakfast Breads

⑤ Muffins, Biscuits, and Scones

6 Smoothies, Jams, and Preserves

Introduction

"TOS! JUS! OLK!" our two-year-old ordered as she slapped the high-chair tray in front of her. She wanted toast, juice, and milk, and Mom better hurry up! I still kid her with this memory, even though Susanna has two of her own in college right now.

When I was growing up, breakfast was usually *puuro* (Finnish for porridge). This typically meant oatmeal, but there was variety, too: Cream of Wheat, Malt-O-Meal, and Wheatena were often found warming in a pot on the woodstove's top. In years to come, I would throw a handful of raisins, nuts, or berries from the field or forest—or whatever was available—into my bowl of *puuro* and top it off with fresh cream or whole milk. The only sweetener I preferred, if any, was honey or maple syrup. One of my favorite breakfasts today is cooked wild rice with nuts, dried fruits, and butter (you'll find the recipe in this book). Sometimes I sweeten it with agave syrup. During the past few years, breakfast has often morphed into lunch or something we call "brunch"—perhaps a special event on the weekend with friends and family. Once I was planning a party and thought that we could blend breakfast into both lunch and supper and call it "blupper." I still would serve traditional breakfast food.

One recent favorite of mine is a "free-form" smoothie. When I find bargain bananas in the produce department, they are usually just at the stage that fruit flies love and can't be kept a day longer. So I grab them, pull off the peels, and slip them into a large freezer bag (well apart so they won't freeze together); then I remove them one at a time for my breakfast smoothie. Likewise, berries are great to freeze. I love the combination of blueberries, raspberries, and bananas along with a bit of yogurt (flavored or not), a handful of sunflower seeds, and even a dollop of peanut or almond butter. Whirl the whole thing up and I have a quick, healthy, delicious breakfast. If there isn't enough liquid to work the blades of the blender, I'll pour in an inch or two of orange juice. You can adapt this recipe-less breakfast to use whatever fruits or berries you have on hand—perfect if breakfasting solo.

The word *breakfast* comes, of course, from the idea of "breaking the fast." Presumably, one has slept (or at least not eaten) for eight hours or so, and by then it is time to "break the fast": it's time to eat something. The advantage of a balanced and interesting breakfast is that you have all day to burn it off. Some nutritionists say you don't need to even count calories at breakfast for that reason; what you consume during the rest of the day (the snacks, the loaded noon and evening meals) is responsible if you are putting on a few pounds. A skimpy breakfast only encourages overeating later in the day.

I'm reminded of an old nutritional adage: "Eat breakfast like a king, lunch like a prince, and dinner like a pauper." What does that mean? According to many health professionals, we perform our daily activities more efficiently, our bodies run smoother, and our cognitive skills are sharper if we have had a good breakfast.

I do acknowledge that many of us are in a time bind first thing in the morning—but there's nothing wrong with keeping it simple! Just try to have some kind of protein (for longer term, sustained energy), some kind of carbohydrate (for quick energy and fiber), and fruit or fruit juice (for that pick-me-up energy). That can boil down to a basic breakfast of eggs, bread, and orange juice or fresh fruit. Or, cooked or dry cereal, dried fruit and nuts, milk, and fresh fruit. Skip the sugar-coated cereal and frosted doughnuts, please!

Ideally, breakfast includes as many of the vital nutrients as possible to get your day revved up (that's what we mean by "breakfast like a king"). Some say that people who do not eat breakfast are more likely to be overweight or obese. In any case, a good breakfast can kickstart your metabolism for the day. It can be a meal that's quick to put together, like a healthy and great-tasting breakfast of hot oatmeal (which you can cook overnight in a crock pot) with nuts, honey, fresh fruit or dried raisins, cranberries, prunes, or apricots, and yogurt to make a delicious treat that will supercharge your metabolism without weighing you down.

REVIEWING MY OWN COOKBOOKS, several of which are Scandinavian themed, I selected many of my favorite breakfasts for *Breakfast with Beatrice*. These recipes are just as interesting to me now as when I first wrote the books. I remember especially the grand breakfasts in Scandinavia and Finland, the amazing expanse of breads (mostly whole grain), cheeses, fish (including a variety of herrings), gravlax, cold cuts, and fresh fruits in season, mostly berries. In Helsinki, I once counted eighty-eight items on the breakfast bread and butter table. Breakfasts in private homes are much simpler: crisp breads, very slightly sweet breads, butter, viili or yogurt, homemade fruit juices. I fondly remember strawberry juice, made with a Finnish steam process juicer called the Mehu-Liisa.

Here at home in Minnesota, we have friends who make waffles for supper—a quick, easy, and delicious option particularly when kids are involved. Kids love to cook waffles themselves. In the Scandinavian countries, heart-shaped cream waffles are a standby snack at any time of day. I was surprised to see that they were often packed in school lunches along with fresh fruit, cheese, and other healthy options.

I am, by nature, a lover of bread for breakfast. Not just muffins, waffles, pancakes, and coffee cakes, but real, serious bread! I like all kinds of bread—especially the kind that is almost a meal in itself, like dark, soured rye or crunchy whole grain breads that cry out for robust cheeses to go with them. And of course one of my favorites is aromatic, freshly baked cardamom bread, or *pulla*.

What follows in *Breakfast with Beatrice* are many of my pancakes, waffles, scones, French toasts, muffins, breads, buns, rolls, parfaits, and creative spins on cooked cereals. Ideas for breakfast come to me everywhere. When I encountered breakfast parfaits (granola, berries, and yogurt layered in a parfait glass) on a buffet line on a cruise ship, I knew this would be a simple way to add variety to my breakfasts at home. The parfaits can be prepared a day early, assembled in canning jars, and refrigerated so they are ready to grab when you're on the run. We all need motivation and tools to create a healthy lifestyle, and learning how to prepare breakfasts that are delicious is a part of that. While it's always fun to plan breakfasts for guests, we need to treat ourselves as special guests too. It's surprising what a difference that can make in the day that follows.

So, go ahead—enjoy your favorite foods at breakfast!

1

Pancakes
and
Waffles

Swedish/Finnish Pancakes

These are so light that Swedes say they should "fly off the griddle."

1 cup all-purpose flour
1 tablespoon sugar
¾ teaspoon salt
3 eggs
2 to 3 cups milk

FOR SERVING
Lingonberry (or other jam or fresh fruit)
Slightly sweetened whipped cream
Powdered sugar

Whisk the flour, sugar, salt, eggs, and 2 cups milk together. Ideally, let batter rest for 2 hours or so. Batter should be the consistency of thick cream. Dilute with the additional milk, if necessary.

To make the pancakes, heat the pancake pan and coat with butter (or with cooking spray). Tilt and turn the pan to coat the bottom completely. Spoon 1 to 2 tablespoons batter to make "dollar" cakes, or ¼ to ⅓ cup batter to make 6-inch cakes.

Serve immediately with lingonberry, whipped cream, and powdered sugar.

Note: If these are made in a small Swedish pancake pan, it will yield about three dozen little pancakes. Call them "Plättar" or "Plettüjä." Made in a large 6-inch version, call them "Flapjacks" and you'll get about 16. Either way, the kids eat them as quickly as I can make them!

Puffy Apple Pancake

This basic pancake has been a family favorite of ours for years. I grew up thinking it was Finnish, only to find out that almost every nationality claims a puffy oven pancake as its own. Sometimes we bake it without the apples and then add fresh fruit to the center of the big, puffy shell that it forms. This is a great Sunday morning brunch dish.

¾ cup (3 to 4 large) beaten eggs
¾ cup milk
¾ cup all-purpose flour
1 tablespoon sugar
¼ teaspoon salt
2 tablespoons butter

2 medium-sized tart cooking apples, peeled, cored, and thinly sliced

FOR SERVING
Powdered sugar
Slightly sweetened whipped cream

In a bowl or blender, measure the eggs, milk, flour, sugar, and salt. Mix until all the flour is incorporated and the batter is smooth. Let stand for 30 minutes.

Preheat the oven to 450°F.

Put the butter into an 11-inch ovenproof skillet or shallow baking pan (preferably with sloping sides). Place in the oven as the oven heats. When the butter is melted, pour the batter into the hot pan. Cover the batter with the apple slices.

Bake for 15 minutes or until the pancake is puffy and brown around the edges. Dust with the powdered sugar and cut into quarters to serve. Pass the whipped cream at the table.

MAKES 4 SERVINGS

Blinis (Linnit)

Karelian Finns traditionally serve these yeast-risen pancakes with mäteen-mäti, *which is the roe of ling cod, on Shrove Tuesday, the day before Ash Wednesday and the beginning of Lent. They are often made with buckwheat in the batter; then their name is* tattariblinit. *They should be served with fresh caviar and sour cream, chopped onion, and a sprinkling of freshly ground allspice.*

½ package (1½ teaspoons) active
    dry yeast
¼ cup warm water (105°F to 115°F)
1 cup milk, scalded and cooled to
    lukewarm

2 cups all-purpose flour or 1½ cups
    all-purpose flour plus ½ cup
    buckwheat flour
2 tablespoons sugar
3 eggs, separated
6 tablespoons melted butter
½ teaspoon salt

In a large bowl, dissolve the yeast in the warm water. Let stand 5 minutes. Add the milk, 1 cup of the flour, and sugar to the mixture. Cover and let rise in a warm place until foamy, about 30 minutes. Beat in the egg yolks. Stir in the butter, salt, and remaining flour, mixing well. Whip the egg whites until stiff and fold into the batter. Let rise in a warm place another 30 minutes.

Heat a plättar pan or pancake griddle until a drop of water sputters on it. Coat with butter. Make small pancakes using 2 to 3 tablespoons of the batter for each cake. Cook on both sides until golden brown, about 2 minutes in all. Serve hot.

MAKES ABOUT 25 PANCAKES

Lise's Danish Pancake Balls

For this recipe you need a Danish aebelskiver pan with round indentations. The pans are usually made of cast iron. My friend Lise uses a metal knitting needle to turn the aebelskiver over. Some people like to fill them with apple-sauce, while others prefer to leave them plain.

1 cup milk	1½ cups all-purpose flour
½ cup melted butter	2 teaspoons baking powder
3 eggs, separated	Applesauce (optional)
2 tablespoons sugar	Powdered sugar

Heat the milk to lukewarm. Whisk in the butter, egg yolks, and sugar. Turn into a bowl and add the flour and baking powder, whisking until well blended and no lumps remain. Whip the egg whites until stiff and fold into the mixture.

Heat aebelskiver pan over medium-high heat until a drop of water sizzles when dripped into the pan. Put about ½ teaspoon butter into each indentation. Spread it around. Spoon in 1 tablespoon of the batter and let it cook about 30 seconds. If using applesauce, drop 1 teaspoon applesauce in the center and top with more aebelskiver batter to cover the applesauce. When the bottoms are browned, turn the cakes over and cook on that side until browned. Remove from pan and place on serving plate. Dust with powdered sugar.

MAKES 20 PANCAKES

Baked Pancake (Pannukakku)

A puffy baked pancake is popular in all of the Scandinavian countries. The proportion of eggs to milk to flour varies according to individual tastes. Some people like a custardy pancake with less egg and milk in relation to the flour, and some like a heavier, rib-sticking variety. My personal favorite is this one, which turns out a crispy, high-sided, golden shell that is a perfect cradle for fresh fruit and whipped cream. It can also be served with just a squeeze of lemon and powdered sugar. The proportions are easy to remember and to scale up or down—an equal measure of flour, eggs, and milk with a touch of sugar and a touch of salt. For baking, a large, slope-sided paella pan or a large slope-sided frying pan with a handle that can go into the oven is ideal. Another option is to bake the pancakes in four 9-inch pie pans.

1½ cups all-purpose flour
1½ cups milk
6 eggs
1 tablespoon sugar
1 teaspoon salt
About ½ cup butter for the baking
** pan or pans**

TOPPING
Powdered sugar and lemon wedges or
1 cup whipping cream, whipped
2 tablespoons powdered sugar
Fresh fruit

In a bowl, whisk together the flour, milk, eggs, sugar, and salt until no lumps remain. Let stand 30 minutes.

Preheat oven to 450ºF. Put butter into 1 large (14- to 16-inch) slope-sided pan (with 4-quart capacity) or into four 9-inch pie pans and preheat in the oven until butter is melted. Brush entire pan with the butter. Pour in the pancake batter. Bake for 15 to 20 minutes until edges are puffed high and golden.

Serve immediately! The pancake will settle quickly, so have the eaters ready at the table. Sprinkle the pancake with powdered sugar and squeeze lemon over, or spoon fresh fruit onto individual servings and top with whipped cream sweetened with powdered sugar.

MAKES 4 SERVINGS

Buttermilk Pancakes or Waffles

As one of the earliest forms of baking, pancakes were once called hearth cakes. The Dutch settlers brought both pancakes and their "waffre" irons to America. The original irons had long handles so the waffles could be baked over an open fire. Pancakes and waffles were served not only for breakfast, but for supper and noon meals.

2 eggs

1 cup buttermilk

½ teaspoon baking soda

1¼ cups all-purpose flour

1 tablespoon sugar

1 teaspoon baking powder

½ teaspoon salt

2 tablespoons melted shortening or vegetable oil

Butter or fat

If making pancakes, heat a heavy griddle slowly while mixing batter. In a large bowl, beat eggs. In a small bowl, mix buttermilk and baking soda. Add to eggs. In a medium-sized bowl, combine flour, sugar, baking powder, and salt. Stir into egg mixture. Blend in shortening or oil.

For pancakes: Heat griddle until drops of water dance on it. Brush with butter or fat. Spoon ¼ cup batter for each cake onto hot griddle. Cook until golden on each side. Makes 16 (4-inch) pancakes.

For waffles: Heat waffle iron. Spoon batter into heated waffle iron. Close iron. Bake until golden. Makes 8 (6- to 8-inch) waffles.

Blueberry Pancakes

Add ½ to 1 cup fresh or frozen blueberries to batter just before cooking pancakes. Cook as above.

Sweet-Milk Pancakes or Waffles

Substitute fresh milk for buttermilk. Omit baking soda and use an additional ½ teaspoon baking powder. For lighter pancakes, separate eggs and make batter using yolks. Beat egg whites until stiff; fold into batter. Cook as above.

Southern Corn Cakes

In place of all-purpose flour, use a combination of ¾ cup cornmeal and ¼ cup all-purpose flour. Cook as above.

variations continued on next page ▶

Swedish Pancakes

Substitute fresh milk for buttermilk. Omit baking soda and reduce flour to ½ cup. Cook as above. Pancakes will be thin and lacy. Fill with berries and whipped cream.

Coconut Waffles

Add 1 cup flaked coconut to batter. Cook as above. Serve with coconut syrup and whipped cream.

Pecan Waffles

Spoon batter into a heated waffle iron. Sprinkle with chopped pecans. Close iron. Bake until golden.

Note: Coconut syrup is often used in mixed drinks and can be found in the beverage section of supermarkets. It makes an excellent topping for waffles and pancakes.

Icelandic Stone Cakes

These pancakes are named "stone cakes" because historically they are said to have been baked on hot stones. They're actually very light, since they are raised with yeast. You may wish to mix this batter the night before and refrigerate it, then bake the cakes the next morning for breakfast.

1 package (3 teaspoons) active dry yeast	1 teaspoon freshly ground cardamom
1½ cups heated milk (105°F to 115°F)	1 egg
1 tablespoon sugar	2 cups all-purpose flour
1½ teaspoon salt	Additional milk or water, if necessary

In a large bowl, sprinkle the yeast over the warm milk; then sprinkle on the sugar. Let stand until yeast is dissolved into the milk. Add the salt, cardamom, egg, and flour. Whisk until smooth. Cover and let rise until bubbly. Or, cover and refrigerate until the next morning.

Heat pancake pan over medium-high heat and spread with butter. If batter is stiff, add milk or water to achieve pouring consistency. Spoon ¼ cup batter onto pan for each cake. Cook on both sides until golden. Serve hot with lingonberry jam and cream.

MAKES ABOUT 20 PANCAKES

Apple Walnut Pancakes

Serve these with cinnamon sugar and melted butter.

1 cup whole wheat flour
1 cup unbleached all-purpose flour
1 teaspoon salt
2 teaspoons baking powder
1 tablespoon brown sugar, light or dark

2 cups milk
2 eggs, well beaten
2 tablespoons vegetable oil
1 cup pared and diced apple
½ cup chopped walnuts

In a large bowl, combine whole wheat flour, all-purpose flour, salt, baking powder, and brown sugar. In a smaller bowl, combine milk, eggs, and oil. Pour liquid ingredients into dry ingredients and stir just until mixed. Add the apples and walnuts. Preheat griddle to 375°F. Spoon 4 to 5 tablespoons of batter at a time to make pancakes. Grease griddle lightly if necessary. Cook 1 to 2 minutes on each side until golden. Serve hot.

MAKES TWELVE 4-INCH PANCAKES

Potato Pancakes

There are dozens of variations of the potato pancake throughout Scandinavia. At the Göta Hotel on the banks of the Göta Canal in central Sweden, they make theirs with coarsely shredded potatoes held together in a thin pancake batter consisting of eggs, milk, and flour. They are delicious served with crisp bacon, sour cream, and lingonberries or strawberry jam.

8 medium-sized baking potatoes, pared
    and coarsely shredded
½ cup flour
2 tablespoons chopped chives
1 cup milk

1 egg
1 teaspoon salt
½ teaspoon freshly ground pepper
½ pound thick sliced bacon
Lingonberries or cranberries

Rinse the potatoes in cold water and drain well. Place in a large bowl and mix in the flour, chives, milk, egg, salt, and pepper. In a heavy, preferably nonstick skillet, over medium heat, cook the bacon until crisp. Remove the bacon slices from the skillet and drain. Hold the bacon slices on a plate lined with a paper towel until ready to use. Spoon out all but 2 teaspoons of the bacon fat from the skillet.

Place the skillet over medium heat and spoon about ¼ cup of the potato mixture into the pan and flatten slightly to make a pancake. Cook until golden and crisp, about 3 or 4 minutes on each side. Repeat this procedure with the remaining batter. Keep cooked pancakes warm until ready to serve.

Serve with the crisp bacon on top and lingonberries or whole, cooked, or canned cranberries on the side.

MAKES 6 SERVINGS

Pumpkin Pecan Waffles

A cheerful Halloween breakfast to get everyone in the mood, or ideal anytime during the autumn season. These are great topped with cinnamon-spiced whipped cream or pure maple syrup.

2 cups all-purpose flour
3 teaspoons baking powder
2 teaspoons pumpkin pie spice
½ teaspoon salt
3 large eggs, separated

1½ cups milk
½ cup fresh, cooked, or canned puréed pumpkin
½ cup melted butter
1 cup chopped pecans

Preheat a waffle iron. In a large bowl, stir together the flour, baking powder, pumpkin pie spice, and salt. In a medium bowl, beat the egg yolks with the milk, pumpkin, and butter. Add the liquids to the dry ingredients, mixing until well blended. Stir in the nuts. In another bowl, beat the egg whites until stiff and fold into the batter. Grease the hot waffle iron and pour on 1 cup of the batter. Close and cook for 3 to 5 minutes, until golden brown. Repeat with the remaining batter. Keep the cooked waffles warm in a 300°F oven.

MAKES ABOUT TWENTY 4-INCH WAFFLES

Heart-shaped Cream Waffles

The traditional Scandinavian waffle iron makes individual heart-shaped waffles. (A regular waffle iron may not create waffles that are this attractive, but they will taste just as good, although they may be slightly thicker and not quite so light.)

⅔ cup all-purpose flour
1 teaspoon freshly ground cardamom
3 eggs
¼ cup sugar
⅔ cup sour cream

3 tablespoons melted butter
Butter for brushing the iron
Powdered sugar
Jam or fresh berries
Whipped cream (optional)

Stir flour and cardamom together and set aside. In small bowl of electric mixer, beat the eggs and sugar together at high speed for 10 minutes, until mixture forms ribbons when beaters are lifted.

Sprinkle flour mixture over eggs; stir the sour cream until smooth and add to the mixture, folding until batter is smooth. Fold in the melted butter.

Place the waffle iron over medium heat and heat until a drop of water sizzles on the grid, turning over once to heat both sides. Brush the grids with butter and spoon in the batter. Cook, turning once, until golden brown; then remove from iron and sprinkle with powdered sugar. Serve immediately with tart lingonberry or other jam or fresh berries and whipped cream.

Or, cook waffles in a standard electric waffle iron as manufacturer of the iron directs.

MAKES 4 SERVINGS

Sweet Cream Waffles

Here is another favorite waffle recipe, which uses sweet, rather than sour, cream.

3 eggs
1 cup whipping cream
⅔ cup all-purpose flour
2 tablespoons water
3 tablespoons melted butter

Butter for brushing the iron
Powdered sugar
Jam or fresh berries
Whipped cream (optional)

In small bowl of electric mixer, beat the eggs for 10 minutes at high speed until very light. Whip the cream and fold into the eggs. Sift the flour over and fold into the mixture along with the water and melted butter.

Place the waffle iron over medium heat and heat until a drop of water sizzles on the grid, turning over once to heat both sides. Brush the grids with butter and spoon in the batter. Cook, turning once, until golden brown; then remove from iron and sprinkle with powdered sugar. Serve immediately with tart lingonberry or other jam or fresh berries and whipped cream.

Or, cook waffles in a standard electric waffle iron as manufacturer of the iron directs.

MAKES 4 SERVINGS

Healthy Oatmeal Nut Waffles

Just throw all the ingredients but the rolled oats and nuts into the blender or food processor, and you're ready for waffles!

2 cups milk
2 eggs
1½ cups whole wheat pastry flour or
    regular whole wheat flour
⅓ cup melted butter or oil

2 teaspoons baking powder
2 tablespoons brown sugar, light or dark
1 cup old-fashioned rolled oats
1 cup chopped walnuts or pecans

Put milk, eggs, flour, butter, baking powder, and brown sugar into blender or food processor with plastic or steel blade in place. Process until blended. Add the oats and nuts. Stir to blend. Cook in preheated waffle iron until waffle stops steaming and is golden (approximately 5 minutes). Excellent with homemade jam, honey, or fruit syrups.

MAKES 4 TO 6 SERVINGS

Bread and Bacon Waffles

This is quick and easy!

Heat the waffle iron. Line up bread slices, regular thickness. Arrange on each slice one strip of bacon cut into two parts. Place into the waffle iron with the control set at medium, and toast until brown. This will take about 3 minutes. If you lift the lid before the bacon is sealed to the bread, the bacon will curl and spoil the effect. Serve with maple syrup.

2 SLICES BREAD AND 2 SLICES BACON PER SERVING

Coconut Waffles

1½ cups all-purpose flour
1 tablespoon sugar
1 teaspoon baking powder
½ teaspoon salt
2 eggs, separated
1 cup buttermilk

½ teaspoon baking soda
¼ cup melted butter
1 cup toasted coconut, plus more for
    topping
Coconut syrup
Whipped cream

Preheat waffle iron. In a large bowl, combine flour, sugar, baking powder, and salt. In another bowl, mix egg yolks, buttermilk, baking soda, and butter. Whip egg whites until stiff. Blend liquids into dry ingredients. Fold in the egg whites and toasted coconut. Spoon into waffle iron and bake until golden. Serve with warmed coconut syrup, toasted coconut, and whipped cream.

MAKES 8 WAFFLES

Chocolate Waffles, Strawberries, and Cream

1 cup buttermilk pancake mix
¼ cup unsweetened dark cocoa
⅔ cup milk
2 tablespoons corn oil

1 egg
Whipped cream
Sliced fresh strawberries

Preheat waffle iron. In a medium bowl, combine pancake mix and cocoa; blend well. Add milk, oil, and egg. Stir until dry ingredients are moistened. Bake in hot waffle iron until golden. Top with whipped cream and strawberries.

MAKES 6 WAFFLES

Carrot Date Nut Waffles

1½ cups all-purpose flour
1 tablespoon sugar
2 teaspoons baking powder
½ teaspoon salt
½ teaspoon cinnamon
½ cup chopped walnuts

½ cup shredded carrots
½ cup chopped dates
1½ cups milk
½ cup vegetable oil
3 eggs, separated
Maple syrup

Preheat waffle iron. Combine flour and next seven ingredients. In another bowl, combine milk, oil, and egg yolks. Stir into flour mixture just until moistened. Beat egg whites until stiff. Fold into batter. Ladle into hot waffle iron. Cook waffles until golden. Serve hot with maple syrup.

MAKES 6 WAFFLES

Orange Nut Waffles

4 eggs
2 cups orange juice
2 tablespoons lemon juice
2 teaspoons grated orange rind (zest)
2 cups all-purpose flour
4 tablespoons yellow cornmeal

1 teaspoon baking soda
1 teaspoon baking powder
¾ teaspoons salt
2 tablespoons melted butter
Maple syrup

Preheat waffle iron. In a large bowl, beat the eggs until fluffy. Add the juices and orange zest. In another bowl, stir the flour, cornmeal, soda, baking powder, and salt together. Add liquids to the dry ingredients; stir just until blended. Add the melted butter. Bake in the heated waffle iron. Serve hot topped with maple syrup, or with a poached egg and bacon, if desired.

MAKES 6 LARGE WAFFLES

Cinnamon Apple Waffles

1¼ cups all-purpose flour
2 teaspoons baking powder
¾ teaspoon salt
2 tablespoons sugar
1 teaspoon cinnamon
3 eggs, separated

4 tablespoons vegetable oil
1½ cups apple cider
1½ cups coarsely shredded apples
Lemon juice
Apple or maple syrup

Preheat waffle iron. In a bowl, combine the flour, baking powder, salt, sugar, and cinnamon. Beat egg yolks with the oil and apple cider. Combine liquids with the dry ingredients. Mix the shredded apple with the lemon juice and blend into the batter. Beat the egg whites until stiff and fold into the batter. Spoon into hot waffle iron. Bake until golden. Serve hot with apple or maple syrup.

MAKES 4 TO 6 MEDIUM WAFFLES

Banana Pecan Waffles

½ cup all-purpose flour
¼ teaspoon cinnamon
Pinch nutmeg
¾ teaspoon baking powder
¼ teaspoon baking soda
Pinch salt
1 teaspoon sugar
1 egg, separated

¼ cup sour cream
⅓ cup milk
¼ cup melted butter
½ cup mashed ripe banana
6 tablespoons chopped toasted pecans
Ice cream
Maple syrup

Preheat waffle iron. In a bowl, combine flour, cinnamon, nutmeg, baking powder, soda, salt, and sugar. In another bowl combine the egg yolk, sour cream, milk, butter, and banana. Stir in the pecans and the dry ingredients; blend well. Beat egg white until stiff and fold into the batter. Spoon into hot waffle iron. Bake until golden. Serve with a scoop of ice cream and maple syrup.

MAKES TEN TO TWELVE 4-INCH WAFFLES

Crispy Three-Grain Waffles

1 cup all-purpose flour
1 cup uncooked quick rolled oats
½ cup yellow cornmeal
2 tablespoons baking powder
½ teaspoon salt

2 eggs
½ cup melted butter
3 cups buttermilk
Maple syrup

In a large bowl, combine the flour, oats, cornmeal, baking powder, and salt. (Yes, it is 2 tablespoons baking powder!) Add the eggs, butter, and buttermilk and stir until smooth. Let batter stand for 15 minutes. It will bubble up a lot in this time. Meanwhile, preheat the waffle iron. Cook the waffles until light golden brown. Serve hot with maple syrup.

MAKES TWELVE 4-INCH WAFFLES

Whole Wheat Waffles

1 cup all-purpose flour
¾ cup whole wheat flour
1 tablespoon brown sugar
3 teaspoons baking powder
1 teaspoon salt

1½ cups milk
⅓ cup shortening, melted
2 eggs, separated
Butter
Maple syrup

In a large bowl, stir together the flours, sugar, baking powder, and salt. In a small bowl, whisk together the milk, shortening, and egg yolks. Add liquids to the dry ingredients, blending thoroughly. Beat egg whites until stiff. Fold into the batter. Bake in preheated waffle iron until golden. Serve with butter and maple syrup.

MAKES EIGHT 4-INCH WAFFLES

Light and Crispy Waffles

2 cups all-purpose flour
3 teaspoons baking powder
¾ teaspoon salt
2 tablespoons sugar
3 eggs, separated

1¾ cups milk
½ cup vegetable oil
Butter for brushing the iron

Stir together flour, baking powder, salt, and sugar. Beat egg whites until stiff. In another bowl, beat yolks with milk and oil. Add yolk mixture to the dry ingredients, blending well. Fold in the egg whites. Preheat waffle iron; brush lightly with butter. Spoon ½ cup batter into heated waffle iron and cook. Serve hot.

MAKES 8 WAFFLES

Belgian Waffles

2 cups all-purpose flour
2 tablespoons sugar
½ teaspoon nutmeg
¼ teaspoon salt
1 cup milk

1 cup whipping cream
5 eggs, separated and at room
    temperature
¼ cup melted butter
Whipped cream and sliced strawberries

Preheat waffle iron. Combine dry ingredients in a large bowl. Beat milk, cream, egg yolks, and butter together. Stir into dry ingredients just until moistened. Whip egg whites until stiff. Fold into batter just until blended. Ladle into hot waffle iron and cook until steam stops, 3 to 5 minutes. Keep waffles warm in oven. Serve with whipped cream and sliced strawberries.

MAKES 3 WAFFLES

2

Savory Breakfast and Casserole Dishes

Piperade Pie

Piperade is a classic dish of the Basque region of France, made with toma-toes and sweet peppers cooked in olive oil. Ham, bacon, onions, garlic, and other vegetables are often added, and when bound with eggs, the mixture makes a great omelet. Here, I've turned it into a quichelike pie.

Pastry for a single-crust pie
**½ cup grated sharp cheddar cheese or
  aged Swiss cheese**
2 tablespoons olive oil
**1 small red bell pepper, seeded, stemmed,
  and coarsely chopped**
**1 small yellow bell pepper, seeded,
  stemmed, and coarsely chopped**
1 medium onion, coarsely chopped
¼ cup chopped scallions (green onions)

2 garlic cloves, minced or mashed
**6 plum tomatoes, peeled, seeded, and
  chopped**
**1 tablespoon chopped fresh basil or
  1 teaspoon dried**
1 teaspoon salt
1 teaspoon freshly ground black pepper
⅛ teaspoon dried red pepper flakes
3 whole eggs, lightly beaten
3 egg whites, lightly beaten

Preheat the oven to 450°F. Prebake the pie shell in a 9-inch pie pan and while the crust is still hot, sprinkle the cheese evenly over the bottom. Lower the oven temperature to 350°F.

In a large nonstick skillet, heat the oil. Add the red and yellow peppers, onion, and scallions and cook over medium heat, stirring, for 10 minutes, until soft but not brown. Add the garlic, tomatoes, basil, salt, pepper, and red pepper flakes. Cook 10 minutes or until the liquid evaporates. Cool 15 minutes; then stir in the eggs and egg whites, and spread the mixture in the pastry shell. Bake at 350°F for 30 minutes, until set, or until a knife inserted just off center comes out clean. Serve at room temperature, cut into wedges.

MAKES 6 TO 8 SERVINGS

Zucchini Quiche

This is perfect for a summertime Sunday brunch served with sausages and a platter of fresh fruit.

Pastry for a single-crust pie
¼ cup freshly grated Parmesan cheese
¼ cup shredded sharp cheddar cheese
½ cup seasoned dry bread crumbs
2 eggs, separated
1½ cups sour cream

2 tablespoons chopped chives
2 tablespoons all-purpose flour
1 teaspoon salt
½ teaspoon freshly ground black pepper
1½ pounds zucchini, cut in ¼-inch slices

Roll out the pastry to fit into an 11-inch tart pan with a removable bottom.

Preheat the oven to 450°F. Mix the cheeses with the bread crumbs. Sprinkle ½ cup of the mixture evenly over the bottom of the pastry.

Beat the egg yolks, sour cream, chives, flour, salt, and pepper together. Beat the egg whites until stiff and fold into the egg mixture.

Arrange one-third of the zucchini slices over the cheese mixture in the pastry-lined pan. Cover with one-third of the egg mixture. Repeat layering until the zucchini and egg mixture are used up.

Bake for 10 minutes; reduce the oven temperature to 325°F and bake for 40 minutes more or until the pie is set. Cool for at least 15 minutes and cut into wedges to serve, either warm or at room temperature.

MAKES 6 TO 8 SERVINGS

Crab and Mushroom Quiche

This recipe lends itself well to variation. If I have a lot of bits and ends of various kinds of cheese on hand, I substitute them for the Swiss cheese. Sometimes I include herbed cream cheese, such as Boursin, in place of part of the cottage cheese.

Pastry for a single-crust pie
2 tablespoons butter

½ pound sliced fresh mushrooms
4 eggs

1 cup sour cream
1 cup small-curd low-fat cottage cheese
½ cup freshly grated Parmesan cheese
¼ cup all-purpose flour
¼ teaspoon salt

Freshly ground black pepper
Freshly grated nutmeg
4 drops hot pepper sauce
2 cups shredded Swiss cheese
½ pound lump crabmeat, picked over

Preheat the oven to 450°F. Partially prebake the pastry in a 9-inch porcelain quiche pan or a 10-inch pie pan. Lower the oven temperature to 350°F.

In a heavy skillet, heat the butter and sauté the mushrooms until they are tender and the liquid has evaporated, 5 to 10 minutes.

In a large bowl, blend the eggs, sour cream, cottage cheese, Parmesan cheese, flour, salt, pepper, nutmeg, and hot pepper sauce.

Sprinkle half the Swiss cheese into the pastry shell. Top with the mushrooms and crabmeat. Spoon the cottage cheese mixture over, and top with the remaining Swiss cheese. Bake for 45 minutes or until a knife inserted near the center comes out clean. The quiche should be puffed and lightly browned. Let it stand for at least 5 minutes before cutting into wedges. Serve hot or at room temperature.

MAKES 8 SERVINGS

....

Ham and Cheese Pie

....

This is a great pie to make when you have leftover cooked ham after a holiday meal. My husband takes chilled wedges of it in his lunch bag, and it's just delicious served with a freshly grated horseradish sauce or crème fraîche flavored with curry.

Pastry for a single-crust pie
1 tablespoon coarse-grain mustard
1 tablespoon butter
1 cup chopped fresh mushrooms
1 cup chopped scallions (green onions)
¼ cup chopped fresh parsley
½ cup heavy whipping cream or undiluted
    evaporated milk

1 cup shredded provolone or mozzarella
    cheese
¼ cup freshly grated Asiago, Parmesan,
    or Romano cheese
3 large eggs, lightly beaten
2 cups (¾ pound) ground cooked ham,
    turkey ham, or smoked turkey breast
1 large tomato, cut into 12 wedges

Preheat the oven to 450°F. Roll out the pastry and fit it into a 9- or 10-inch quiche pan or pie pan. Prebake the pie shell until pale golden and dry.

Brush the inside of the baked shell with the mustard. Lower the oven temperature to 350°F.

In a large, nonstick skillet over medium heat, melt the butter and sauté the mushrooms and scallions for 5 minutes, or until tender.

Turn the vegetables into a mixing bowl and add the parsley, cream, half of the shredded provolone or mozzarella, the grated asiago, eggs, and ham. Mix well.

Turn the filling into the pie shell and smooth the top.

Bake for 35 to 40 minutes, until a knife inserted in the center of the pie comes out clean. Remove the pie from the oven and arrange the tomato wedges over the top. Sprinkle with the remaining shredded provolone or mozzarella. Return to the oven for 5 to 10 minutes longer, until the tomatoes are hot and the cheese is melted. Serve chilled, at room temperature, or warm, cut into wedges.

MAKES 6 TO 8 SERVINGS

Bacon and Egg Quiche Lorraine

Pastry for a single-crust pie
¼ pound bacon
2 eggs

¾ cup cream or milk
½ teaspoon salt
Dash of cayenne pepper

Make the pastry and divide it into two parts. Roll out each part and line two individual-size (4-inch) pie pans with the pastry.

Preheat the oven to 400°F. Cook the bacon until crisp, drain, and crumble into the pastry-lined pans. Beat the eggs, stir in the cream or milk, and add salt and cayenne pepper. Pour the egg mixture over the bacon. Bake for 20 to 25 minutes or until filling is set in the center. Serve hot.

TO SERVE FOUR: *Double all quantities and make four individual quiches. Or line a 9-inch pie pan with pastry for a single-crust pie; double filling ingredients, and pour into the pastry-lined pan. Bake at 400°F for 15 minutes; lower heat to 350° and bake an additional 20 to 25 minutes or until pie is set in the center.*

TO SERVE SIX: *Triple all ingredients and make six individual quiches. Or line a 10-inch round pie pan, or a square pan 9 × 9 × 2 inches deep, with the pastry. Triple the filling ingredients and pour into the pastry-lined pan. Bake at 400°F for 15 minutes; lower heat to 350°F and bake an additional 25 to 30 minutes or until pie is set in the center.*

Baked or Shirred Eggs

4 eggs
4 tablespoons milk or cream

Salt and pepper

Butter two baking dishes or 10-ounce custard cups generously. Break two eggs into each, and add 2 tablespoons milk or cream to each dish. Sprinkle with salt and pepper. Place on baking sheet, cover, and bake at 325ºF for 20 minutes or until eggs are as firm as you like them.

SERVES 2

Note: When baking eggs for more than two people, you may wish to put all the eggs in one casserole. The eggs on the outer side of the casserole will cook more quickly than those in the center; this variation may work out well if either of you likes your eggs at different degrees of doneness.

Bacon Shirred Eggs

Line the baking dishes with crisp crumbled bacon before adding the eggs.

Cheese Shirred Eggs

Line the buttered baking dishes with shredded cheese of your choice before adding the eggs.

Creamy Scrambled Eggs

4 to 6 eggs
¼ cup cream

½ teaspoon salt
Pepper to taste

Break the eggs into a bowl and beat with a fork until the yolks are broken. Add the cream and salt. Pour into the top of well-buttered double boiler or into a well-buttered frying pan set at low heat. Cook, stirring occasionally, until the mixture is set. Allow about 20 minutes for cooking, depending on the number of eggs used. Try to avoid cooking too quickly, as this makes the egg whites tough rather than creamy.

For a brunch party, scrambled eggs can be cooked over a hot-water bath in the chafing dish.

SERVES 2

Poached Eggs on Toast

1½ quarts water
2 tablespoons vinegar or
   1 tablespoon salt

4 eggs
Buttered toast

Lightly grease a 2-quart saucepan, and add the water and vinegar or salt. Bring the water to a gentle boil. Break the eggs into a saucer and slip them, one at a time, into the water. Reheat water to simmering; remove from heat and cover. Let stand 5 minutes or until eggs are as firm as you like them. Remove the eggs from the water with a slotted spoon or slotted pancake turner. Slip two eggs onto a piece of buttered toast for each serving.

TO SERVE FOUR, SIX, OR MORE: *Simply cook two eggs per person, and serve as directed above.*

Poached Eggs on Spinach

Serve the poached eggs on cooked, buttered, well-drained spinach.

Poached Eggs on Hash

Serve the poached eggs on hot fried patties of corned beef hash.

Poached Eggs on Horseback

Serve a poached egg on a cooked hamburger patty.

Poached Eggs in Puff Nests

2 eggs
1 cup béchamel sauce*

½ cup shredded Swiss cheese
2 large cream puffs**

Poach and drain the eggs. Make the béchamel sauce and add the cheese. Cut the top ⅓ off the cream puffs and insert a poached egg in each. Place cream puff tops over the eggs, and cover with sauce. Heat in a 450ºF oven for 5 minutes. Serve immediately.

* For Béchamel Sauce: Melt 2 tablespoons butter in a saucepan and stir in 2 tablespoons flour over medium heat, stirring until the flour is lightly browned. Gradually add ½ cup warmed chicken broth and ½ cup light cream. Cook, stirring constantly, until smooth and thick. Add salt to taste. Makes 1 cup.

** For Cream Puffs: In a saucepan, combine 1 cup water, ¼ teaspoon salt, 1 teaspoon sugar, and ½ cup butter. Heat until butter is melted. Bring mixture to a full, rolling boil and add 1 cup

all-purpose flour all at once. Stir briskly until the flour absorbs all the liquid. Remove from heat and beat until very smooth and pasty. Beat in 4 eggs, one at a time, beating until mixture is very smooth again and shiny. Let cool about 15 minutes. Preheat the oven to 400°F. Shape paste into 12 balls, and place on a parchment-covered baking sheet, making them as high as possible, using about ¼ cup paste for each one. Bake for 35 minutes until golden and lightweight. Poke a hole into each puff to allow steam to escape as puffs cool.

MAKES 12 PUFFS. Use 2 for this recipe and freeze the rest for another use.

Eggs Benedict for Two

Eggs Benedict in bed—what a luxury! But who's going to cook 'em?

2 eggs
2 slices ham
1 English muffin

Butter
Hollandaise sauce*

Poach the eggs until done to your liking. Meanwhile, heat the ham in a frying pan, and toast and butter the English muffin. Make the hollandaise sauce. To assemble, place a ham slice on each half of the muffin. Top ham with egg, and pour the hollandaise sauce over all.

* Fill a pot with 3 cups of water and bring to a simmer. Turn off the heat. Meanwhile, in a mixing bowl that will fit over the pot of water, combine 4 egg yolks, a pinch of salt, and 1 tablespoon of lemon juice. Whisk ingredients together until pale and slightly thickened. Put the bowl over the hot water and continue to whisk until the yolks are able to coat the back of a spoon. Slowly whisk in 1 cup melted butter a little at a time, whisking constantly. If butter is added too quickly, the sauce will not emulsify. Thin sauce with warm water if it becomes too thick. Once all of the butter is added, season to taste with salt, pepper, and lemon juice. Hold over hot water for up to 30 minutes.

Note: You may wish to make the hollandaise sauce ahead—or you may choose to serve Eggs Benedict when you have some hollandaise left over. Simply reheat the sauce slowly over warm water, stirring, to keep it smooth. If heated too quickly, it will separate. If it should separate, process it in the blender to rehomogenize it.

MAKES 2 SERVINGS

Samsøe Soufflé

You can prepare this soufflé, freeze it, then bake it later—but it will have a coarse texture.

1 cup half-and-half
¼ cup all-purpose flour
2 tablespoons butter
1 cup shredded Samsøe, Jarlsberg,
    or Swiss cheese

½ teaspoon salt
¼ teaspoon white pepper
4 eggs, separated
⅛ teaspoon cream of tartar

Butter a 1- to 1½-quart soufflé dish; set aside. In a medium saucepan, combine half-and-half and flour. Beat with a whisk until smooth. Over medium heat, bring mixture to a boil, stirring with a whisk. Add butter. Cook and stir until mixture thickens. Stir in cheese, salt, and white pepper. In a small bowl, beat egg yolks until blended. Stir in about ½ cup cheese sauce. Stir egg yolk mixture into remaining cheese sauce; set aside. In a medium bowl, beat egg whites until frothy. Add cream of tartar; continue beating until the whites form short, soft, but distinctive peaks; tips of peaks will bend over. Fold into cheese sauce. Pour cheese mixture into prepared dish. Bake or cover and freeze. To bake immediately, preheat oven to 375°F. Bake 30 to 35 minutes or until puffed and golden. Soufflé will be soft in the center. To bake after freezing, preheat oven to 350°F. Remove cover from soufflé dish; place frozen soufflé in pre-heated oven. Bake 45 to 60 minutes.

MAKES 4 SERVINGS

Spinach Soufflé

1 cup cooked spinach
1 tablespoon butter
1 tablespoon flour
½ cup milk
⅛ teaspoon salt

2 egg yolks, slightly beaten
¼ cup shredded Swiss cheese
½ teaspoon salt
Dash of cayenne pepper
2 egg whites, beaten stiff

Drain the spinach well and press through a wire strainer or whirl in blender until puréed.

In a small pan, melt the butter; add the flour, mixing until smooth. Blend in the milk and salt. Cook over medium heat, stirring, until thick and smooth. Remove from heat, and add the spinach, egg yolks, and cheese. Add salt and cayenne pepper. Fold in the egg whites. Pour into two well-buttered individual soufflé dishes, 1½ cup size, or into one small soufflé dish, 3 to 4 cup size. Bake at 375ºF for 20 to 25 minutes or until soufflé is puffed and the edges are tinged with a golden color. Serve immediately! This means *immediately,* for soufflés begin to fall as you take them out of the oven. It's best to have the guest ready and waiting at the table.

TO SERVE FOUR: *Double all quantities and bake in individual soufflé dishes. If one large dish is used, it should hold 1 to 1½ quarts.*

TO SERVE SIX: *Triple all quantities and make six individual soufflés; or use a large 2-quart soufflé dish and bake 15 minutes longer.*

Souffléed Grits

Native Americans taught the early settlers how to prepare hominy, which turned out to be an important basic food. It was and still is made with yellow dent corn or the standard field corn, which when dried has a "dent" in the top of each kernel. According to the old method, the corn was dried on the plant. When it was completely dry, it was picked and stored for processing later in the fall. Early settlers used lye made from wood ashes to treat the hominy. The dried corn was soaked in water with the lye until the grains puffed up to triple or quadruple their original size. The corn was then boiled for 2 hours or until the hulls slipped off. Next, it went through several soakings with fresh water, after which it could be drained and frozen, or dried and ground into a meal.

To serve it plain and buttered, the hominy is soaked overnight in fresh water. Then it is boiled until all the water has evaporated, buttered while hot, and served in place of potatoes. Ground hominy is called grits *and has a texture slightly coarser than cornmeal.*

5 cups water	½ cup whipping cream
1 cup hominy grits	1 teaspoon salt
2 eggs, separated	¼ teaspoon white pepper

Boil water in a medium-sized saucepan. Stir in grits. Cook over low heat 25 to 30 minutes, stirring occasionally. Cool. Preheat the oven to 350°F. Grease a 1-quart casserole. Blend egg yolks into cooked grits. Add cream, salt, and pepper. In a medium-sized bowl, beat egg whites until they stand in peaks; fold into the grits. Spoon the mixture into the greased casserole. Bake 35 to 40 minutes or until puffed and golden. Serve immediately.

MAKES 4 SERVINGS

Swedish Farmer's Omelet

The winter version of this omelet may include only onions and potatoes. In the summertime, Swedes add garden vegetables as they come into season.

¼ cup butter
1 medium-sized sweet onion, sliced
4 medium-sized potatoes, peeled
    and diced
1 cup finely diced ham
2 tablespoons fresh chives, minced
1 teaspoon dried dill weed
6 eggs

½ cup milk
1 teaspoon salt
½ teaspoon pepper
1 cup shredded mild farmer's cheese (such
    as Bondost) or jack cheese
1 tomato, peeled and sliced
1 green pepper, seeded and sliced
1 cup sour cream (optional)

In a 10-inch nonstick, broiler-proof omelet pan, melt the butter over medium heat. Add the onion and potatoes. Sauté for 15 to 20 minutes, until the potatoes are tender. Add the ham, chives, and dill.

Beat together the eggs, milk, salt, and pepper and pour over the sauté. Cover and cook over low heat for 15 to 20 minutes, until set. Sprinkle with half the cheese.

Preheat the broiler. Top the omelet with the tomato, green pepper, and remaining cheese. Broil until the cheese melts. Serve with sour cream, if desired.

MAKES 6 SERVINGS

Norwegian Baked Cheese Omelet

Cheese is the backbone of the Scandinavian breakfast. It is so quick, I sometimes make this omelet for a late-night supper, too.

4 eggs
¼ cup water
½ teaspoon salt
2 tablespoons butter
4 whole green onions, sliced
1 cup diced cooked ham

1 red bell pepper, seeded and sliced into
    thin rings
12 ounces regular or low-fat Jarlsberg
    cheese, cut into ½-inch cubes
Chopped parsley, for garnish

Preheat the oven to 400ºF. Whisk together the eggs, water, and salt. In a heavy, oven-proof casserole or frying pan, melt the butter. Add the onions, ham, and bell pepper and sauté over medium heat for 3 to 4 minutes, until the onions are bright green and the pepper is hot. Pour the egg mixture over the sauté and sprinkle with the cheese cubes. Bake for 15 to 20 minutes, until the egg mixture is set and the cheese is melted. Garnish with chopped parsley.

MAKES 4 SERVINGS

Seafood Omelet

One Swedish cook I know serves this omelet as the hot course after a cold smorgasbord. It is as delicious at room temperature as it is hot, and if you reheat it as directed, it will puff up a second time.

½ cup butter
1 cup flour
2 cups milk
8 eggs, lightly beaten
¼ teaspoon salt
¼ teaspoon nutmeg
8 ounces fresh or frozen crab claws, for
    garnish (optional)
Fresh dill, for garnish
Thinly sliced lemon, for garnish

FILLING
¼ pound freshly cooked lobster or
    crabmeat
1½ cups heavy whipping cream and
    seafood stock
2 tablespoons butter
2 tablespoons flour
2 tablespoons dry sherry
Salt
Cayenne pepper

Grease a 9 × 13-inch jelly-roll pan and line it with parchment paper. Butter the paper generously and sprinkle it with flour. Set aside. Preheat the oven to 400°F.

Melt the butter in a saucepan. Add the flour and stir over medium heat for 1 minute. Add the milk, whisking briskly, and cook over low heat until the mixture is very thick and smooth. Remove from the heat and beat in all of the eggs at once, then the salt and nutmeg. Pour the mixture into the prepared pan and bake for 30 minutes, or until puffed and golden.

To prepare the filling, drain the juices from the lobster or crabmeat into a 2-cup or larger measuring cup. Add the heavy cream to equal 1¼ cups. Melt the butter in a saucepan. Add the flour and cook over medium heat, stirring, for 2 minutes. Stir in the stock-and-cream mixture. Cook, stirring, until thickened and smooth. Season with the sherry, and with salt and cayenne pepper to taste. Keep the filling warm.

Place a strip of waxed paper on a work surface and invert the baked omelet onto it. Remove the parchment paper from the bottom of the omelet. Spread the omelet with three-fourths of the filling. Using the waxed paper to lift the omelet, roll it up jelly-roll style, starting at a narrow end. Place the rolled omelet on a heatproof serving dish, seam side down. You may serve the omelet immediately or hold it, covered, at room temperature, for up to 1 hour before serving. To reheat before serving, place the rolled omelet in a 400°F oven for 5 to 8 minutes. Before serving, top the omelet with the remaining filling. Garnish with crab claws (optional), dill, and lemon slices.

MAKES 6 TO 8 SERVINGS

French Omelet

4 eggs
4 tablespoons water

½ teaspoon salt
Butter

For best results, use an omelet pan 6 inches in diameter. Beat the eggs, water, and salt together with a fork. Heat the omelet pan until a drop of water sizzles, and butter it generously. Pour in the egg mixture all at once. Lower the heat, lift up the pan, and with a fork or spatula lift the omelet around the edges to allow uncooked mixture to run onto the bottom. Tilt and shake the pan to keep the omelet loose from the pan. When the mixture no longer flows freely, the omelet is done. The omelet should *not* be browned, as this causes the egg to become overcooked and rubbery, and also results in an off-flavor. "Roll out," or fold, the omelet onto a warm plate. Divide into two portions.

TO SERVE FOUR: *Make two omelets.*
TO SERVE SIX: *Make three omelets.*

Cheese Omelet

Make a French Omelet and sprinkle the surface with ½ to ¾ cup shredded cheddar, jack, or Swiss cheese before folding or rolling out onto a serving plate.

Spanish Omelet

Make a French Omelet and sprinkle the surface with ½ cup shredded jack or cheddar cheese and 1 chopped peeled tomato. Add Tabasco sauce to taste before folding or rolling out onto a warm serving plate.

Mexican Omelet

Make a French Omelet and sprinkle the surface with ½ cup shredded jack cheese, 1 peeled and chopped tomato, and 1 chopped, canned green chili pepper before folding or rolling out onto a serving plate.

Puffy Rice Omelet

2 eggs, separated	**1 tablespoon flour**
1½ teaspoons water	**½ cup milk**
¼ teaspoon salt	**½ cup shredded sharp cheddar cheese**
½ cup cooked rice	**Salt**
2 tablespoons butter	**Pepper**

Preheat the oven to 350ºF. Beat the egg yolks until thick and stir in the water, salt, and rice. Beat the egg whites until stiff but not dry. Fold the egg whites into the egg yolk and rice mixture. Melt half the butter in a 6-inch ovenproof frying pan, and pour in the egg mixture. Cook over medium to low heat until golden brown on the bottom. Bake for 20 minutes or until the omelet is set.

Meanwhile, melt the remaining butter and blend in the flour. Stir in the milk, and cook until thickened and smooth. Add the cheese and stir until melted. Add salt and pepper to taste. To serve, turn the omelet out onto a hot platter, fold in half, and pour the hot cheese sauce over it. Divide into two portions.

TO SERVE FOUR: *Double all quantities, making an omelet twice as big.*
TO SERVE SIX: *Triple all quantities, but divide the mixture between two pans to bake (remember to butter them well), unless you have a very large frying pan that is ovenproof.*

Puffy Omelet

Your electric frying pan is handy for this type of omelet.

4 eggs, separated
4 tablespoons water

½ teaspoon salt
Butter

Put the egg whites into a bowl, add the water and salt, and beat until they are stiff. Beat the yolks thoroughly; then fold them into the whites. Heat butter in an 8-inch frying pan until a drop of water sizzles. Pour in the egg mixture, and cook over low heat until the bottom is set and very slightly golden. Cover and cook for 5 minutes or until set. Crease through the center, fold over, and roll onto a serving plate. Serve with your choice of sauce.

TO SERVE FOUR: *Double the quantities and use a 10-inch frying pan.*
TO SERVE SIX: *Triple the quantities and use a 12-inch frying pan, or simply make the basic omelet three times.*

Alternate method: Make the omelet as directed, except after it is cooked on the bottom, finish cooking it by baking in a 350ºF oven for 10 to 15 minutes or until lightly golden.

Baked Artichoke and Shrimp Omelet

Artichokes and shrimp add elegance as well as flavor!

1 (9-ounce) package frozen
    artichoke hearts or 1 (8½-ounce)
    can artichoke hearts
6 eggs
½ teaspoon salt
⅛ teaspoon cayenne pepper

2 tablespoons olive oil
¾ cup chopped green onions
1 cup cooked peeled shrimp
½ cup whipping cream
¾ cup shredded Swiss or Jarlsberg cheese
¼ cup grated Parmesan cheese

Preheat the oven to 400ºF. Butter a 1½-quart casserole or quiche dish. Cook frozen artichoke hearts according to package directions; drain. Or, rinse, drain, and quarter canned artichoke hearts. In a medium bowl, beat eggs, salt, and cayenne pepper. In a medium skillet, heat oil. Add green onions; sauté 5 minutes or until wilted. Add artichokes; sauté 2 to 3 minutes longer. Remove from heat; add shrimp and cream. Pour into egg mixture; mix well. Pour into buttered casserole. Sprinkle with cheeses. Bake, uncovered, 15 to 20 minutes or until a knife inserted in the center comes out clean.

MAKES 4 SERVINGS

Hätäleipä Baked with Ham and Cheese

The topping turns this quick-to-bake bread into a meal. This dish is perfect for casual entertaining when you want something new and delicious to serve. To round out the meal, combine this with a crisp green salad and beer or wine. Or you might serve it along with a hearty split pea or Yankee bean soup. The amounts of ham and cheese are variable according to what you have on hand. Of course, the more toppings you use, the more satisfying the dish, but if you're short on one or the other, don't let that stop you! In fact, you might substitute summer sausage, Thuringer, or another pre-cooked meat.

1 recipe Hätäleipä (see page 97)
1 to 2 cups cubed cooked ham

1 to 2 cups shredded or cubed Swiss, jack, or cheddar cheese

Prepare the bread dough and spread it out onto the prepared baking sheet, shaping the dough into a circle 10 inches in diameter. Let the dough rise for 30 minutes. Press ham into the dough. Preheat the oven to 400°F. Bake for 15 minutes, remove from oven, and top with the cheese. Return the bread to the oven for 5 to 10 minutes, until the bread is browned and the cheese is melted. Cool 5 minutes; then cut into wedges to serve.

MAKES 8 SERVINGS

Swedish Bacon Bake

Prepare this omelet the night before and bake it at the last minute.

1 pound sliced bacon
½ pound sliced mushrooms
3 tablespoons butter (optional)
2 tablespoons cornstarch
2 cups half-and-half

18 eggs
1 teaspoon salt
½ teaspoon dried leaf tarragon
1½ cups shredded Emmentaler or Jarlsberg cheese

Butter a shallow 2- to 3-quart casserole dish; set aside. Cut bacon slices in half. In a large skillet, cook bacon over medium heat until crisp. Drain on paper towels and set aside. Increase heat to high. Pour off all but about 3 tablespoons of the bacon drippings. Sauté mushrooms in bacon drippings until mushrooms are lightly browned, about 3 minutes. Or, if desired, melt butter in a large skillet; sauté mushrooms in melted butter. Stir in cornstarch until evenly distributed. Slowly stir in half-and-half until blended. Cook and stir until thickened. In a large bowl, beat eggs until blended. Stir in 1 or 2 cups mushroom mixture. Stir egg mixture into remaining mushroom mixture. Scramble over medium heat just until eggs begin to set; do not cook completely. Stir in salt and tarragon. Pour partially cooked egg mixture into prepared casserole dish. Sprinkle cheese over top. Overlap cooked bacon slices around the edge. Cover and refrigerate overnight, if desired, or bake immediately. To bake immediately, preheat the oven to 300ºF. Bake 30 minutes or until casserole is heated through and cheese is melted. To bake after being refrigerated, preheat the oven to 300ºF; bake 45 minutes.

MAKES 8 TO 10 GENEROUS SERVINGS

Salted Salmon

This simple-to-prepare dish is popular in all Scandinavian countries.

2 pounds fresh salmon fillet
½ cup chopped fresh dill or 2 tablespoons
    dried dill weed, crumbled
¼ cup salt

¼ cup sugar
¼ teaspoon ground white pepper
¼ teaspoon ground allspice

Rinse salmon; dry with paper towels. Place in a 13 × 9-inch glass dish. Sprinkle with half of the dill. In a small bowl, combine the salt, sugar, white pepper, and allspice. Sprinkle half of mixture over fish; turn fish over and sprinkle with remaining salt mixture. Top with remaining dill. Cover with plastic wrap; refrigerate 24 hours. If a compact texture is desired, place a 12 × 7-inch dish on top of the fish. Place several cans of food in the top dish for weight. Occasionally spoon juices over fish. To serve, drain fish and cut diagonally in ⅛-inch slices. Arrange on a platter.

MAKES 12 APPETIZER SERVINGS

Farmhouse Breakfast Sausage

When farmers did their own butchering, there were lots of scraps left over and these were made into sausages. Sausages are basic to many cuisines, but especially German, Swiss, Dutch, French, and Scandinavian. The taste of the sausages reflected the flavorings favored by each ethnic group. Today, about the only sausage people might make at home is from game, or just for the fun of it. For the uninitiated, the first thought would be that sausage should be made of very lean meat; not true. For juiciness, the meat should be at least 30 percent fat. If you purchase a pork butt roast, the fat percentage is about right. Grind it yourself, or ask the butcher to do it for you. Then have some fun seasoning and flavoring your own sausages.

2 pounds fresh pork butt, coarsely ground
1½ teaspoons dried leaf thyme
1 teaspoon dried sage leaves, crumbled
1 teaspoon salt
¾ teaspoon freshly ground black pepper
¼ teaspoon cayenne pepper
About 2 ounces salted sausage casings (optional)

In a large bowl, blend pork, thyme, sage, salt, black pepper, and cayenne pepper. Refrigerate overnight for flavors to blend. Shape into patties. Cook in a heavy skillet over medium heat until cooked through, turning once.

For link sausages, purchase salted sausage casings from the meat market. Soak in cold water to remove salt; then slip end of casing over faucet in kitchen sink. Run cold water through to flush out the inside of the casings. This is more easily done if casings are cut into 20- to 24-inch lengths. Put meat mixture into a sausage-stuffing machine or into a large pastry bag with a ½- to 1-inch tip. Slip casings over end of pastry tip and press meat into casings; tie the ends with string. If sausage is hard to press into casings, add water to meat mixture to soften it.

MAKES 2 POUNDS OF SAUSAGE

Note: Sausage casings are available from the butcher; extra casings may be frozen.

Fresh Pork Sausage

Scandinavians are experts at making sausage. The practice goes back to when almost everybody lived on a farm and every family had its own "house pig." The pig was butchered in the fall so that the hams could be cured and smoked for Christmas dinner. The remainder of the meat was used for a variety of fresh cuts. The scraps and bits ended up in meat loaves, meatballs, pâtés, and sausages.

In this day and age, when most people buy their sausages, if you don't want to go through the trouble of pressing the meat into sausage casings, you can simply fry it up in patties. This sausage mixture has a smooth, almost creamy texture. Store uncooked links or patties in the freezer until you are ready to cook them.

2½ pounds ground pork
2 teaspoons salt
¼ teaspoon pepper
¼ teaspoon ground ginger
¼ teaspoon ground cloves

Pinch of ground nutmeg
¼ cup instant potato flakes
2 cups milk
Sausage casings (optional)

Place the pork, salt, pepper, ginger, cloves, nutmeg, and potato flakes in the large bowl of an electric mixer or in a large food processor fitted with a steel blade, and mix until blended. Set the mixer or processor on high speed and slowly beat in the milk until the mixture is very light and pale pink in color.

Press the mixture into sausage casings (available from any butcher or meat market) and tie the ends with string, or shape the mixture into patties. Brown the sausages in a heavy skillet, turning occasionally, until cooked through, about 10 minutes.

MAKES APPROXIMATELY 3 POUNDS OF SAUSAGE

Hash-browned Potatoes

The white potato is native to South America and was cultivated thousands of years ago in Peru. The Spanish explorers found the Incas cultivating this tuber and called it patata. The Incan name was "papa." The potato arrived in North America via Europe and was one of the earliest of the cultivated crops of the new settlers in New England. This is a "hash-house favorite."

3 cups diced cooked or raw potatoes

Salt and freshly ground black pepper to taste

¼ cup minced onion (optional)

¼ cup minced fresh parsley or fresh spinach (optional)

¼ cup half-and-half (optional)

2 to 4 tablespoons butter or bacon drippings

In a large bowl, combine potatoes, salt and pepper, onion and parsley or spinach, if used. Stir in half-and-half, if used. In a slope-sided, preferably nonstick skillet, heat 2 tablespoons butter or drippings. Add potatoes. Cook over medium heat until potatoes are browned and bottom is crusty, lifting potatoes at first until they are well-coated. Reduce heat and cook until potatoes are tender, if using raw potatoes. Add more butter or drippings, if necessary, to keep potatoes from sticking. Slide potatoes out onto a plate; then invert and slide from the plate back into the skillet, browned-side up. Brown 5 to 10 minutes, shaking skillet constantly. Slide out onto a warm platter. Cut into wedges to serve.

MAKES 6 SERVINGS

Cream Cheese and Salmon Smørrebrød

Use your own homemade Salted Salmon (page 36) or purchase it at a delicatessen.

4 slices pumpernickel or other rye bread

4 teaspoons butter, softened

2 ounces cream cheese, softened

3 ounces thinly sliced smoked or salted salmon

16 paper-thin cucumber slices

Cut crusts from bread. Spread 1 teaspoon butter on each piece of bread, covering completely. Cut each buttered slice in half crosswise; trim to make 4 × 2-inch rectangles. Spread each with cream cheese, covering completely. Top each with salmon, laying salmon flat. Top each with 2 cucumber slices, gathering slices in a mound.

MAKES 8 SANDWICHES

Ham and Egg Smørrebrød

Ham and vegetables make this smørrebrød as colorful as a garden of flowers.

6 slices whole wheat bread
7 teaspoons butter, softened
1 egg, thoroughly beaten
6 thin slices cooked ham

6 butter or leaf lettuce leaves
12 paper-thin cucumber slices
6 tomato slices
Parsley or watercress

Cut crusts from bread. Spread 1 teaspoon butter on each slice of bread, covering completely; set aside. Over low heat, melt remaining teaspoon butter in a skillet or omelet pan that measures 8 inches across the bottom. Add beaten egg; swirl pan until egg covers bottom of pan. Cook only until egg is set and the surface feels dry. Cut into ½-inch strips; let cool. Roll ham slices into cones. Gather lettuce leaves in ruffles. Place each ruffled leaf on 1 end of each slice of buttered bread. Place 1 ham cone on part of each slice not covered with lettuce. Loosely roll up cooled egg strips. Place 1 rolled egg strip inside wide end of each ham cone. Cut each cucumber and tomato slice from center to outer edge, cutting through peel. Twist cucumber slices and tomato slices and place on top of ham. Garnish with parsley or watercress.

MAKES 6 SANDWICHES

The Veterinarian's Breakfast

This is named after a Copenhagen veterinarian, or Dyrlaegen, *who ordered it every morning on his way to work.*

1 teaspoon softened butter
1 slice rye bread
1 slice liver pâté
2 tablespoons chilled beef consommé
   aspic, chopped

4 thin slices Danish salami
3 sweet onion rings
1 sprig fresh dill

Spread the butter to the edges of the rye bread. Top with the liver pâté and beef consommé aspic. Arrange the salami so that the outer edges completely hide the bread and the meat overlaps in the center of the sandwich. Arrange the onion rings on top and place a sprig of fresh dill in the center of the onion rings.

MAKES 1 SERVING

The Golden Sunrise

The combination of blue cheese, tomato, and egg yolk is a Danish favorite, but you can substitute a tablespoon of hollandaise sauce for the egg yolk. When using an eggshell for garnish, before cracking it, wash the egg in soapy water, rinse, and pat dry.

1 teaspoon softened butter
1 slice French bread
4 thin slices blue cheese
1 slice tomato

1 uncooked pasteurized egg yolk, or
    1 tablespoon hollandaise sauce, in a
    half of an eggshell

Spread the butter to the edges of the bread. Arrange the cheese slices to completely hide the bread. Place the tomato slice on top. Place the egg yolk in a half of a washed eggshell, or spoon hollandaise sauce into the shell and nest it on top of the tomato slice.

MAKES 1 SERVING

Fancy Brunch Torte

Perfect for the morning when guests sleep late and breakfast runs into lunch (that's how brunch got its name). Make this torte up to two days ahead and keep it in the refrigerator. It tastes great chilled or warmed; we end up heating a slice at a time in the microwave as the breakfasters arrive on the scene. With a bowlful of strawberries to spoon onto the plate and a steaming cup of coffee in hand, a memorable day has begun.

5 eggs
1 tablespoon chopped fresh chives
1 tablespoon minced fresh parsley
1 teaspoon dried tarragon leaves
½ teaspoon salt
2 tablespoons extra-virgin olive oil

2 large red peppers, seeded and cut into
    1-inch pieces
2 cloves garlic, minced or pressed
2 bunches (10 ounces each) fresh spinach,
    washed and stemmed
¼ teaspoon freshly grated nutmeg
¼ teaspoon salt

¼ teaspoon freshly ground pepper

1 (15-ounce) package frozen puff pastry, thawed

½ pound Swiss cheese, thinly sliced

½ pound cooked ham, thinly sliced

1 egg, beaten, for glaze

Preheat the oven to 350°F. In a large bowl, whisk together the eggs, chives, parsley, tarragon, and salt. Brush a nonstick 8-inch skillet with some of the olive oil. Place over medium-high heat. Pour half of the egg mixture into the skillet. With a spatula, lift the omelet from the skillet so that the uncooked egg can run under the cooked egg. After about 30 seconds, there should be no more uncooked egg on top of the omelet. Flip it over and brown the other side. Slide out onto a plate. Repeat with the remaining mixture and make another omelet. Place the second omelet onto a plate and reserve.

Add the remaining oil to the skillet and add the red peppers; stir-fry over moderately high heat until the peppers are crisp-tender. Remove and reserve. Add the garlic and spinach, and sauté for 2 to 3 minutes. Season with the nutmeg, salt, and pepper; then remove from the skillet and reserve.

Coat an 8-inch springform pan with nonstick spray. Roll out one of the pieces of puff pastry on a lightly floured surface to fit the bottom and sides of the pan; trim corners and patch together to fill in holes as needed.

Layer the ingredients into the pastry: Place one omelet on the bottom. Top with half the spinach, half the cheese, half the ham, and all of the red bell pepper. Top that with half the ham, half the cheese, half the spinach, and the second omelet. Roll the remaining pastry out to fit over the top. Trim to make an 8-inch circle and seal the edges to the bottom crust. Make fancy cutouts with the scraps. Brush the top of the torte with beaten egg and place the cutouts on top. Make slits on the top with the tip of a knife. Place the pan on a baking sheet.

Bake for 1 hour and 15 minutes or until the top is golden brown. Cool to room temperature on a wire rack.

MAKES 8 SERVINGS

Cheese Casserole

A crustless quiche!

8 Swedish anchovy fillets

2 cups shredded Gouda or Jarlsberg cheese

4 eggs

2 cups half-and-half

2 tablespoons chopped fresh parsley

Butter a 9- or 10-inch quiche pan or shallow casserole dish. Preheat the oven to 350ºF. Arrange anchovies over bottom of prepared pan or dish. Sprinkle cheese over top. In a medium bowl, beat eggs; stir in half-and-half. Pour egg mixture over cheese and anchovies. Bake 25 minutes or until golden brown around edges. Sprinkle with parsley. Serve hot or cool.

MAKES 6 SERVINGS

Country Egg and Ham Brunch

Assemble this breakfast casserole the night before, and while it bakes in the morning there's time to set out plates, make coffee, stir up juice, and cut fruit. It is possible to de-fat this old classic with modern-day products: use egg substitute in place of the whole eggs, skim milk instead of whole, and omit the butter. Turkey ham is low in fat, and you can substitute low-fat cheese for the whole-milk cheddar.

12 eggs, beaten

9 slices whole wheat bread, crusts removed, cut into ½-inch squares

4 tablespoons butter, cut into pieces

3 cups milk

6 green onions or scallions, chopped, including green tops

¼ cup chopped green bell pepper

¼ cup chopped red bell pepper

1 pound diced cooked ham or turkey ham

2 cups shredded sharp cheddar cheese

¼ teaspoon freshly ground pepper

Chopped fresh herbs (such as basil, chervil, or parsley)

Butter a 13 × 9-inch baking dish. In a large bowl, combine until well blended the eggs, bread, butter, milk, green onions or scallions, green bell pepper, red bell pepper, ham, and cheese. Season with the pepper.

Pour the mixture into the prepared dish, checking to see that all the ingredients are evenly distributed. Cover and refrigerate overnight or bake immediately.

Preheat the oven to 300ºF. Uncover the casserole and bake for 1 hour or until set.

Garnish with the fresh chopped herbs and serve immediately.

MAKES 8 TO 12 SERVINGS

French Egg Casserole

Do you ever have extra hard-cooked eggs left over? At Eastertime, for instance? Here's a French egg casserole that tastes as if the eggs were cooked just for it. In fact, that's exactly what I do.

4 hard-cooked eggs
4 slices bacon, cooked crisp
1 cup medium white sauce*
1 cup shredded sharp cheddar cheese

Dash of garlic powder
Pinch each of thyme, marjoram, and basil
1 tablespoon chopped fresh parsley
4 tablespoons buttered bread crumbs

Peel the eggs and cut into thin slices. (Actually, you can use more eggs if you like, depending on how many you have on hand, but don't exceed 8 for this amount of sauce.)

Drain and crumble the bacon. Make the white sauce, and add the cheese, garlic powder, thyme, marjoram, basil, and parsley to it. Pour a bit of the sauce into each of two individual casseroles, *au gratin* dishes, or 12-ounce custard cups. Add a layer of egg slices, then a few bacon crumbles, then more sauce. Continue layering until ingredients are used up, ending with the sauce. Sprinkle the top with buttered bread crumbs. Bake at 350ºF for 20 minutes or until bubbly around the edges and the crumbs are browned.

* For a simple white sauce: Combine 2 tablespoons butter and 2 tablespoons all-purpose flour. Stir together and add 1 cup milk. Bring to a boil, whisk, and salt to taste.

Note: To make buttered bread crumbs, heat 1 tablespoon butter until melted. Toss bread crumbs in the melted butter until evenly coated.

Savory Pots de Crème Suisses

Juicy red strawberries and cinnamon muffins are perfect with this!

4 egg yolks
2 cups half-and-half
1 cup shredded Swiss cheese

¼ teaspoon salt
Dash of cayenne pepper

Preheat the oven to 300ºF. In a small bowl, beat egg yolks. In a medium, heavy saucepan, bring half-and-half just to a simmer. Add cheese, salt, and cayenne pepper. Stir until cheese melts. Add a small amount of cheese mixture to egg yolks; then return egg mixture to saucepan. Stir over low heat until blended. Butter 4 individual custard cups. Divide egg mixture between buttered custard cups. Place in a medium baking pan. Add enough hot water to pan to come halfway up sides of custard cups. Bake 15 to 20 minutes or until set in center. Serve warm.

MAKES 4 SERVINGS

Eggs Baked in Wild Rice Nests

The flavor of wild rice blends well with lightly baked egg.

²⁄₃ **cup uncooked wild rice**
2 cups hot water
1 teaspoon salt
1 cup shredded Swiss or Jarlsberg cheese
8 eggs
2 tablespoons butter

8 smoky, fully cooked link sausages,
  sliced
½ cup whipping cream
½ cup fresh bread crumbs
1 tablespoon melted butter

Rinse wild rice in 3 changes of hot tap water or until water is no longer cloudy. In a medium saucepan, bring 2 cups water and salt to a boil; stir in rice. Return to a boil. Cover and reduce heat to low. Cook 35 minutes or until rice is tender and has absorbed all the liquid. Preheat the oven to 350°F. Butter a shallow 1½-quart casserole or 11 × 7-inch or 8-inch-square baking dish. Spread rice over bottom of buttered casserole. Sprinkle with half of cheese. Make 8 evenly spaced indentations in rice and cheese. Carefully crack 1 egg into each indentation. Pierce egg yolks but do not stir; dot with 2 tablespoons butter. Arrange sausage slices around eggs. Pour cream over all. Sprinkle with remaining cheese. In a small bowl, combine bread crumbs and 1 tablespoon melted butter; sprinkle over cheese in casserole. Bake, uncovered, 15 to 25 minutes or until cheese is melted and eggs are set to your liking.

MAKES 4 SERVINGS

Mushroom Brunch Casserole

Great for a Sunday brunch with sliced melon and fresh muffins.

2 tablespoons butter

½ pound sliced fresh mushrooms

1 bunch green onions, chopped

1 medium green bell pepper, chopped
(optional)

12 slices seven-grain or whole wheat
bread, crusts removed

2 cups shredded cheddar cheese

8 eggs, beaten

3 cups milk

1 tablespoon chopped fresh parsley

1 teaspoon Dijon-style mustard

1 teaspoon salt

¼ teaspoon black pepper

10 bacon slices, crisp-cooked, crumbled

1 tomato, peeled, seeded, and diced

Generously butter a shallow 3-quart casserole or 13 × 9-inch baking dish. In a large skillet, melt the butter. Add mushrooms, green onions, and green pepper, if desired; sauté about 10 minutes or until liquid has evaporated. Remove from heat. Arrange 6 bread slices in bottom of buttered casserole. Top with half of cheese, all mushroom mixture, then with remaining bread slices. Top bread with remaining cheese. In a large bowl, beat eggs, milk, parsley, mustard, salt, and pepper. Pour over bread mixture in casserole. Sprinkle bacon and tomato evenly over top. Cover and refrigerate several hours or overnight. Preheat the oven to 325°F. Bake, uncovered, 50 minutes to 1 hour or until a knife inserted in center comes out clean. Let stand 5 minutes before serving.

MAKES 12 SERVINGS

Egg Scramble with Turkey Ham

Turkey ham has fewer calories than ham made from pork.

6 thick bread slices, crusts removed,
cubed

1 pound turkey ham, cut in ½-inch cubes

2 cups cheddar cheese, cubed

8 eggs

2 cups milk

½ teaspoon dried leaf thyme

½ teaspoon dry mustard

The day before you plan to serve this casserole, butter a shallow 3-quart casserole or 13 × 9-inch baking dish. Sprinkle bread cubes, turkey ham, and cheese evenly over bottom of buttered casserole. In a large bowl, beat eggs, milk, thyme, and mustard. Pour egg mixture over ham mixture in casserole. Cover and refrigerate overnight.

Preheat the oven to 325ºF. Bake casserole, uncovered, 1 hour or until edges are lightly browned and a knife inserted in the center comes out clean.

MAKES 8 SERVINGS

Swiss Egg and Cheese Bake

You'll find this a delicious and practical dish when you have Sunday morning guests!

6 eggs	**2 tablespoons butter**
⅓ cup milk	**1 cup diced cooked ham**
½ teaspoon salt	**1 cup shredded Swiss or Gruyère cheese**
¼ teaspoon white pepper	**¼ cup fine fresh bread crumbs**
1 teaspoon dried leaf tarragon	

Preheat the oven to 400ºF. Butter a shallow 1- to 1½-quart casserole or 8-inch-square baking dish. In a medium bowl, beat eggs, milk, salt, white pepper, and tarragon. In a large skillet, melt butter. Add egg mixture. Cook and stir over medium heat until just starting to set. Spoon mixture into buttered casserole. Sprinkle with ham, cheese, and bread crumbs. Bake, uncovered, 10 minutes or until top is golden.

MAKES 6 SERVINGS

Tex-Mex Strata

Corn tortillas take the place of bread in this strata.

½ pound fresh bulk pork sausage, mild, regular, or hot	**1 cup shredded jack cheese**
⅔ cup chopped green onions	**4 eggs, beaten**
⅓ cup chopped green bell pepper	**2 cups milk**
12 (6-inch) corn tortillas	**½ teaspoon salt**
1½ cups shredded cheddar cheese	**½ cup tomato sauce**
	1 (4-ounce) can diced green chilies

Butter an 8-inch-square baking dish. In a large skillet, cook the sausage, green onion, and green pepper until sausage is crumbly and no longer pink. Drain off fat; set sausage mixture aside. Arrange 4 tortillas in the bottom of the buttered baking dish. Sprinkle with half of the sausage mixture and half of the cheddar cheese. Top with 4 more tortillas, remaining sausage mixture, and remaining cheddar cheese. Top with remaining tortillas. Press tortillas down firmly over layers to remove air spaces and even out mixture in dish. Top with jack cheese. In a medium bowl, beat milk, eggs, salt, tomato sauce, and green chilies. Pour over layers in baking dish. Cover and refrigerate several hours or overnight. Remove from refrigerator 1 hour before baking. Preheat the oven to 325ºF. Bake, uncovered, 40 to 45 minutes or until a knife inserted near the center comes out clean. Let stand 10 minutes before serving.

MAKES 6 SERVINGS

Baked Oat or Rye Porridge

Cooked grains in their simplest form have always been the mainstay of rural Scandinavian cuisine. While perfect for breakfast, they are also often served for dessert with a fruit sauce poured over each serving. And leftover porridge can be pressed into a dish and chilled, then sliced, fried in butter, and served with strawberry jam and butter. This steaming porridge, baked all night in a slow oven, is wonderful on a chilly spring morning.

6 cups water
2 cups old-fashioned rolled oats, steel-cut oats, or cracked rye berries (available in health food stores)
¼ to ½ teaspoon salt

Lingonberry or cranberry preserves or cinnamon and sugar
Butter
Cream or milk

Combine the water, oats (or rye), and salt in a 2½-quart baking dish. Cover tightly. Place the dish in a pan filled with enough hot tap water to reach halfway up the sides of the dish, and place in the oven. Set the oven at 250ºF. Bake overnight, or for about 8 hours.

Serve hot with lingonberry or cranberry preserves or cinnamon and sugar, butter, and cream or milk.

MAKES 8 SERVINGS

Spiced Wild Rice Porridge
with Nuts and Fruit

Keep cooked wild rice in the refrigerator or freezer so that you can make this tasty and easy—and nutritious—breakfast.

2 cups cooked wild rice*
¼ cup heavy cream
2 tablespoons honey or maple syrup
Pinch of salt
½ cup dried fruits, raisins, cranberries, apples, or diced dried apricots

½ cup coarsely chopped toasted pecans, almonds, or walnuts
1 teaspoon freshly ground cardamom
½ teaspoon cinnamon

In a medium saucepan, combine the rice, cream, honey, and salt. Cook, stirring, over medium heat for about 5 minutes or until mixture is hot. Stir in the dried fruit, nuts, cardamom, and cinnamon. Serve hot with additional cream or milk.

MAKES 2 SERVINGS

* To cook wild rice, rinse ⅔ cup wild rice until water runs clear. Place into a saucepan and add 2 cups water. Bring to a boil, lower heat to simmering, cover, and cook for 30 to 35 minutes until rice has absorbed the water and is tender to the bite. This yields 2 cups cooked wild rice.

Scandinavian Fruit Soup

In the United States, we think of fruit soup as a dessert, but in Scandinavia it is offered on winter breakfast buffets, along with thick cream, which is poured over each serving.

¾ cup dried apricots or peaches
¾ cup dried pitted prunes
2 tablespoons golden raisins
2 tablespoons dark raisins
1 tablespoon currants
1 (3-inch) cinnamon stick
1 teaspoon grated orange peel
3 tablespoons quick-cooking tapioca

4 cups apple juice, cranberry juice, or water
¼ cup sugar
1 tart red apple, peeled, cored, and cut into 1-inch chunks
Heavy whipping cream

Cut the apricots (or peaches) and prunes into quarters and place in a 2½-quart saucepan. Add the golden and dark raisins, currants, cinnamon stick, orange peel, and tapioca. Add the juice or water and let stand for 1 hour. Stir in the sugar. Place over moderate heat and heat to boiling; then reduce the heat and simmer, stirring occasionally, for 30 minutes or until the fruit is tender and the soup is thickened. Add the apple and cook for 10 minutes or until the apple is tender. Remove from heat and cool. Pour the soup into a serving bowl, cover, and chill. Serve with cream.

MAKES 6 SERVINGS

3

Pastries and Coffee Cakes

Cottage Cheese Pastry

Use this lovely, flaky pastry for sweet or savory pies.

1 cup cold, firm butter

2 cups all-purpose flour

1 cup small-curd cottage cheese

1 to 2 tablespoons ice water, if needed

In a large bowl, cut butter into flour until mixture is crumbly and pieces are about the size of peas. Stir in cottage cheese until mixture forms a crumbly dough. Knead lightly to shape into a ball, adding ice water a few drops at a time, if necessary. Chill 30 minutes before rolling out.

MAKES ENOUGH PASTRY FOR A 9-INCH DOUBLE-CRUST PIE

Cream Twists

Not a cookie, bread, or cake, but a favorite pastry, buttered and served warm with coffee.

1 cup sugar

1 egg

1 cup heavy whipping cream

1 cup sour cream

1 teaspoon salt

2 teaspoons baking powder

1 teaspoon vanilla

3½ cups all-purpose flour

In a large bowl, combine sugar, egg, and whipping cream; beat until light and fluffy. Add sour cream, salt, baking powder, and vanilla, and beat again until light and fluffy. Slowly stir in flour, making a stiff dough. Turn out onto a lightly floured board. Knead only long enough to make a smooth ball. Wrap in plastic wrap; refrigerate overnight. Preheat the oven to 450ºF. Lightly grease a large baking sheet; set aside. Turn out dough onto a lightly floured board. Cut into fourths. Refrigerate 3 portions. Cut remaining portion into 12 equal pieces. Roll each piece between your hands to make an 8-inch rope. Shape each into a figure 8. Pinch ends to seal. Arrange shaped dough, 2 inches apart, on prepared baking sheet. Bake 6 to 8 minutes or until lightly browned. Cool slightly. Repeat with remaining dough. Place warm rolls in a container with a tight cover to keep them soft and puffy. Wipe moisture from inside of lid as it gathers, so rolls do not become wet. Freeze, if desired. Serve warm.

MAKES 48 ROLLS

Austrian Carnival Doughnuts ("Krapfen")

Austrians observe the tradition of Fasching, or Carnival, for about two weeks before the beginning of the solemn Lenten season. During this time of merrymaking, they traditionally enjoy rich pastries such as these wonderful jam-filled doughnuts, similar to bismarks. Rather than frying the doughnuts, you can bake them, which results in a different texture and crust.

4 cups all-purpose flour
1 package (2¾ teaspoons) active
    dry yeast
3 tablespoons sugar
1 teaspoon salt
1 cup milk

3 tablespoons butter or vegetable oil
2 eggs
About 6 tablespoons apricot, strawberry,
    or plum jam
Vegetable oil, for deep frying
Powdered sugar, for dusting

In a large bowl with an electric mixer, or in the food processor with the dough blade in place, combine the flour, yeast, sugar, and salt.

Heat the milk in a small saucepan over medium-high heat to scalding; then pour into a bowl and add the butter or oil, whisking until the butter is melted. Whisk in the eggs. Add the liquids to the dry ingredients all at once, and mix or process until the dough is soft, smooth, and satiny. Cover and let rise in a warm place until doubled, about 1 hour.

Cover a large cutting board with a clean, woven tea towel and dust with flour. Turn the dough out onto another lightly floured surface and roll out to ⅓-inch thickness. Using a plain, round cookie or biscuit cutter about 2½ inches in diameter, press the dough lightly just to mark off circles on half the rolled-out dough. From the other half of the dough, cut out the same number of rounds as you've marked. Place 1 teaspoon jam on the center of each of the marked rounds. Place the cut-out round over the jam. With the cutter, cut through the top and bottom rounds, following the top round as a guide, thus sealing the edges and separating the doughnuts. Place the cut-out doughnut on the floured, cloth-covered board. Cover and let rise until doubled, about 30 minutes.

In a large heavy pot or deep fryer, heat the oil to 380°F. Lower the doughnuts into the oil with a slotted spoon and cook about 2 minutes until the bottoms are golden brown. Turn the doughnuts over and cook about 2 minutes longer until the second side is browned. Remove with a slotted spoon and cool on a wire rack placed over paper towels. Dust with powdered sugar.

MAKES ABOUT 18 DOUGHNUTS

Note: Although it isn't traditional, I prefer to bake the krapfen. Preheat the oven to 400°F. Place the filled doughnuts on a parchment-covered or lightly greased baking sheet instead of on the floured, cloth-covered board. Let stand, covered, until doubled, about 30 minutes Bake for 10 to 15 minutes, until golden. Cool on a wire rack. Glaze with Lemon Icing.

LEMON ICING
1 cup powdered sugar
2 tablespoons fresh lemon juice
1 tablespoon butter, at room temperature
Water, if necessary

Stir the powdered sugar, lemon juice, and butter together in a small bowl to make a smooth icing. If necessary, add water 1 teaspoon at a time, and mix until smooth.

Jelly Doughnuts

This recipe is from Marge Portella, who says she makes these every year for her family at Hanukkah.

2 packages (5½ teaspoons) active dry yeast
3½ tablespoons sugar, divided
¾ cup milk, scalded and cooled to warm (105°F to 115°F)
2½ cups all-purpose flour
2 large egg yolks
Pinch of salt
Pinch of cinnamon
1½ tablespoons butter
Vegetable oil, for deep frying
Red fruit jelly, such as raspberry, strawberry, or currant
Sugar, for rolling

In a small bowl, dissolve the yeast and 2 tablespoons of the sugar in the milk. Sift the flour into a large bowl; make a well in the center. Add the yeast mixture, egg yolks, salt, cinnamon, butter, and remaining sugar. Mix until stiff. Turn out onto a floured surface and knead until smooth and elastic, about 5 minutes. Cover and let rise for 1 hour or until doubled.

On a lightly floured surface, roll out the dough to about ½-inch thickness. With a cookie or biscuit cutter, cut into 2-inch rounds. Reroll the scraps and cut additional circles. Cover the rounds and let rise for 15 minutes.

In a deep, heavy saucepan or in a deep fryer, heat the oil to 375°F. Lower the dough-nuts into the oil with a slotted spoon, and cook on one side for 2 minutes; turn over and cook until brown on the second side, about 1 to 2 minutes longer. Remove and drain on several thicknesses of paper towels.

Make a small opening on the top of each doughnut and insert a small spoonful of jelly into the doughnut. Roll in sugar. These are best eaten immediately.

MAKES 30 TO 35 DOUGHNUTS

Yeast-raised Doughnuts

Across the country, but especially in small towns, you're likely to find the locals enjoying "dunkers" and coffee in the morning. To some, dunkers mean yeast-raised doughnuts such as these, but to others they may be Cake Doughnuts, as in the next recipe. Either variety may be dusted with pow-dered sugar, cinnamon sugar, or glazed with a variety of frostings.

1 package (3 teaspoons) active dry yeast	1 egg
¼ cup warm water (105°F to 115°F)	¼ cup melted butter
¼ cup sugar	3 to 3½ cups all-purpose flour
1 teaspoon salt	Vegetable oil for frying
½ teaspoon nutmeg	Powdered sugar, cinnamon sugar, or
1 cup milk, scalded and cooled to	powdered sugar glaze
lukewarm	

In a large mixing bowl, dissolve the yeast in the warm water. Add the sugar and let stand 5 minutes, until the mixture becomes foamy. Add the salt, nutmeg, milk, egg, butter, and 2 cups of flour. Beat by hand until smooth, or use electric mixer and beat at low speed for 3 minutes until satiny. Stir in the remaining flour to form a stiff dough. Cover and let rise in a warm place until doubled, about 1 to 1¼ hours.

Dust work surface with flour. Turn dough onto the surface. With floured hands, pat dough out until it's smooth and an even thickness. With rolling pin, roll out to ½-inch thickness. Cut with floured doughnut cutter and place on a flour-dusted bak-ing sheet in a warm place until light and doubled in size, about 45 minutes.

In a skillet or large saucepan, heat 2 to 3 inches of oil to 375°F. Lift doughnuts into the oil. Fry about 1 minute on each side or until golden brown. Drain on paper towels.

While still warm, dust with sugar or dip in glaze.

MAKES 24 DOUGHNUTS

Long Johns

Roll dough out to make a ½-inch-thick square. Cut into 1½ × 4-inch rectangles. Let rise and fry as directed for doughnuts. Frost with one of the suggested glazes.

Bismarks

Roll dough to ½-inch thick and cut with a 2- or 3-inch cookie cutter (no hole in the center). Let rise and fry as directed for doughnuts. Fit a pastry bag or cake decorating tube with a metal tip with a ¼-inch opening. Fill bag or tube with strawberry or raspberry jelly. Make a hole in the edge of the warm fried bismark with the tip and force the jelly into the center of the bismark; you will be able to squeeze about 1 tablespoon jelly into each. Dust with powdered sugar or frost with vanilla-flavored powdered sugar glaze.

Cake Doughnuts

2¼ cups all-purpose flour
½ cup sugar
1½ teaspoons baking powder
½ teaspoon baking soda
¼ teaspoon salt
¼ teaspoon nutmeg

½ cup buttermilk
2 tablespoons vegetable oil
½ teaspoon vanilla
1 egg, slightly beaten
Vegetable oil for frying
Powdered sugar or cinnamon sugar

In a large mixing bowl, blend the flour, sugar, baking powder, baking soda, salt, and nutmeg. In a measuring cup, blend the buttermilk, vegetable oil, vanilla, and egg. Stir liquid ingredients into the dry ingredients, just until dry ingredients are moistened.

Heat 2 to 3 inches oil in a skillet or saucepan to 375°F.

Dust work surface with flour and turn dough out onto it. Knead lightly until dough is no longer sticky. Roll dough out to about ½-inch thickness. Cut with floured doughnut cutter. With a pancake turner, transfer doughnuts into the oil and fry 1 minute on each side, until golden brown. Drain on paper towels. Dust while warm with powdered sugar or cinnamon sugar.

MAKES 15 DOUGHNUTS

Icelandic Crullers

A favorite coffeebread in Iceland, these are served with morning coffee or afternoon "tea," which turns out also to be coffee. They are a fried bread shaped much like Norwegian fattigman.

4 cups all-purpose flour	⅓ cup sugar
4 teaspoons baking powder	1 egg
1 teaspoon salt	¾ cup milk
2 teaspoons freshly ground cardamom	Vegetable oil for frying
½ cup softened butter	Powdered sugar

In a large bowl, combine the flour, baking powder, salt, and cardamom. Make a well in the center of the dry ingredients and add the butter, sugar, egg, and milk. With a spoon, stir until a dough forms.

Turn dough out onto a floured surface and roll out to ⅛-inch thickness. Cut into strips ¾-inch wide and about 3 inches long to make parallelograms and cut diagonally, using a pastry wheel and a ruler. Make a slit in the center of each cruller and pull one pointed end through the slit.

Heat oil to 375°F. Lower crullers into oil and fry until golden brown, about 1 to 2 minutes on each side. Remove from oil and drain on paper towels. Dust with powdered sugar.

MAKES 48 CRULLERS

Danish Dream Cream Rolls

These rolls are an easy version of Danish pastry, made with a refrigerated dough; they have a creamy vanilla filling in the center.

¼ cup warm water (105°F to 115°F)	¼ cup milk, lukewarm
1 package (3 teaspoons) active dry yeast	3½ cups all-purpose flour
1 tablespoon sugar	¼ cup sugar
3 egg yolks	½ teaspoon salt
1 cup whipping cream	½ cup firm butter

FILLING
2 eggs
3 tablespoons sugar
3 tablespoons all-purpose flour
1 cup milk
1 teaspoon vanilla

GLAZE AND DECORATION
1 slightly beaten egg
1 tablespoon milk
Pearl sugar or crushed sugar cubes
Raspberry jam or strawberry jam

In a small bowl, combine the water, yeast, and 1 tablespoon sugar; stir and let stand a few minutes until the yeast foams. Add the egg yolks, cream, and milk; set aside.

In a large bowl, or in the work bowl of a food processor, combine the flour, sugar, and salt. Slice butter into ¼-inch pieces and add to the flour. With a pastry blender, or with on/off pulses of food processor, blend until butter is in pea-sized pieces. Pour liquid mixture over flour; blend just until flour is moistened. Cover and refrigerate 12 to 24 hours.

To prepare the cream filling, in a bowl, whisk together the eggs and sugar. In a saucepan, whisk together the flour and milk. Heat the milk mixture to simmering, whisking all the time to keep the mixture smooth; cook until thickened and smooth. Whisk a portion of the hot milk mixture into the eggs; then return the entire amount to the saucepan; cook 1 minute longer. Cover and chill thoroughly. Add the vanilla.

Mix the egg and milk together to make a glaze.

Remove dough from the refrigerator. Turn out onto a floured board. With the side of a rolling pin, pound the dough until it is about 1 inch thick. Roll out as thin as possible and fold into thirds. Roll out again to make layers stick together. Fold into thirds again so that the dough makes a fat square.

Pound with the side of a rolling pin again to flatten the dough. Roll out to make a rectangle 15 × 35 inches. Cut into 5-inch squares.

Spoon about 1 tablespoon of the cream filling onto the center of each square. Fold corners toward the centers of the squares, enclosing the filling within the packets.

Cover a baking sheet with parchment paper or lightly grease it. Place the filled squares on the baking sheet. Brush with the glaze and sprinkle with pearl sugar or crushed sugar cubes. Let rise until puffy, 30 to 45 minutes. Preheat the oven to 400ºF. Bake for 15 minutes or until golden. Spoon jam on top of each hot roll.

MAKES 21 ROLLS

Lemon Pastry

This is one of my all-time favorite pastries for pies. The combination of egg and lemon juice makes it tender and flaky.

2 cups all-purpose flour	1 egg, lightly beaten
½ teaspoon salt	2 teaspoons fresh lemon juice
¾ cup chilled butter, cut in ½-inch slices	4 to 5 tablespoons ice water

Stir the flour and salt together. Cut the butter into the flour until the mixture resembles coarse crumbs.

With a fork, stir the egg, lemon juice, and 2 tablespoons of the ice water together. Sprinkle the liquid over the flour mixture and mix just until the pastry holds together, adding more water if needed. Knead the dough in the bowl for 2 or 3 strokes—just until the dough makes a smooth ball. Cover and chill for 30 minutes or until firm, and use as directed in recipes.

MAKES ENOUGH PASTRY FOR 1 DOUBLE-CRUST PIE

Classic Danish Pastry

Known as "Danish" the world over, except in Denmark, where it is "Vienna bread," this is the Danes' classic coffeebread. Light, buttery, only slightly sweet, and delicately perfumed with cardamom, the dough encases a small amount of well-flavored nut or fruit filling. This is the original method of preparing the basic dough; a soft yeasted dough is rolled out with a layer of butter, which when folded and rolled creates layers of flaky sweet pastry. A faster method follows.

1½ cups butter, chilled	½ teaspoon freshly crushed cardamom seed (optional)
2 packages (5½ teaspoons) active dry yeast	½ teaspoon salt
½ cup warm water (105°F to 115°F)	2 eggs, at room temperature
½ cup heavy cream or undiluted evaporated milk, warmed	¼ cup sugar
	3¾ to 4 cups all-purpose flour

Slice butter into lengthwise pieces and place between sheets of plastic wrap. Roll out to make an 8-inch square. Refrigerate while preparing and chilling the yeast dough.

In a large bowl, dissolve the yeast in the warm water. Let stand 5 minutes. Add the cream or milk, cardamom seed if used, salt, eggs, and sugar. With a spoon, beat in 3 cups flour; continue beating until smooth and elastic. Stir in ½ cup more flour and beat again until smooth, about 2 minutes. Dough will be soft. Cover and chill at least 30 minutes or up to 8 hours.

Turn chilled dough out onto a floured board and roll out to make a 16-inch square. Unwrap the chilled butter and place over half the pastry, Step 1. Fold uncovered half over the butter and press edges to seal together, Step 2. Roll dough out to make as large a square as possible, bursting bubbles as they show up and resealing holes. Fold into thirds, making 3 layers, Step 3. Dust with additional flour if necessary. Turn dough and roll again to make a long, narrow shape, Step 4. Fold from the short sides into thirds; dough will end up about square. Repeat rolling out and folding the dough in the same manner 3 more times. Chill between steps if necessary to keep the dough cold and to keep the butter from melting. Chill 30 minutes before shaping. During the last chilling, get out the baking sheets and fillings. (You may prepare the dough to this point a day in advance and finish shaping and filling it the next day.) For filling, shaping, and baking, follow directions in the recipes that follow.

MAKES ABOUT 24 SERVINGS

Quick Method Danish Pastry

Here is a quick method for making Danish. Rather than folding and rolling a layer of butter into a yeast dough, the butter is first cut into the dough as in making pie crust. I like this method of making the dough and refrigerating it overnight. You can get by without the folding and rolling, but I like to do it a couple of times to flatten out the pieces of butter that are mixed into the yeast dough.

3¾ to 4 cups all-purpose flour
1½ cups butter, chilled
2 packages (5½ teaspoons) active
    dry yeast
½ cup warm water (105°F to 115°F)
½ cup heavy cream or undiluted
    evaporated milk

½ teaspoon freshly crushed cardamom
    seed (optional)
½ teaspoon salt
2 eggs, at room temperature
¼ cup sugar

Measure 3½ cups flour into a bowl, or into the work bowl of a food processor with the steel blade in place. Cut the butter into ¼-inch slices and add to the flour. Process or cut the butter into the flour until the butter is about the size of kidney beans.

In a large bowl, dissolve the yeast in the warm water. Let stand 5 minutes. Stir in the cream or milk, cardamom seed, salt, eggs, and sugar.

Turn the flour-butter mixture into the liquid ingredients, and with a rubber spatula mix carefully just until the dry ingredients are moistened. Cover and refrigerate 4 hours, overnight, or up to 4 days.

Turn dough out onto a lightly floured board; dust with flour. Pound and flatten to make a 16- to 20-inch square. Fold into thirds, making 3 layers. Turn dough around and roll out again. Fold from the short sides into thirds. This should result in a perfect square. Repeat folding and rolling again if you wish. Wrap and chill the dough 30 minutes or as long as overnight. For filling, shaping, and baking, follow directions in the recipes that follow.

MAKES ABOUT 24 SERVINGS

Danish Pastry Braid

To make this mock braid, you start out with one batch of the basic Danish Pastry dough. The braid is shaped by slashing the edges of the rolled-out dough, and the resulting strips are folded over the filling.

1 recipe Danish Pastry, Classic or
    Quick Method

BUTTERCREAM FILLING
¼ cup soft butter
1 cup powdered sugar
1 teaspoon almond extract
1 cup pulverized almonds
1 (3-ounce) package almond paste
1 egg white

GLAZE
1 slightly beaten egg
2 tablespoons milk or water
Pearl sugar or crushed sugar cubes for
    topping
Chopped or sliced almonds for topping

ICING
1 cup powdered sugar
2 to 3 teaspoons warm water
½ teaspoon almond extract

Cover baking sheets with parchment paper or lightly grease and dust them with flour.

Divide chilled dough into two parts. Roll out each part to make a rectangle 12 x 16 inches. Place strips on prepared baking sheets.

To make the filling, cream the butter and sugar until light. Blend in the almond extract, almonds, almond paste, and egg white.

Spread filling down the length of the center of the strip. Cut slanting strips at ¾-inch intervals along both sides up toward the center using a fluted pastry wheel. Fold strips over the filling in a crisscross manner.

Preheat the oven to 400°F.

Let rise for 15 to 30 minutes, just until the pastry appears puffy. It will not double. Beat the egg with the milk or water to make a glaze and brush the pastry lightly with it. Sprinkle with sugar and/or chopped almonds.

Bake about 15 minutes or until golden.

Frost, if desired, with almond water icing. Blend the sugar, water, and almond extract until smooth and thin enough to drizzle over the braids.

MAKES 2 FILLED BRAIDS

Danish Birthday Pretzel

I have served this pretzel with birthday candles pressed into the top of the twist. It's perfect for a breakfast birthday party!

1 recipe Danish Pastry, Classic or
   Quick Method

FILLING AND DECORATION
¼ cup soft butter
½ cup powdered sugar
1 cup almond paste
1 cup almonds, pulverized

½ cup raisins or currants
½ teaspoon almond extract
1 egg
1 slightly beaten egg white for brushing
   the pretzel
Granulated or pearl sugar for topping
Chopped almonds for topping

Cover 1 large baking sheet with parchment paper or lightly grease it.

Roll pastry out on a lightly floured surface to make a 12-inch square. Fold into thirds and roll out, stretching it as you are rolling it, to make a 24-inch-long strip. Fold into thirds again lengthwise and roll to flatten the layers together.

To prepare the filling, cream together the butter, powdered sugar, almond paste, pulverized almonds, raisins, almond extract, and egg to make a smooth paste. Spread filling down the length of the strip of dough. Roll up, jelly-roll fashion, from the long side to make a long, narrow roll. Pinch seam to seal.

Continue rolling the strip of dough to stretch it out to about 48 inches in length. Brush all sides of the roll with egg white and roll in sugar and chopped almonds until well coated on all sides.

Place roll on the parchment paper curved like a U, with the ends even. About 5 inches from the ends, loop sides of the U around each other and tuck ends under the closed part of the U to make a simple pretzel shape. Let rise in a warm place for about 40 minutes. It will not double. Preheat the oven to 375°F. Bake for 20 to 30 minutes or until just golden. Do not overbake.

MAKES 1 LARGE PRETZEL, 12 SERVINGS

Danish Envelopes

Envelopes may be made either as a large pastry that can be cut up for serving or as individual pastries.

1 recipe Danish Pastry, Classic or Quick Method

FILLING AND DECORATION
1 cup raspberry or apricot preserves
½ cup almond paste
1 slightly beaten egg
Powdered sugar

Cover 2 large baking sheets with parchment paper or lightly grease them. Roll pastry out on a lightly floured surface to make a 20-inch square. For large pastries, cut into 4 equal squares. Place on baking sheets.

Mix the preserves and almond paste until blended. Spoon ¼ of the mixture across the center of each of the squares. Fold over 2 opposite corners to partially cover the filling, and pinch together to fasten. Place 2 envelopes, 4 inches apart, on each prepared baking sheet. Let rise in a cool place for 30 to 45 minutes or cover with plastic wrap and refrigerate overnight.

Preheat oven to 375°F. Brush pastries with beaten egg. Bake 20 to 25 minutes or until puffed and golden. Sprinkle with powdered sugar and serve warm.

For individual pastries, cut rolled-out dough into 4-inch squares. Dot each square with the mixture of preserves and almond paste. Fold 2 opposite corners of each square over to partially cover the filling. Place on prepared baking sheets 2 inches apart.

Let rise in a cool place for 30 to 45 minutes, or cover with plastic wrap and refrigerate overnight. Bake at 375°F for 8 to 10 minutes until golden. Sprinkle with powdered sugar and serve warm.

MAKES 4 LARGE PASTRIES OR 25 INDIVIDUAL PASTRIES

Danish Pecan Snails

Snails are usually filled with almond paste or a cinnamon and sugar mixture. Pecans are a Danish American invention. And a good one!

1 recipe Danish Pastry, Classic or
   Quick Method

1 teaspoon cinnamon
1 slightly beaten egg

FILLING
½ cup softened butter
1 cup light or dark brown sugar, packed
1 cup finely chopped pecans

ICING
1 cup powdered sugar
3 to 4 teaspoons hot coffee

Place paper cupcake liners in 24 muffin cups.

Roll the pastry out on a lightly floured surface to make a 20-inch square. Spread with the butter. Sprinkle with the brown sugar, pecans, and cinnamon.

Roll up jelly-roll fashion. Cut into 24 slices. Place slices with cut side up into each of the muffin cups.

Let rise in a cool place for 30 to 45 minutes, or cover with plastic wrap and refrigerate overnight.

Preheat the oven to 375°F. Brush pastries with beaten egg. Bake 20 to 25 minutes or until puffed and golden.

Mix the powdered sugar with the coffee. Drizzle the icing over the hot pastries. Serve warm.

MAKES 24 SNAILS

Danish Bearclaws or Cockscombs

These pastries have many names. Sometimes they're called "scrubbing brushes." Scandinavian Americans are more likely to call these "bearclaws," but some Danes insist that they look like the comb on a rooster!

1 recipe Danish Pastry, Classic or
   Quick Method

FILLING AND DECORATION
1 egg white
½ cup almond paste

¾ cup powdered sugar
1 slightly beaten egg
Pearl sugar or crushed sugar cubes for
   topping
Sliced almonds for topping

Cover 2 large baking sheets with parchment paper or lightly grease and flour them.

On a lightly floured surface, roll the chilled pastry out to make an 18 × 16-inch rectangle. Cut lengthwise into 4 strips.

In a small bowl, beat the egg white, add the almond paste and powdered sugar, and mix until smooth and blended.

Spread about 2 tablespoons filling down the center of each strip. Fold strips lengthwise to enclose the filling. Roll lightly to flatten and seal the edges. Cut each strip into 4-inch lengths. Make 7 cuts on each of the 4-inch lengths, cutting from the sealed edge toward the center. Place pieces on the prepared baking sheets, curving them slightly to separate the slits.

Let rise in a cool place until puffy, or cover with plastic wrap and refrigerate overnight.

To bake, preheat the oven to 400ºF. Brush pastries with beaten egg; then sprinkle generously with sugar and almonds. Bake 5 to 8 minutes or until golden. Remove from baking sheets and cool on wire rack. Serve warm.

MAKES 16 BEARCLAWS

Danish Fruit-filled Packets

These may be shaped and filled as individual pastries or as larger ones that are cut into individual servings.

**1 recipe Danish Pastry, Classic or
    Quick Method**

FILLING
1 cup dried apricots or dried prunes
2/3 cup water
1/3 cup sugar

1 slightly beaten egg
Sliced almonds

ICING
1/2 cup powdered sugar
2 1/2 teaspoons milk

In small saucepan, simmer the apricots or prunes in the water for 30 minutes, covered, until soft. Cool, mash or chop the fruit, add the sugar, and chill.

Cover 2 large baking sheets with parchment paper or lightly grease them. Preheat the oven to 375°F.

For 4 large pastries, roll pastry out on lightly floured surface to an 18-inch square. Cut into 4 squares. Place 2 squares on each prepared baking sheet. Roll again lightly to bring the squares back to a 9-inch width.

Place 1/4 of the filling on the top of each square. Fold the corners toward the center and press down well. Brush with egg. Sprinkle with sliced almonds. Let rise for 15 to 30 minutes until puffy. Bake for 15 to 20 minutes or until golden.

To make the icing, mix powdered sugar and milk until smooth. Drizzle the icing over the hot pastries.

To serve, cut pastries into 4 quarters.

For 25 individual pastries, roll pastry out on lightly floured surface to make a 20-inch square. Cut into 4-inch squares. Dot the center of each square with filling. Fold in the corners of each toward the center and press down well. Place on the prepared baking sheets. Brush with egg and sprinkle with sliced almonds. Let rise 15 to 30 minutes until puffy. Bake 8 to 10 minutes or until just golden. Drizzle the icing over the hot pastries.

MAKES 4 LARGE PASTRIES OR 25 SMALL PASTRIES

Finnish Blueberry Squares

In the summertime, when Finns spend a month or so at their summer cottages, they enjoy picking wild blueberries. This yeast-crusted blueberry pie is eaten for breakfast and with morning coffee.

1 package (3 teaspoons) active dry yeast
¼ cup warm water (105°F to 115°F)
1 egg
½ cup sugar
1 teaspoon salt
½ cup milk, scalded and cooled to
    lukewarm

½ cup softened or melted butter
3¼ cups unbleached all-purpose flour

TOPPING
4 cups fresh blueberries or frozen un-
    sugared blueberries
1 cup sugar
1 tablespoon cornstarch

In a large bowl, dissolve the yeast in the warm water. Let stand 5 minutes. Add the egg, sugar, salt, and milk. Stir in the butter and 2 cups of the flour. Beat until smooth. Add the remaining flour and beat again until the dough is stiff but smooth. Cover and let rise in a warm place until doubled, about 1 to 3 hours.

Preheat the oven to 400°F. Grease a 15 × 10-inch jelly-roll pan and dust with flour. Dump dough from bowl onto the prepared pan. With flour-dusted hands, press dough into the pan to line it evenly, pressing it enough so that it extends about 2 inches over the edges of the pan.

In a bowl, combine the blueberries and half the sugar with the cornstarch. Pour mixture onto the dough-lined pan in an even layer. Lift extended dough edges up over the berries to partially cover the berries, making an uneven edge.

Let rise 30 minutes. Preheat the oven to 400°F. Bake for 20 to 25 minutes or until crust is golden and filling is bubbly. Serve from the pan cut into squares.

MAKES ONE 15 × 10-INCH OPEN-FACED PIE, 12–16 SERVINGS

Buttery Berry Squares

The blueberry is favored for this special pastry. However, you may also use lingonberries, strawberries mixed with chopped rhubarb, or chopped apples.

2½ cups all-purpose flour
½ teaspoon baking powder
½ cup sugar
1 cup softened butter
1 egg
1 tablespoon lemon juice

FILLING AND TOPPING
2 cups fresh blueberries, lingonberries, or a mixture of sliced strawberries and chopped rhubarb, or diced fresh apple
4 tablespoons sugar (more if using tart fruit)
Grated rind of 1 lemon
Lemon juice to taste
2 tablespoons cornstarch
4 tablespoons sugar for topping

Preheat the oven to 375°F. Lightly grease and flour a 15 × 11-inch jelly-roll pan.

In a food processor or a large bowl, combine the flour, baking powder, and sugar. Blend in the butter with a pastry blender or use on/off pulses of the food processor until the mixture resembles coarse crumbs. Combine the egg and the lemon juice. Add to the crumbly mixture, tossing to blend evenly, until dough will hold together. Chill 30 minutes, if necessary.

Reserve about 1/3 of the dough. Roll the remaining dough out to fit the jelly-roll pan, covering the bottom and sides evenly. (This is a rather rich and crumbly dough, but just press to patch the pieces together in the pan.)

Combine the berries, sugar, lemon juice and rind, and cornstarch. Mix to blend well. Turn mixture into the pan and spread out evenly.

Roll out reserved dough and cut into strips. Place strips in a crisscross fashion over the filling, sealing strips to the edges. Sprinkle the top with additional 4 tablespoons of sugar.

Bake for 25 to 30 minutes or until the crust is a light golden brown. Cut into squares to serve.

MAKES ONE 15 × 11-INCH PAN

Pennsylvania Dutch Apfelstrudel

Fruit-enclosed pastries are natural to the Pennsylvania Dutch. Apfelstrudel in its original form is made with a thinly stretched dough filled with a mixture of apples, sugar, and spices. Raisins, nuts, chopped candied citron, or cherries are sometimes added to the strudel. To stretch the strudel dough, it is helpful to have at least two extra sets of hands (invite your friends to a "strudel stretch").

PASTRY
3 cups all-purpose flour
2 eggs
½ teaspoon salt
3 tablespoons oil
¾ cup warm water
½ cup plus 1 tablespoon melted butter
Toasted bread crumbs or cinnamon sugar

APPLE FILLING
10 large tart apples, pared, cored, and
    sliced
2 tablespoons lemon juice
1 cup sugar
2 teaspoons cinnamon
Nutmeg

To prepare pastry, put flour into a large bowl and make a well in the center. Combine the eggs, salt, oil, and water. Whip mixture with a fork until blended, and pour into the well of flour. Stir until a soft dough forms. Pick up the dough with one hand and slap it into the bowl or onto a breadboard about 100 times, or until it becomes very elastic and is no longer wet and sticky but leaves the board and your hands clean. The dough is very sticky in the beginning, but as you work with it, it becomes less sticky. Let dough rest for 5 to 10 minutes.

Cover a table with a clean tablecloth or sheet (a round table about 5 feet in diameter is ideal). Dust lightly with flour. Dust the ball of dough with flour, and place it in the center of the cloth. Roll out the dough with a rolling pin to make a circle about 20 inches in diameter.

Starting with one person stretching the dough, reach under the dough with palms up. Turn hands sideways making fists of your hands, and very slowly rotate fists outward under the dough to stretch it. When it is about 24 inches in diameter, set the dough back onto the cloth.

At this point, it is helpful to have several sets of hands working. Very carefully, hands under the dough with palms up and fingers straight out (not curved upward), stretch the dough evenly and very slowly from the center outward. Keep pulling evenly in all directions until it is tissue-thin and almost transparent. It should be about as thin as the membrane of an egg. The dough should be 4 to 5 feet in diameter. A thick edge will remain; cut it away with a knife and save it for making noodles.

Preheat the oven to 400ºF.

Brush dough all over with ½ cup melted butter and sprinkle with toasted bread crumbs or cinnamon sugar.

To make the filling, put the apple slices in a mixing bowl. Sprinkle with the lemon juice, sugar, cinnamon, and a dash of nutmeg. Toss lightly.

Sprinkle filling over ⅔ of the dough, leaving ⅓ free (this will be the end of the roll). Fold the 2 sides perpendicular to the free end about 4 or 5 inches over the filling, to hold it in the ends when the strudel is rolled.

Starting with the filled end, gently lift the cloth to roll the strudel, rolling toward the empty end. Place the roll on a buttered baking sheet, bending it into a horseshoe or wreath shape. Brush it with about 1 tablespoon melted butter, and bake for 35 to 45 minutes or until golden brown.

MAKES 10 TO 12 SERVINGS

For cherry filling

Combine two 16-ounce cans drained, pitted sweet cherries with ½ cup sugar, 1 cup raisins, 1 cup finely chopped toasted almonds, 1 teaspoon grated lemon peel, and 1 teaspoon cinnamon. Mix well.

Apple Strudel Squares

The ever-present apple has brought out the apple cookery and bakery of the cooks of every country that has settled in the United States. Some classics have evolved over the years into desserts that are a bit easier to make than the original. This is a strudel that is made with a flaky pastry that lines a jelly-roll pan, with a filling not unlike the classic apple pie.

PASTRY
3 cups all-purpose flour
1 teaspoon salt
1 cup chilled butter

½ cup water
1 egg
1 tablespoon cider vinegar

FILLING

3 pounds (about 11 or 12 medium to large)
    tart cooking apples
2 cups sugar
6 tablespoons all-purpose flour
2 teaspoons cinnamon
¼ teaspoon salt

½ cup chopped pecans
¼ cup butter

GLAZE

2 tablespoons melted butter
1 cup powdered sugar
½ teaspoon vanilla
Milk

Preheat the oven to 375°F.

Mix 3 cups flour with 1 teaspoon salt in a large bowl. Cut in the butter until it is about the size of peas. Combine the water, egg, and vinegar. Add to the flour mixture and mix with a fork until the dough holds together in a ball. Divide the dough in half.

Roll out half the dough and fit onto an ungreased 11 × 17-inch jelly-roll pan.

Pare, core, and slice the apples, and arrange over the crust in the pan. Combine the sugar, flour, cinnamon, and salt. Sprinkle mixture over the apples. Sprinkle with the nuts. Dot with butter. Roll out the remaining dough. Place over the top of the apples. Seal the edges. Make several slits on top, and bake 1 hour or until golden.

To prepare the glaze, combine the melted butter, the powdered sugar, vanilla, and enough milk to make a thin glaze. Drizzle over the warm pastry.

MAKES 16 SERVINGS

....

Kolaches

....

The coffee break on a Midwestern farm often is accompanied by this Bohemian pastry, which may have a filling of poppy seeds, cream cheese, berries, or fruit and is served warm from the oven, dribbled with a thin powdered-sugar frosting.

PASTRY

1 (8-ounce) package cream cheese
1 cup butter, at room temperature
2 cups all-purpose flour

POPPY-SEED FILLING

½ cup poppy seeds, ground
⅓ cup sour cream or sweet cream
1 tablespoon butter
1 tablespoon honey
¼ cup chopped almonds

1 teaspoon grated lemon rind
1 tablespoon candied orange peel
¼ cup golden raisins
2 tablespoons sugar
1 tablespoon cornstarch
2 tablespoons red currant jelly

1 egg, beaten with 2 tablespoons milk
2 tablespoons granulated sugar
1 cup powdered sugar
2 tablespoons hot water or coffee
¼ teaspoon vanilla

In a bowl, cut the cream cheese into the butter and flour until the mixture forms a stiff pastry. Chill 3 hours or overnight.

To make the poppy-seed filling, combine all the ingredients in a 2-quart saucepan. Stir over medium heat until mixture comes to a boil. Boil 1 minute. Cool.

Preheat the oven to 400°F.

Roll dough out to ⅛-inch thickness, and cut into 18 squares. Divide filling between the squares. Lift 2 opposite corners up over the filling to make a packet, with the other 2 ends open. Press to seal. Place on a lightly greased baking sheet. Brush with egg-and-milk mixture and sprinkle with granulated sugar. Repeat until all of the *kolaches* have been filled. Bake 10 to 13 minutes or until golden.

Combine the powdered sugar, water or coffee, and vanilla. Drizzle over the warm *kolaches*.

MAKES 18 KOLACHES

For apple filling

Pare, core, and slice 4 medium tart apples. Heat ¼ cup butter in a frying pan and add apples. Sauté over medium heat until tender-crisp, about 5 minutes. Sprinkle with ½ cup sugar and cool. Add ½ teaspoon cinnamon.

New Orleans Beignets

These are the favorite deep-fried doughnuts served at the Café du Monde near the New Orleans French Market. These should be served with espresso or café au lait.

2 tablespoons vegetable shortening
¼ cup granulated sugar
¼ teaspoon salt
½ cup boiling water
½ cup undiluted evaporated milk
1 package (3 teaspoons) active dry yeast

¼ cup warm water (105°F to 115°F)
1 egg
3¾ cups all-purpose flour
Vegetable oil for frying
Powdered sugar

In a large mixing bowl, blend the shortening with the granulated sugar, salt, and boiling water. Add the milk and cool to lukewarm. Dissolve the yeast in the warm water, and add the sugar mixture to the yeast mixture. Stir in the egg and 3 cups flour. Beat until very smooth. Stir in enough of the remaining flour to make a soft dough. Place in a greased bowl, and turn to grease the top of the dough. Cover and refrigerate 2 to 4 hours.

Roll chilled dough, a small portion at a time, to ¼-inch thickness; cut into 2-inch squares. Do not allow to rise before frying. Fry in oil heated to 370ºF to 375ºF. Brown on one side for 2 minutes; turn and brown the other side 1 minute. Drain. Dust with powdered sugar and serve hot.

MAKES ABOUT 4 DOZEN DOUGHNUTS

Dutch Fruit Fritters

Apples are the fruit used most often, but bananas, peaches, or other fruits that are in season can be made into fritters.

Corn or peanut oil for frying
1 cup all-purpose flour
1 teaspoon baking powder
½ teaspoon salt
¼ teaspoon nutmeg

2 tablespoons granulated sugar
2 eggs
⅓ cup milk
Sliced apples, bananas, and/or peaches
Powdered sugar

Begin heating oil to 375ºF.

In a mixing bowl, combine the flour, baking powder, salt, nutmeg, and granulated sugar. Add eggs and milk. Beat with whisk until smooth. Dip fruit into batter and drop into hot oil. Fry about 3 minutes, turning once during that time, until golden. Drain, and sprinkle with powdered sugar. Serve hot.

MAKES ABOUT 18 FRITTERS

Orange Date Nut Cake

We often have drop-in guests, and it is our custom to serve coffee and something to go with it. This is the perfect cake for the occasion. It's great to take along on a picnic, too.

1½ cups sugar, divided
¾ cup butter, at room temperature
2 eggs, beaten
2 teaspoons grated orange zest
2½ cups all-purpose flour
1 teaspoon baking powder

1 teaspoon baking soda
1 cup chopped pitted dates
1 cup chopped walnuts
1 cup buttermilk
1 cup fresh orange juice

Preheat the oven to 350°F. Butter a 13 × 9-inch baking pan or a 10-inch fluted tube pan.

In a large mixing bowl, cream ¾ cup of the sugar and the butter together until smooth. Add the eggs and beat until light. Stir in the orange zest. In another bowl, mix the flour, baking powder, and baking soda together. Put the dates and walnuts into another small bowl and mix with 1 tablespoon of the flour mixture. Add the flour mixture and buttermilk alternately to the creamed mixture and beat until batter is light. Fold in the dates and nuts. Turn the batter into the prepared pan.

Bake for 35 to 40 minutes for the 13 × 9-inch cake, or 55 to 60 minutes for the tube pan, or until a wooden skewer inserted into the center of the cake comes out clean.

Meanwhile, combine the orange juice and the remaining sugar in a small saucepan. Heat to simmering over medium heat; pour simmering syrup over the hot cake when you take it out of the oven.

Cool the cake in the pan on a wire rack. Invert the tube cake onto a serving plate or cut squares from the 13 × 9-inch cake.

MAKES ABOUT 16 SERVINGS

Blueberry Cream Cheese Coffee Cake

Remember this coffee cake when you want to serve something extra special for brunch on a summer morning. The buttery crust encases a cream cheese layer with fresh blueberries and an almond streusel topping baked into it.

2¼ cups all-purpose flour
1 cup sugar, divided
¾ cup butter, at room temperature
1½ teaspoons baking powder
¼ teaspoon salt
¾ cup sour cream

2 large eggs
1 teaspoon almond extract
1 (8-ounce) package cream cheese, at
  room temperature
2 cups fresh blueberries
½ cup slivered almonds

Preheat the oven to 350°F. Lightly grease the bottom and sides of a 10-inch spring-form pan and dust with flour.

In a large mixing bowl, mix the flour and ¾ cup of the sugar. With a pastry blender or fork, cut in the butter until the mixture resembles coarse crumbs. Reserve 1 cup of the mixture.

Add the baking powder, salt, sour cream, 1 of the eggs, and the almond extract to the remaining flour mixture. Mix until a stiff dough forms. Press the dough over the bottom and 2 inches up the sides of the pan; it will be about ¼ inch thick on the sides.

In a small bowl, with an electric mixer, beat the cream cheese, remaining ¼ cup sugar, and remaining egg until well blended. Pour the mixture over the dough in the pan and spread evenly. Arrange the blueberries over the top. Mix the almonds with the reserved crumb mixture and sprinkle over the blueberries.

Bake for 50 to 55 minutes or until the filling is set and the crust is golden brown. Cool 15 minutes; then remove sides of the pan and finish cooling. Serve warm.

MAKES 12 TO 16 SERVINGS

Autumn Fruit Kuchen

When plums, nectarines, peaches, pears, and apples are in season, this is one of my favorite coffee cakes to bake. Serve it hot out of the oven for breakfast, brunch, coffee break, or dessert. The kuchen batter is a cross between a pastry and a cake. Tender and delicious, it is made without leavening. Kuchen is the German word for "cake," but we have come to know it as a yeast-risen fruit- or cheese-filled cake that is often served for breakfast.

½ cup butter, at room temperature
½ cup sugar
3 eggs

½ teaspoon vanilla
1 cup all-purpose flour
⅛ teaspoon salt

FRUIT TOPPING

14 to 16 purple plums, halved and pitted; or 3 large apples, peeled, cored, and cut into 1-inch-thick slices; or 3 large pears, peeled, cored, and thickly sliced; or 3 large ripe nectarines or peaches, peeled, pitted, and thickly sliced

¼ cup sugar

1 tablespoon butter, cut into tiny pieces

Preheat the oven to 375ºF. Butter and flour an 11-inch round tart pan with a removable bottom or a 9-inch square cake pan.

In a large bowl, cream the butter with the sugar until smooth; beat in the eggs until light and fluffy. Stir in the vanilla, flour, and salt. Spread the batter evenly in the prepared pan.

Press the fruit evenly into the batter, sprinkle with the sugar, and dot with the butter.

Bake for 40 minutes or until a wooden skewer inserted in the center of the cake comes out clean. Serve warm or cool on a wire rack. Serve with a topping of slightly sweetened whipped cream, if desired. The kuchen can also be frozen, well wrapped. Thaw and reheat in a 300ºF oven for 10 to 15 minutes.

MAKES 12 SERVINGS

Norwegian Coffeebread

Cardamom-perfumed, this cake brings back memories of Norway to those who have visited there. It is often cut into slices, spread with butter, sugar, and jam, or topped with nøkkelost, a favorite Norwegian cheese that is spiced with cloves. Or the bread may be topped with thin shavings of caramel-colored gjetost, another favorite Norwegian cheese. Gjetost is a sweet-tasting cheese made by slowly boiling off the liquid from the whey left from the manufacture of butter and cheese. The traditional version of gjetost was made entirely of goat's milk whey. Today, however, most of the gjetost exported from Norway is made largely of cow's milk whey with just a small percentage of goat's milk whey.

2 packages (5½ teaspoons) active
   dry yeast
½ cup warm water (105°F to 115°F)
1½ cups milk, scalded and cooled
   to lukewarm, or 1 (12-ounce) can
   undiluted evaporated milk
¼ cup sugar

½ teaspoon salt
1 teaspoon freshly ground cardamom
3 tablespoons softened or melted butter
4 to 4½ cups unbleached all-purpose
   flour
Melted butter to brush on loaves

In a large bowl, dissolve the yeast in the warm water. Let stand 5 minutes. Stir in the milk, sugar, salt, cardamom, and butter.

Stir in 3 cups of the flour and beat batter until glossy. Stir in 1 cup more flour. Let stand 15 minutes, covered.

Turn dough out onto a floured surface. Clean the bowl, lightly oil it, and set aside.

Knead dough until it is smooth and glossy, about 10 minutes. Place in the oiled bowl, turn over to oil the top of the dough, cover, and let rise in a warm place until doubled, about 1 hour.

Lightly oil a work surface. Turn dough out onto it and divide into 2 equal parts. Shape into smooth round loaves.

Dust baking sheets with flour (do not grease them), or cover with parchment paper. Place loaves on the baking sheets with the smooth sides up. Let rise in a warm place until almost doubled.

Preheat the oven to 375°F. Brush loaves with melted butter. Bake for 30 to 35 minutes or until golden and loaves sound hollow when tapped. Brush again with butter and cool on racks.

MAKES 2 ROUND LOAVES

Cardamom Coffeebread

Although this bread is the basic yeast coffeebread of all Scandinavia, the name I give it is Finnish because of my own bias. The Swedes call it vetebröd, *Norwegians call it* hvetebröd, *the Danes call it* hvedebrød, *and the Icelandics call it* hveitibraud. *All of these names mean "wheat bread."*

The Finns who settled in the United States in the early 1900s brought this recipe with them. At that time, the Finnish word for wheat was nisu *rather than* vehnä, *the modern name. (The Finnish language has been "Finnicized" since the early part of this century, and all words that were too "Swedish" such as* nisu *have been changed to more correct Finnish, which for wheat is "vehna.") But many American Finns still call this bread "nisu," and the debates become heated! Where I grew up, we called this bread "biscuit." Saturday was the day we baked biscuit so that it would be fresh for Sunday morning's coffee. My Finnish aunt, Ida Luoma, who was born and raised in Finland and emigrated to become the wife of my uncle Edward in 1930, adamantly explains that "biscuit" is totally wrong. She says, "Ei se ole biskit-tiä, se on pulla!" (It isn't biscuit, it is pulla!) The name pulla arises from the Swedish bollar, which is translated as "bun." But pulla is most often shaped into a braided loaf. All very confusing!*

2 packages (5½ teaspoons) active
   dry yeast
½ cup warm water (105°F to 115°F)
1 teaspoon sugar
1½ cups (12-ounce can) undiluted
   evaporated milk
½ to 1 cup sugar
2 teaspoons salt

1½ teaspoons ground cardamom or seeds
   of 12 cardamom pods, crushed
4 eggs, at room temperature
7 to 8 cups all-purpose flour
½ cup melted butter

GLAZE
1 slightly beaten egg
2 tablespoons milk

In a large bowl, dissolve the yeast in the warm water; add 1 teaspoon sugar, stir, and let stand for 5 minutes until yeast foams. Empty the milk into a pan and warm just to between 105°F and 115°F. Add the milk, sugar according to sweetness desired, salt, cardamom, eggs, and half the flour to the yeast mixture. Beat with an electric mixer or spoon until dough is smooth and shiny. Beat in the melted butter. Add remaining flour 1 cup at a time until dough is stiff but not dry. Cover and let rest for 15 minutes. Turn out onto a lightly floured surface and knead until satiny and smooth, about 10 minutes. Wash bowl, lightly oil it, and add dough to bowl, turning to oil the top of the dough. Cover and let rise in a warm place until doubled, about 1 to 1½ hours. Turn risen dough out onto a work surface and divide into 3 portions.

Then divide each portion into 3 parts. Roll out to make strands about 24 inches long. Make 3 braids, using 3 strands each. Place on lightly greased baking sheets. Cover and let rise until doubled, about 1 hour.

Preheat the oven to 375°F. Mix egg and milk to make a glaze and brush braids with the mixture. Bake for 20 to 25 minutes or until golden, or until a wooden skewer inserted in the center comes out clean.

MAKES 3 LOAVES

Danish Butter Crown

To make this pastry like bread, you need a tube pan 10 to 12 inches in diameter.

1¼ cups chilled butter

3 cups all-purpose flour

2 packages (5½ teaspoons) active
    dry yeast

¼ cup warm water (105°F to 115°F)

½ cup milk, at room temperature

½ teaspoon freshly crushed cardamom
    seed

2 eggs, at room temperature

1 teaspoon salt

¼ cup sugar

FILLING AND DECORATION

½ cup sugar

½ cup butter, at room temperature

½ cup almond paste

1 teaspoon almond extract

½ cup sliced almonds

Powdered sugar

Cut butter into ¼-inch slices; add to flour in work bowl of food processor with metal blade in place. Process using on/off pulses until butter is the size of kidney beans; or with a fork or pastry blender, cut butter into flour.

Turn mixture into a large bowl and chill. Measure yeast into a bowl. Add warm water; let stand 5 minutes. Add milk, cardamom, eggs, salt, and sugar and mix well. Pour liquid mixture over flour-butter mixture and fold together carefully just until flour is moistened. Cover and refrigerate 4 hours to overnight.

Turn dough out onto lightly floured surface; dust with flour. Pound and flatten to a 20-inch square. Fold dough into thirds. Turn dough so short side faces you. Roll dough out a little and fold into thirds again. (Chill dough if necessary.)

To prepare filling, cream the sugar, butter, almond paste, and almond extract until blended. Spread dough with the filling and roll up. Cut into 8 equal slices.

Butter 10-inch bundt pan or fancy tube pan. Sprinkle bottom of pan with sliced almonds. Place dough slices cut side down into the pan, spacing them evenly.

Let rise until almost doubled. Preheat the oven to 375ºF. Bake for 45 to 55 minutes or until golden. Dust with powdered sugar and serve warm.

MAKES 1 COFFEE CAKE

Icelandic Coffee Wreath

The Icelandics have a practical and down-to-earth approach to all of their cooking and baking, but they are exceptionally skilled at making wonderful things to go with coffee.

2 packages (5½ teaspoons) active
    dry yeast
½ cup warm water (105°F to 115°F)
1 egg
¼ cup butter
⅓ cup sugar
¼ teaspoon salt
⅓ cup sour cream
2½ to 3 cups unbleached all-purpose flour

FILLING
1 cup almond paste
1 egg
2 tablespoons sugar
1 tablespoon cinnamon
1 teaspoon vanilla
½ cup raisins
1 tablespoon grated orange peel

GLAZE
1 slightly beaten egg
2 tablespoons milk
Pearl sugar or crushed sugar cubes

In a large bowl, dissolve the yeast in the water and let stand 5 minutes. Add the egg, butter, sugar, salt, and sour cream. Beat in 2 to 2 ½ cups of the flour to make a stiff dough. Cover and let rise in a warm place until doubled, about 1 hour.

Sprinkle the surface with remaining flour. Turn dough out onto surface and roll out to make a square about 20 to 24 inches across.

To make the filling, blend the almond paste, egg, sugar, cinnamon, and vanilla. Spread this mixture over the rolled-out dough to within ½ inch of the edge of the dough. Sprinkle with the raisins and orange peel. Roll dough up, jelly-roll fashion, enclosing the filling.

Cover a baking sheet or a 16-inch pizza pan with parchment paper or lightly grease it. Place roll on the pan in the shape of a wreath and seal ends together. With a pair of scissors, clip the wreath and lift the cut dough back over the wreath decoratively. Let rise 1 hour or until puffy. Preheat oven to 400°F.

To make glaze, mix the beaten egg well with the 2 tablespoons milk. Brush wreath with the mixture and sprinkle with the pearl sugar. Bake for 20 to 30 minutes or until golden.

MAKES 1 COFFEE RING

Swedish Tea Ring

More likely to be served with coffee than with tea, this cinnamon-and-cardamom-flavored bread baked in a wreath shape is a classic. The refrigerator yeast dough is my own invention. It is a no-knead dough that produces a light-textured yeast bread.

2 packages (5½ teaspoons) active dry yeast
1 cup warm water (105°F to 115°F)
½ cup melted butter
½ cup sugar
3 slightly beaten eggs
1 teaspoon salt
1 teaspoon ground cardamom (optional)
4 to 4½ cups all-purpose flour

½ cup softened butter
½ cup sugar
1 tablespoon cinnamon
1 cup blanched almonds, finely chopped (optional)

GLAZE
1 cup powdered sugar
2 tablespoons hot coffee or milk
½ teaspoon almond extract

In a large bowl, dissolve the yeast in the warm water and let stand 5 minutes. Stir in the ½ cup melted butter, ½ cup sugar, the eggs, salt, cardamom, and 4 cups of flour until the dough is smooth. Cover and refrigerate 2 to 24 hours.

Turn dough onto a floured surface and roll out to make a 20- to 24-inch square. Spread with a thin layer of softened butter right to the edge. Mix ½ cup sugar and the cinnamon and sprinkle over the butter. Sprinkle the almonds over the cinnamon sugar. Roll up as for a jelly roll.

Grease a baking sheet and place the roll on the sheet, shaping it into a ring. Pinch ends together to close the circle. With scissors, cut almost through the ring at ½-inch intervals. Turn each piece so that the cut side is exposed. Let rise until almost doubled.

Preheat the oven to 375ºF. Bake for 15 to 20 minutes or until just golden. While ring bakes, mix the glaze ingredients. Brush while hot with the glaze.

MAKES 1 LARGE RING

Sister's Coffee Cake

"Sister's cake" is sometimes translated as "nun's cake," a translation that is a bit misleading. A better translation of sister might be "deaconess," the Lutheran equivalent of nun. Although I have found a cake by this name in every Scandinavian country, there has been no consistency as to what the cake is actually like. The only similarity they have with each other is that they are all made with good ingredients and make wonderful eating! This variety is from Norway and the cake is made of cinnamon rolls baked side by side in a pan.

2 packages (5½ teaspoons) active
    dry yeast
1 cup warm water (105°F to 115°F)
½ cup melted butter
½ cup sugar
3 slightly beaten eggs
1 teaspoon salt
4½ to 5 cups all-purpose flour

FILLING
½ cup softened butter
½ cup brown sugar, packed
1 tablespoon cinnamon

GLAZE
1 slightly beaten egg
2 tablespoons milk

In a large bowl, dissolve the yeast in the warm water and let stand 5 minutes. Stir in the melted butter, sugar, eggs, salt, and 4½ cups flour until dough is smooth. Cover and refrigerate 2 to 24 hours.

Turn dough out onto a floured surface and roll out to make a 24-inch square. Spread with a thin layer of soft butter right to the edge. Mix the brown sugar and cinnamon, and sprinkle mixture over the butter. Roll up as for a jelly roll.

Grease two 9-inch square pans or 10-inch tube pans. Cut the roll into 2-inch pieces and place them cut sides up in the pans evenly spaced, dividing the cut rolls between the two pans.

Let rise, covered, until almost doubled, about 45 minutes to 1 hour. Mix the egg and milk to make a glaze and brush the tops of each cake with the glaze.

Preheat oven to 375ºF. Bake for 30 to 35 minutes or until a skewer inserted in the center comes out clean. Let stand 5 minutes in pan before unmolding. Serve warm.

MAKE 2 COFFEE CAKES

Boston Cake

The Scandinavians seem to think that this cake is traditional to Boston. But a Bostonian might not recognize it any more than an Austrian would recognize Wienerbrød.

1 package (3 teaspoons) active dry yeast
¼ cup warm water (105°F to 115°F)
¼ cup milk
2 eggs
⅓ cup sugar
½ teaspoon salt

¼ cup softened butter
2 to 2½ cups unbleached all-purpose flour

FILLING
¼ cup softened butter
½ cup sugar
1 tablespoon cinnamon

In a large bowl, dissolve the yeast in the warm water; add the milk, eggs, sugar, salt, and butter. Beat in the flour until the dough is smooth and satiny. Cover and let rise in a warm place until doubled, about 1 hour.

Dust dough in bowl lightly with flour and gather into a ball. Turn out on a lightly floured surface and pat out to make a 14-inch square. Spread with soft butter. Combine the sugar and cinnamon and sprinkle over the butter. Roll up jelly-roll fashion.

Butter a 12-cup ring mold or bundt pan. Cut dough into 8 equal pieces. Place each cut piece with cut side down into the pan, spacing them evenly.

Cover and let rise until almost doubled. Preheat the oven to 375ºF and bake 25 to 30 minutes or until golden. Invert onto serving plate.

MAKES 1 COFFEE CAKE

Finnish Coffeebread "Pizza"

This old-fashioned quick and delicious coffeebread has been made by Finnish bakers for generations! The "pizza" part is my own idea because that's just how this coffee cake is made. The yeast dough is rolled out on a baking sheet, the toppings go on, it rises a bit and is baked. Saturday is usually baking day in a Finnish household. Often a Finnish homemaker will take a portion of the pulla dough and roll it out, spread it with toppings, and bake it for morning coffee. This recipe is perfect for a large crowd or coffee open house. It freezes well cut into squares and stacked in plastic containers ready to reheat and serve.

2 packages (5½ teaspoons) active
    dry yeast
½ cup warm water (105°F to 115°F)
1 egg
½ cup sugar
1 teaspoon salt
1 cup milk, scalded and cooled to
    lukewarm
¼ cup softened or melted butter
4 cups unbleached all-purpose flour

TOPPING AND DECORATION
1 cup blanched almonds
¾ cup sugar
¾ cup softened butter
½ cup all-purpose flour
1 cup sliced or slivered almonds
1 cup powdered sugar
2 tablespoons milk

In a large bowl, dissolve the yeast in the warm water. Let stand 5 minutes. Add the egg, sugar, salt, and milk. Stir in the butter and 2 cups of the flour. Beat until smooth. Add the remaining flour and beat again until smooth. Cover and let rise in a warm place until doubled, about 1 hour.

To prepare the topping, grind the blanched almonds in a food chopper with a fine blade, or place in a food processor with steel blade in place. Process until pulverized. Add the sugar, butter, and flour and process until mixture is a smooth paste.

Preheat the oven to 400ºF. Grease two 17 × 14-inch baking sheets. Divide dough into 2 parts and place each on a baking sheet. Pat out to rectangle 16 × 12 inches. Spread each with half the topping mixture. Sprinkle with additional sliced or slivered almonds. Bake for 20 minutes or until crust is golden. Remove from oven and drizzle with icing made by mixing the powdered sugar and milk together. Serve immediately.

MAKES 2 COFFEE CAKES

Norwegian Cinnamon Wreath

A rich, buttery dough is rolled up, filled with cinnamon and sugar, and made into a wreath. The wreath is slashed only about ½ inch into the bread, just enough to expose a layer or two of cinnamon filling.

2 packages (5½ teaspoons) active dry yeast
1 cup warm water (105°F to 115°F)
½ cup melted butter
½ cup sugar
3 slightly beaten eggs
1 teaspoon salt
1 teaspoon ground cardamom (optional)
4½ to 5 cups all-purpose flour

FILLING
½ cup softened butter
½ cup sugar
1 tablespoon cinnamon
1 cup dark raisins

GLAZE
1 egg
2 tablespoons milk

In a large bowl, dissolve the yeast in the warm water; let stand 5 minutes. Stir in the melted butter, sugar, eggs, salt, cardamom, and 4½ cups flour until the dough is smooth. Cover and refrigerate 2 to 24 hours.

Turn dough out onto a floured surface and roll out to make a 20-inch square. Spread with a thin layer of softened butter right to the edge. Mix sugar and cinnamon and sprinkle over the butter. Sprinkle the raisins over the cinnamon sugar. Roll up as for a jelly roll.

Cover a baking sheet with parchment paper or lightly grease it. Place the roll on the sheet and pinch the ends together to make a ring.

Let rise in a warm place until almost doubled. Mix egg and milk to make a glaze and brush ring with the mixture.

Preheat the oven to 375°F.

With a sharp knife, make diagonal cuts spaced about 2½ inches apart, about ½ inch into the risen loaf.

Bake for 15 to 20 minutes or until just golden.

MAKES 1 LARGE RING

Streusel Raspberry Coffee Cake

This is a delicate, buttery cake with raspberries and a crunchy streusel topping.

1½ cups all-purpose flour
½ cup sugar
2 teaspoons baking powder
1 egg
½ cup melted butter
½ cup milk
1 cup fresh or frozen whole unsweetened
    raspberries

STREUSEL TOPPING
¼ cup chopped pecans
¼ cup brown sugar, packed
¼ cup all-purpose flour
2 tablespoons melted butter

Preheat the oven to 375°F. Butter a 9-inch square cake pan.

In a large bowl, stir together the flour, sugar, and baking powder. In a small bowl, mix the egg, butter, and milk. Stir the liquids into the dry ingredients just until blended. Spoon half the mixture into the prepared pan. Top with the raspberries and then spoon the remaining dough over them.

In another bowl, combine the pecans, brown sugar, and flour. Stir in the melted butter until the mixture resembles moist crumbs. Sprinkle it over the top of the dough in the pan.

Bake for 25 to 30 minutes or until the topping is golden.

MAKES ONE 9-INCH SQUARE CAKE

Walnut Pear Coffee Cake

Chunks of pear are moist bits atop a sour cream coffee cake. The top is crisp with a crumbly brown sugar and nut layer.

¼ cup butter, at room temperature
½ cup sugar
½ teaspoon vanilla
1 egg
1 cup all-purpose flour
½ teaspoon baking powder
½ teaspoon baking soda
¼ teaspoon salt
½ cup sour cream
1 large ripe Bose or red Bartlett pear,
    peeled and cut into ½-inch cubes

CRISP TOPPING

¼ cup brown sugar, packed

¼ cup all-purpose flour

1 teaspoon cinnamon

2 tablespoons softened butter

½ cup chopped walnuts

Preheat the oven to 350°F. Butter a 9-inch springform or square baking pan.

Cream the butter and sugar until blended; beat in the vanilla and egg until light. In a separate bowl, stir the flour, baking powder, soda, and salt together and add to the creamed mixture along with the sour cream, blending well. Spread the batter in the prepared pan and sprinkle the pears over evenly, pressing them into the batter slightly.

Mix the topping ingredients together until blended and crumbly, and sprinkle over the pears.

Bake for 45 to 50 minutes or until the top is browned and it tests done. Cool and cut into squares.

MAKES ONE 9-INCH ROUND OR SQUARE CAKE

....

Apple Pie Coffee Cake

....

Topped with sautéed apple slices, this cake is heavenly with morning coffee or even for dessert, served with a pouf of whipped cream.

1¼ cups all-purpose flour

½ cup sugar

1 teaspoon baking powder

¼ teaspoon baking soda

¼ teaspoon salt

1 teaspoon cinnamon

½ cup butter, at room temperature

½ cup milk

1 egg

1 teaspoon vanilla

TOPPING

½ cup all-purpose flour

½ cup plus 2 tablespoons sugar

3 tablespoons butter

2 cups sliced tart apple (2 medium)

1½ teaspoons cinnamon

¼ teaspoon ground nutmeg

Preheat the oven to 350°F. Grease and flour a 9-inch springform or square baking pan.

Combine the flour, sugar, baking powder, soda, salt, and cinnamon together in a large bowl. With an electric mixer, blend in the butter until the mixture is crumbly. In another bowl, mix the milk, egg, and vanilla until blended and stir into the flour mixture until the batter is well mixed. Turn into the prepared baking pan and spread evenly.

For the topping, combine the flour, ½ cup of the sugar, and 2 tablespoons of the butter until the mixture looks like coarse crumbs. Sprinkle half of the mixture over the batter in the pan.

In a heavy skillet, melt the remaining 1 tablespoon of butter and add the apple slices; sauté for 2 to 3 minutes on high heat, just until the apples are cooked, stirring constantly. Sprinkle the 2 tablespoons of sugar over them and add the cinnamon and nutmeg. Spread the mixture over the crumbs in the pan. Top with the remaining crumbs. Bake for 1 hour or until the top is golden brown. Remove from the oven and cool for 10 minutes. If using a springform pan, loosen the cake by running a knife around the inside edge of the pan. Remove the ring and finish cooling on a rack with the bottom of the pan still in place.

MAKES ONE 9-INCH ROUND OR SQUARE CAKE

Sour Cream Cinnamon Coffee Cake

Bake this coffee cake in a fancy tube pan such as a bundt pan or kugelhof pan. The cinnamon and nut layer running through the center and covering the top of the cake makes it extra special.

1 cup butter, at room temperature
1 cup sugar
2 eggs
1 cup sour cream, stirred
2 cups all-purpose flour
1½ teaspoons baking powder

½ teaspoon baking soda
1 teaspoon vanilla

FILLING AND TOPPING
¾ cup finely chopped walnuts or pecans
1 teaspoon cinnamon
2 tablespoons sugar

Preheat the oven to 350°F. Butter and flour a 9- or 10-inch fancy tube pan or bundt cake pan.

In a large mixing bowl, beat the butter, sugar, and eggs together until light and fluffy. Blend in the sour cream. In another bowl, combine the flour, baking powder, and soda, and add to the creamed mixture, beating until blended. Add the vanilla. Spoon half the batter into the prepared pan.

For the filling and topping, mix the nuts, cinnamon, and sugar until blended. Sprinkle half the mixture over the batter in the pan. Top with the remaining batter and then the remainder of the nut mixture.

Bake for 45 to 55 minutes or until it tests done. Let cool for 10 minutes; then remove from the pan.

MAKES ONE 10-INCH BUNDT CAKE

Whole Wheat Coffee Cake

Light, not too sweet, and grainy, this coffee cake is best served warm. However, you can bake it and freeze it if you wish.

1 egg
½ cup sugar
½ cup milk
3 tablespoons melted butter
1½ cups whole wheat flour
1½ teaspoons baking powder
½ teaspoon salt

TOPPING
½ cup brown sugar, packed
¼ cup whole wheat flour
¼ cup finely chopped walnuts
3 tablespoons softened butter
1 teaspoon cinnamon

Preheat the oven to 375°F. Grease an 8-inch square cake pan.

In a mixing bowl, beat the egg with the sugar, milk, and butter until light. Stir in the flour, baking powder, and salt, blending well. Turn the mixture into the cake pan.

Stir the topping ingredients together until the mixture is crumbly. Sprinkle the crumbs over the top of the cake. Bake for 20 to 25 minutes or until it tests done and the crumbs are golden brown.

MAKES ONE 8-INCH SQUARE CAKE

Cinnamon Nut Sour Cream Coffee Cake

Quick-to-mix coffee cakes are country favorites. They may be baked in a fancy bundt pan or in an oblong 13 × 9-inch baking pan.

1 cup softened butter

1 cup sugar

2 eggs

1 cup sour cream

2 cups all-purpose flour

1½ teaspoons baking powder

½ teaspoon baking soda

1 teaspoon vanilla

¾ cup chopped walnuts or pecans

1 teaspoon cinnamon

2 tablespoons brown sugar

Preheat oven to 350ºF. Generously grease and flour either a 13 × 9-inch baking pan or a 10-inch bundt pan. In a large bowl, beat the butter and sugar until smooth and light. Add the eggs and beat until light. Blend in the sour cream. In a medium bowl, combine the flour, baking powder and soda. Stir into the egg mixture along with the vanilla. Spoon half of the batter into the prepared pan. In a small bowl, combine the nuts, cinnamon, and brown sugar. Sprinkle half of the nut mixture over batter in the pan. Top with the second half of batter. Sprinkle with the remaining nut mixture. Bake 45 to 55 minutes or until a wooden skewer inserted in the center comes out clean. Cool on a rack 5 minutes. Turn out of pan. Serve warm.

MAKES 10 TO 12 SERVINGS

Pennsylvania Dutch Streusel Coffee Cake

In place of nut mixture, blend together 1 cup packed brown sugar, ¼ cup all-purpose flour, 2 tablespoons cinnamon, ¼ cup melted butter, and 1 cup chopped walnuts or pecans. Use in the same way as nut mixture. Bake as above.

Blueberry Buckle

Omit nut mixture. Turn entire batter into a greased 13 × 9-inch baking pan. Sprinkle with 2 cups fresh or unthawed frozen blueberries. Combine ¾ cup sugar, ½ cup all-purpose flour, ½ teaspoon cinnamon, and ⅓ cup softened butter. Sprinkle over blueberries before baking. Bake as above.

Pineapple Coffee Cake

Omit nut mixture. Turn entire batter into a greased 13 × 9-inch baking pan. Spread top of batter with a mixture of ½ cup softened butter, ½ cup honey, and 1 cup well-drained crushed pineapple.

Pecan Butter Coffee Cake

This is so easy to make, and your guests won't believe it is low in fat too, thanks to the "magic of yeast." The yeast batter is quick to mix, and you spoon it out onto a pecan and butter mixture in the pan.

TOPPING
3 tablespoons butter
3 tablespoons chopped pecans
½ cup sugar
2 tablespoons dark corn syrup
½ teaspoon vanilla

YEAST BATTER
2¼ cups all-purpose flour
¼ cup sugar
1 tablespoon butter, at room temperature
1 teaspoon salt
1 package (3 teaspoons) active dry or
   rapid-rise yeast
¾ cup very warm water (120°F to 130°F)
1 large egg, lightly beaten

Coat a 9-inch square pan with nonstick spray.

Combine the butter, pecans, sugar, and corn syrup in a small saucepan. Heat over medium-low heat and stir until the sugar is dissolved. Remove from the heat and stir in the vanilla. Pour the pecan mixture into the pan.

In a mixing bowl, combine 1¼ cups of the flour, the sugar, butter, salt, and yeast. With an electric mixer, mix 15 seconds, or until the ingredients are blended. Pour in the water and add the egg; mix at medium speed, scraping the sides of the bowl, until the batter is smooth and elastic. Stir in the remaining flour until the mixture is smooth. Spoon the batter into the pan over the pecan mixture. Cover and let rise in a warm place for 45 minutes to 1 hour or until doubled.

Preheat the oven to 375ºF.

Bake the coffee cake for 30 to 35 minutes or until golden brown. Immediately invert the coffee cake onto a heatproof serving plate. Let the pan remain a minute or so over the coffee cake so that the topping can drizzle down over its sides.

MAKES 12 SERVINGS

Maple Pecan Coffee Cake

¾ cup well-packed light or dark brown
   sugar
¼ cup maple syrup
⅓ cup butter, at room temperature

¾ cup coarsely chopped pecans
1 teaspoon vanilla
½ recipe Basic Whole Wheat Refrigerator
   Dough (page 113)

In a small bowl, cream together the brown sugar, maple syrup, and butter. Add the pecans and vanilla. Spread mixture over the bottom of a well-buttered 9-inch round cake pan. Divide dough into 32 equal pieces. (Cut into quarters; cut each quarter into quarters, then cut each piece in half to equal 32 pieces.) Shape each into a smooth ball. Set balls on the pecan mixture in 1 layer, leaving a little space around each. Cover with plastic wrap and let rise in a warm place for 1 to 1½ hours or until doubled. Preheat oven to 350°F. Bake for 25 to 30 minutes. Cool in pan 5 minutes; then invert onto serving dish.

MAKES ONE 9-INCH ROUND COFFEE CAKE

4

Breakfast Breads

Hätäleipä

Hätä means "emergency" in Finnish, and leipä translates to "bread." It's quick to make and delicious to eat. Finns make it when they have run out of ordinary rye bread, because it is so easy to prepare. With just a hint of molasses, the bread has a grainy flavor of coarse rye flour. To serve it, cut the loaf into wedges, then split the wedges. It is wonderful for open-faced sandwiches!

1 package (3 teaspoons) active dry yeast
1 cup warm water (105°F to 115°F)
2 tablespoons light or dark molasses
1 tablespoon oil, melted lard, bacon
    drippings, or melted butter

1 teaspoon salt
½ cup dark or light rye flour
1½ cups bread flour or unbleached all-
    purpose flour
Melted butter to brush top of loaf

In a large bowl, dissolve the yeast in the warm water, add molasses, and then let stand 3 to 5 minutes until yeast foams. Stir in oil, salt, and rye flour. Stir in bread flour; then beat 50 times. Cover a baking sheet with parchment paper or grease generously. Turn the dough out onto the sheet, spreading it into a circle about 8 inches in diameter. Let rise 30 minutes. Preheat the oven to 400°F. Bake for 20 minutes or until center of loaf springs back when touched. Brush the top with melted butter. Serve hot, cut into wedges and split horizontally.

MAKES 1 LOAF, ABOUT 9 INCHES IN DIAMETER

Cornmeal Oat English Muffin Bread

Basically a batter bread, this can be baked in a casserole. However, because the texture of the bread is open, it is ideal for slicing and toasting.

2 packages (5½ teaspoons) active
    dry yeast
2 cups warm water (105°F to 115°F)
½ cup shortening or lard, softened
1 tablespoon sugar
2 teaspoons salt

½ cup yellow cornmeal, preferably stone
    ground
1 cup rolled oats
4 cups bread flour or unbleached all-
    purpose flour
Additional rolled oats to coat loaves

In a large bowl, dissolve the yeast in the warm water. Let stand 5 minutes until yeast foams. Add shortening, sugar, salt, cornmeal, oats, and 1 cup of the bread flour; beat until smooth. Gradually add remaining flour to make a stiff dough, beating well after each addition. Lightly oil a working surface (bread board or clean countertop), and turn dough out onto it. Divide dough into 3 portions. Shape each into a smooth, round ball; then roll each in additional oats to coat evenly. Place into 3 well-greased baking pans. Let rise in a warm place for 50 to 60 minutes or until doubled. Preheat the oven to 350°F. Bake for 40 to 45 minutes or until golden. Remove from pans immediately, and cool on rack. To serve, cut into slices crosswise and toast.

MAKES THREE 5 X 3-INCH LOAVES

Cornmeal Raisin Casserole Bread

The crunchiness of cornmeal, rich flavor of molasses, and chewiness of golden raisins are an irresistible combination in a yeast bread. This bread has a crusty coarseness and is excellent sliced while still warm. You can serve it plain or slathered with butter and a dollop of homemade fruit jelly or jam.

1 cup milk
1 cup water
1 cup yellow cornmeal
3 tablespoons butter
½ cup light (unsulfured) molasses
½ cup warm water (105°F to 115°F)

2 packages (5½ teaspoons) active
   dry yeast
1 teaspoon sugar
2 teaspoons salt
5½ to 6 cups bread flour or unbleached
   all-purpose flour
1 cup golden raisins

In a large saucepan, bring the milk and water to a boil. Remove from heat and add the cornmeal, stirring with a whisk until smooth. Add butter and molasses, and stir until no lumps remain. Cool to lukewarm. In a large bowl, mix the warm water and yeast. Add sugar. Let stand 5 minutes until yeast foams. Add cornmeal mixture, salt, and about half the flour. The batter should be thick, but still soft enough to beat. Beat for 5 minutes with an electric mixer. With a spoon, stir in the raisins and gradually add more flour, stirring until the batter is very stiff. When flour is moistened, cover and let rise until doubled, about 1 hour. Stir down. Divide dough between 2 buttered 9-inch round pans or casseroles, or two buttered 9 × 5-inch loaf pans. Smooth tops of loaves. Cover and let rise in a warm place 45 minutes to 1 hour, until batter reaches tops of the pans. Preheat the oven to 350°F. Bake for 40 to 50 minutes, until loaves sound hollow when tapped. Remove from pans and cool on wire rack.

MAKES 2 LOAVES

Raisin Pumpernickel

Studded with raisins, this compact rye and wheat bread is excellent thinly sliced and topped with a thin slice of cheese, corned beef, or ham. It slices best the day after baking.

2 cups hot water

2 cups nonfat dry milk

4 cups dark seedless raisins

2 packages (5½ teaspoons) active
    dry yeast

½ cup warm water (105°F to 115°F)

2 tablespoons honey

2 tablespoons melted butter or
    vegetable oil

2 teaspoons salt

1½ tablespoons caraway seeds

1 cup unprocessed bran

2 cups medium rye flour or dark rye flour

3 cups whole wheat flour

1 to 1½ cups bread flour or all-purpose flour

GLAZE

1 egg white beaten with 2 tablespoons
    water

Coarse salt

In a large bowl, combine the hot water, dry milk, and raisins. In a small bowl, dissolve the yeast in the warm water; add honey and set aside until yeast foams, about 5 minutes. Add the melted butter, salt, caraway seeds, and bran to the raisin mixture. Add the rye flour, yeast mixture, and 1 cup of the whole wheat flour. Beat until smooth. Slowly add remaining whole wheat flour. Add enough bread flour to make a stiff dough. Cover and let rest 15 minutes. Turn out onto a lightly floured surface and knead, adding more flour as necessary to keep dough from sticking. Knead until smooth, about 10 minutes;* dough may be slightly sticky. Wash bowl, lightly oil it, and add dough to bowl. Turn over to oil the top of the dough, cover, and let rise 1 hour until doubled. Punch down and divide dough into 3 parts. Shape each into a strand about 20 inches long. Braid the strands. Cover the baking sheet with parchment paper or lightly grease it. Place the braid in a tight spiral on prepared sheet. Cover and let rise until about doubled, about 45 minutes. Brush with egg white glaze and sprinkle with coarse salt. Preheat the oven to 350°F. Bake for 55 to 60 minutes or until skewer inserted in the center comes out clean. Cool on rack.

MAKES 1 LARGE LOAF

* Kneading by hand in this recipe can be broken by "resting" periods to make the job easier.

Old-fashioned Oatmeal Bread

Oats give this loaf a nutty flavor. Try it toasted for breakfast with cheese and homemade jam.

⅔ cup old-fashioned rolled oats
2 cups boiling water
½ cup nonfat dry milk
½ cup light brown sugar, tightly packed
½ cup butter or vegetable oil

1 teaspoon salt
1 package (3 teaspoons) active dry yeast
¼ cup warm water (105°F to 115°F)
1 teaspoon sugar
5 to 5½ cups unbleached all-purpose flour

In a large bowl, mix oats and boiling water; stir and let stand 30 minutes. Add dry milk, brown sugar, butter, and salt. In custard cup, dissolve yeast in warm water; add sugar and let stand 5 minutes until yeast foams. When oat mixture has cooled to 105°F to 115°F, add yeast. Stir in all-purpose flour slowly to make a stiff dough. Let rest 15 minutes. Turn out onto lightly floured surface and knead for 10 minutes until dough is smooth and satiny. Wash bowl, oil it, and add dough to bowl. Turn to oil top of dough. Cover and let rise for 1 hour or until doubled. Punch down, divide in half. Shape into loaves. Grease two 8½ × 4½-inch loaf pans. Place shaped dough into pans. Cover and let rise until almost doubled, about 45 minutes. Heat the oven to 375°F. Bake until loaves are golden and sound hollow when tapped, 25 to 30 minutes. Remove immediately from pans and let cool on rack.

MAKES 2 MEDIUM LOAVES

Winter Morning Oatmeal Bread

Steamy oatmeal porridge is one of my family's favorite breakfasts through-out the chilly season. I like to cook an oversupply and use what is left to make yeast bread. This bread is great for toasting, for sandwiches, and for quick meals during the school year. You can use any amount of leftover cooked cereal, from 1 to 3 cupfuls, in this recipe. It is simple to calculate the amount of additional liquid you need in the recipe. If you remember that when you cook oatmeal for breakfast, the formula is 1 part rolled oats to

2 parts water, you know, then, that ⅔ of each cup of leftover cereal can be counted as liquid in the recipe.

2 packages (5½ teaspoons) active
    dry yeast
½ cup warm water (105°F to 115°F)
¼ cup dark or light brown sugar
2 tablespoons melted butter or
    shortening, or oil
1 teaspoon salt
1 to 3 cups cooked oatmeal, cooled to
    105°F to 115°F

Warm water (105°F to 115°F) (1⅓ cups if
    you use 1 cup oatmeal, ⅔ cup water if
    you use 2 cups oatmeal, no additional
    water if you use 3 cups oatmeal)
½ cup additional rolled oats
4 to 5 cups bread flour or unbleached all-
    purpose flour
Honey to brush on tops of loaves
Rolled oats to sprinkle on top of loaves

In large bowl, dissolve the yeast in the warm water; add the brown sugar and let stand 5 minutes until yeast foams. Stir in the butter, salt, oatmeal, and warm water. Whisk until blended. Add the rolled oats and bread flour, 1 cup at a time, beating well to keep mixture smooth, until a stiff dough forms. Let rest 15 minutes. Turn out onto lightly floured surface and knead until smooth and elastic, about 10 minutes. Wash bowl, oil it, and add dough to the bowl; turn over to oil the top lightly, and cover. Let rise in a warm place until doubled. Punch dough down, divide in half, and shape into 2 loaves. Place into 2 greased 8½ × 4½-inch loaf pans and let rise until doubled. Preheat the oven to 375°F. Bake for 30 to 35 minutes or until loaves sound hollow when tapped. Brush hot loaves with honey and sprinkle with rolled oats. Return to oven for 5 minutes or until tops are dry and oats are lightly toasted. Cool on rack.

MAKES 2 LOAVES

Sesame Oat Cinnamon Swirl Loaf

These spicy loaves, rich with cinnamon and sesame seeds, are ideal for a Sunday brunch or afternoon tea. Try this treat toasted on a gray winter morning and see if it doesn't lift your spirits.

1½ cups boiling water
1 cup rolled oats, quick or old-fashioned
½ cup sesame seeds
1 package (3 teaspoons) active dry yeast

½ cup warm water (105°F to 115°F)
½ cup tightly packed dark brown sugar
¼ cup melted butter or margarine
2 teaspoons salt

½ cup whole wheat flour

4 to 4½ cups unbleached all-purpose
   flour

1 tablespoon ground cinnamon

In a large bowl, combine boiling water and rolled oats. Place sesame seeds in small fry pan. Toast over medium heat, stirring frequently, until seeds are golden, 3 to 5 minutes. Stir seeds into the oat mixture. In a separate bowl, dissolve the yeast in the warm water; add brown sugar, and let stand 5 minutes until yeast bubbles. Stir in the butter, salt, and cooled oat mixture. Add the whole wheat flour and beat in the all-purpose flour until mixture makes a stiff dough. Let rest 15 minutes. Turn out onto a lightly floured surface and knead for 10 minutes, until smooth and satiny. Wash bowl, oil it, and add dough to bowl; turn over to oil the top of the dough. Cover and let rise until doubled, about 1 hour. Punch dough down and divide in half. Roll each out to make a rectangle 8 × 12 inches; sprinkle each half with half the cinnamon. Roll up tightly. Seal seams and ends. Grease two 8½ × 4½-inch loaf pans. Place loaves into pans. Let rise until doubled, about 45 minutes to 1 hour. Heat the oven to 375ºF. Bake until loaves are golden and sound hollow when tapped, 30 to 35 minutes. Remove immediately from pans. Cool on wire racks.

MAKES 2 MEDIUM LOAVES

Country Raisin Molasses Oat Loaf

For the busy baker, this refrigerator method is the handiest! This crusty, moist, round loaf rises in the refrigerator—and you shape it into a loaf just after you have mixed the dough.

1 package (3 teaspoons) active dry yeast

1 cup warm water (105°F to 115°F)

2 tablespoons light (unsulfured) molasses

1 egg, slightly beaten

1 tablespoon melted butter or margarine

1 teaspoon salt

½ cup dark raisins

¾ cup rolled oats, quick or old-fashioned

½ cup whole wheat flour

2 to 2½ cups unbleached all-purpose flour

1 egg white

Rolled oats for the top

In large bowl, dissolve the yeast in the warm water; let stand 5 minutes until yeast bubbles. Add molasses, egg, butter, salt, raisins, and rolled oats. Stir in the whole wheat flour. Slowly add the all-purpose flour to make a stiff dough. When dough is stiff, let rest 15 minutes. Turn out onto a lightly floured surface and knead until smooth and elastic, 5 to 8 minutes. Cover baking sheet with parchment paper or grease it lightly. Shape dough into a circle about 8 inches in diameter. Cover tightly with plastic wrap and let stand at room temperature about 20 minutes. Refrigerate for 8 to 24 hours. Uncover dough and let stand at room temperature 30 minutes. Heat the oven to 375ºF. Beat egg white with a fork until foamy. Spread beaten white over bread dough and sprinkle with oats. Bake until evenly browned, 30 to 35 minutes. Remove from baking sheet and cool on wire rack.

MAKES 1 LOAF

Wheat Monkey Bread

This pull-apart loaf is easy to serve.

1 cup milk

¼ cup warm water (110°F)

1 package (3 teaspoons) active dry yeast

2 tablespoons sugar

1½ teaspoons salt

2 tablespoons butter, at room
    temperature

2 eggs

1½ cups whole wheat flour

2 to 2½ cups unbleached all-purpose flour

½ cup melted butter

1 cup wheat germ

Generously butter a 2-quart casserole. In a small saucepan, heat milk until bubbles form around edge of the pan. Remove from heat; cool to 110ºF or until a few drops on your wrist feel warm. Pour the warm water into a large bowl; stir in the yeast and sugar until dissolved. Let stand until foamy, about 5 minutes. Stir in salt, cooled milk, butter, eggs, and whole wheat flour; beat well. Gradually add all-purpose flour, beating to keep mixture smooth. Add enough all-purpose flour to give a stiff dough. Let dough rest 15 minutes. Turn out dough onto a lightly floured surface. Clean and butter bowl. Knead dough 10 minutes or until smooth and satiny, adding all-purpose flour as necessary to keep dough from sticking. Place dough in the buttered bowl, turning to coat all sides. Cover and let rise in a warm place until doubled in size, about 1 hour. Turn out dough onto a lightly oiled surface. Divide dough into quarters. Divide each quarter into quarters to make 16 pieces. Divide each piece into 2 parts, making a total of 32 pieces. Place melted butter and wheat germ in 2 separate small dishes. Roll each piece of dough in melted butter, then in wheat germ. Place dough pieces in even layers in buttered casserole. Cover and let rise in a warm place until doubled in size, 45 minutes to 1 hour. Preheat the oven to 375ºF. Bake for 35 to 45 minutes or until a skewer inserted in center comes out clean. Cool in casserole 5 minutes. Invert onto a serving dish. Pull apart pieces to serve.

MAKES 32 PULL-APART ROLLS

Custard Corn Bake

Try this with maple syrup poured over each serving.

3 eggs

4 cups milk

1 teaspoon salt

1 cup yellow cornmeal

2 teaspoons baking powder

1 tablespoon sugar

2 tablespoons vegetable oil

Preheat the oven to 375ºF. Butter a deep 2-quart casserole. In a large bowl, beat eggs, milk, and salt. In another large bowl, mix cornmeal, baking powder, and sugar. Stir oil and ½ of egg mixture into cornmeal mixture until blended. Turn into the buttered casserole. Pour remaining egg mixture over mixture in the casserole. Bake, uncovered, stirring 3 times during the first 15 minutes. Bake 45 minutes longer or until top is golden and crust has formed.

MAKES 6 SERVINGS

Cinnamon Bubble Bread

As delicious as cinnamon rolls, but quicker to prepare.

1 cup milk

1 cup warm water (110°F)

2 packages (5½ teaspoons) active
    dry yeast

2 tablespoons sugar

2 teaspoons salt

2 tablespoons melted butter

4½ cups all-purpose flour

½ cup melted butter

½ cup sugar

1 tablespoon cinnamon

Generously butter a deep 2-quart casserole. In a small saucepan, heat milk until bubbles form around edge of the pan. Remove from heat; cool to 110ºF or until a few drops on your wrist feel warm. Pour the warm water into a large bowl; stir in yeast and 2 tablespoons sugar until dissolved. Let stand until foamy, about 5 minutes. Add salt, cooled milk, 2 tablespoons butter, and 1 cup of the flour; beat until smooth. Gradually beat in the remaining flour to make a stiff, satiny, smooth dough. Cover and let rise in a warm place until doubled in size, about 45 minutes. Turn out dough onto a lightly oiled surface. Divide dough into quarters. Divide each quarter into quarters to make 16 pieces. Divide each piece into 2 parts, making a total of 32 pieces. Place ½ cup melted butter in a small dish. In another small dish, mix ½ cup sugar and cinnamon. Roll each piece of dough in melted butter, then in cinnamon sugar. Place dough pieces in even layers in buttered casserole. Cover and let rise in a warm place until doubled in size, about 45 minutes. Preheat the oven to 375°F. Bake for 35 to 45 minutes or until browned and a skewer inserted in the center comes out clean. Cool in casserole 5 minutes. Invert onto a serving dish. Pull apart pieces to serve.

MAKES 32 PULL-APART ROLLS

Cinnamon Sally Lunn

A cake-like bread created by Sally Lunn in eighteenth-century Bath, England.

2 packages (5½ teaspoons) active
   dry yeast
¼ cup sugar
5 cups unbleached all-purpose flour
1½ teaspoons salt

2 cups hot milk (125°F)
2 eggs, slightly beaten
⅓ cup melted butter
Cinnamon

In the large bowl of an electric mixer, combine yeast, sugar, 2 cups flour, and salt. Add hot milk; beat at high speed with electric mixer until mixture is smooth and satiny. Add eggs, butter, and remaining flour; beat with mixer until smooth. If batter is too stiff for mixer, beat 100 strokes by hand using a wooden spoon. Cover and let rise in a warm place until doubled in size, about 1 hour. Generously butter a deep 2½-quart casserole or 10-inch tube pan. Generously sprinkle inside with cinnamon so entire surface is dusted. Stir down batter. Turn into prepared casserole. Let rise in a warm place until batter is within 1 inch of top of the pan, about 45 minutes. Preheat the oven to 350°F. Bake for 45 minutes or until bread sounds hollow when tapped with your fingers. Turn bread out of casserole and serve hot.

MAKES 1 LARGE LOAF

Quick Sally Lunn

This yeast-risen coffee cake probably originated in Bath, England, where a woman named Sally Lunn sold tea cakes in the eighteenth century. This quick version is leavened with baking powder instead of yeast.

½ cup butter, at room temperature
⅓ cup sugar
3 eggs, at room temperature
2 cups all-purpose flour

3 teaspoons baking powder
½ teaspoon salt
1 cup milk, at room temperature

Preheat the oven to 425°F. Lightly grease a 10-inch tube pan.

In a large bowl, cream the butter with the sugar until blended. Beat in the eggs until light.

In another bowl, stir together the flour, baking powder, and salt. Add half the dry ingredients to the creamed ingredients alternately with half the milk; then repeat. Stir until the ingredients are just blended. Turn into the prepared pan and bake for 45 to 50 minutes, or until it tests done. Serve while still hot, separating the cake into thick wedges with two forks.

MAKES ONE 10-INCH TUBE BREAD

Coconut Granola Bread

This makes a tightly textured but very tasty bread that's great cut into thin slices for breakfast as well as for tea or coffee breaks. I use low-fat granola, which you can find in the cereal section of the supermarket.

1 package (3 teaspoons) active dry yeast
1 cup warm water (105°F)
1 teaspoon sugar
3 tablespoons instant nonfat dry milk
½ cup honey
¼ cup shredded coconut

¼ cup chopped dates
1 teaspoon salt
2 large egg whites
½ cup whole wheat flour
1 cup low-fat granola cereal
2½ cups bread flour

In a large bowl, dissolve the yeast in the warm water and add the sugar. Stir and let stand for 5 minutes, until the yeast begins to bubble. Add the dry milk, honey, coconut, dates, salt, egg whites, whole wheat flour, and granola cereal. Stir until well mixed.

Stir in bread flour gradually until the dough is stiff but still sticky. Cover the bowl and let the dough stand for 15 minutes.

Turn the dough out onto a lightly floured surface. Shape into a ball and knead for 5 to 6 minutes. Wash the bowl and oil it. Place the ball of dough in the oiled bowl and turn the dough over to oil the top. Cover and let rise in a warm place until doubled, 1½ to 2 hours.

Cover a baking sheet with parchment paper or coat with nonstick spray. Punch the dough down and turn out onto a lightly floured surface. Shape into a fat loaf. Place the loaf with the smooth side up onto the center of the baking sheet. With a sharp knife, score the top of the loaf. Cover and let rise in a warm place for about 1 hour, or until almost doubled.

Preheat the oven to 350°F.

Bake the bread for 45 minutes or until a wooden skewer inserted into the center of the loaf comes out clean and dry. Remove from the pan and cool on a wire rack.

MAKES 1 LOAF (16 SLICES)

Milk and Honey Bread

A basic versatile bread, great for toasting, sandwiches, or to serve with any meal. Shape it into an oblong loaf and bake it in a standard bread pan, or shape it into a round, a braid, or individual buns.

2½ cups milk
1 package (3 teaspoons) active dry yeast
1 teaspoon sugar
1 tablespoon vinegar or lemon juice

2 tablespoons olive or canola oil
3 tablespoons honey
2½ teaspoons salt
5½ to 6 cups bread flour

Heat the milk in a small saucepan over medium-high heat until bubbles begin to form around the edges. Remove from the heat and cool.

In a large bowl, dissolve the yeast and sugar in the warm milk. Let stand until foamy, about 10 minutes.

Add the vinegar, oil, honey, salt, and 2 cups of the flour. Beat well, until the mixture is smooth. Add the remaining flour ½ cup at a time, beating to keep the mixture smooth. When the dough is soft but will hold its shape, turn out onto a lightly floured surface. Cover and let rest for 5 to 10 minutes.

Knead, adding flour 1 tablespoon at a time, for about 5 minutes, until the dough is smooth and satiny. Place in a clean, lightly oiled bowl, turn to oil the top, and cover with a towel or plastic wrap.

Let rise until doubled in bulk, about 1 to 1½ hours. Turn the dough out onto a lightly oiled surface and knead to press out air bubbles. Divide the dough into two equal portions. Form into round or oblong loaves and place into lightly greased baking pans. Or divide the dough into three parts, roll into strands 20 inches long, and braid the three strands together to make a braided loaf. Place on a baking sheet covered with parchment paper. Cover with a towel and let rise in a warm place for 30 to 45 minutes or until doubled.

Preheat the oven to 375ºF. Bake the loaves for 30 to 35 minutes or until a wooden skewer inserted into the center of a loaf comes out clean and dry. Remove from the pans and cool on a wire rack.

MAKES 2 LOAVES (20 SLICES EACH)

Honey Nut Oatmeal Bread

Before this bread goes into the oven, it is spread with honey and chopped nuts.

2 cups boiling milk
1 cup rolled oats, quick or old-fashioned
1 tablespoon lard or shortening
⅓ cup dark molasses
1 teaspoon salt
1 package (3 teaspoons) active dry yeast

¼ cup warm water (105°F to 115°F)
4½ to 5 cups bread flour or unbleached
 all-purpose flour
⅓ cup honey
½ cup chopped walnuts or pecans

In a large bowl, pour milk over the rolled oats; add lard, molasses, and salt. Set aside to cool to lukewarm. In a small bowl, dissolve the yeast in the warm water; let stand until yeast foams, about 5 minutes. Add yeast to cooled oat mixture. Stir in flour gradually, beating to keep dough smooth, and adding flour until a soft, smooth dough forms. Turn out onto a lightly floured surface and knead until smooth and satiny, about 10 minutes. Wash bowl, oil it, and add dough to bowl; turn dough over to oil top of the dough. Cover and let rise until doubled, about 1 to 1½ hours. Cover 2 baking sheets with parchment paper or grease them lightly. Divide dough in half, shape into balls, place balls smooth side up on prepared baking sheets, and press down until dough is about 1 inch thick. Let rise until puffy again, about 45 minutes. Pierce all over with a fork. Spread each loaf with half the honey and half the chopped nuts. Preheat the oven to 350°F. Bake for 30 to 35 minutes or until golden. Cool on rack.

MAKES 2 LOAVES

Buckwheat Raisin Bread

In this bread, the groats are first soaked, then combined with the bread dough along with finely ground buckwheat flour. The sweetness of the raisins balances the tartness of the buckwheat flavor.

½ cup buckwheat groats
1 cup boiling water
2 packages (5½ teaspoons) active
　　dry yeast
1½ cups warm water (105°F)
½ cup dark molasses
3 tablespoons butter, softened or melted

2 tablespoons caraway seeds
1 teaspoon salt
1 cup dark raisins
½ cup buckwheat flour
5 to 5½ cups bread flour or unbleached
　　all-purpose flour
Butter to brush on tops of loaves

In a large bowl, combine the buckwheat groats and boiling water. Set aside for 30 minutes until buckwheat has softened. In a small bowl, combine yeast and the warm water; add molasses and stir; let stand 5 to 10 minutes or until mixture begins to foam. Stir yeast mixture into cooled buckwheat mixture; add butter, caraway seeds, salt, raisins, and buckwheat flour; beat well. Slowly add the bread flour, beating to keep smooth, until a slightly stiff dough forms. Cover and let stand 15 minutes. Turn out onto a lightly floured surface and knead 10 minutes or until dough is springy and smooth; it may be slightly tacky, but should have an even texture. Wash bowl, oil it, and add dough to bowl; turn over to oil top of the dough. Cover and let rise until doubled, about 1 to 1½ hours. Grease two 9-inch round cake pans or 2 loaf pans 9 × 5 inches. Punch dough down. Divide in half and shape into loaves to fit pans. Let rise until doubled, about 45 minutes to 1 hour. Preheat the oven to 375°F. Bake for 35 to 40 minutes. Brush tops of hot loaves with butter. Remove from pans and cool on wire racks.

MAKES 2 LARGE LOAVES

Whole Wheat Brioche

My favorite brioches are shaped with the classic French topknots, but you can shape this dough into small oval loaves or individual breads as well. When you start this dough the day before, you'll discover that the chilled dough is very easy to shape; this version also requires no kneading.

2 packages (5½ teaspoons) active
   dry yeast
½ cup sugar, divided
½ cup warm water (105°F to 115°F)
½ cup milk, scalded
½ cup softened butter
1 teaspoon salt

3 eggs, at room temperature
2 cups whole wheat flour
2 cups bread flour or all-purpose flour

GLAZE
1 egg white
1 tablespoon sugar

In a small bowl, dissolve the yeast and 1 tablespoon of the sugar in the warm water. Let stand 5 minutes, until yeast is foamy. In a large bowl, mix the milk and butter; stir until butter is melted. Add the salt, eggs, and whole wheat flour, mixing until smooth. Stir in the yeast mixture. Beat well. Beat in the bread flour to make a stiff dough. Cover with plastic wrap; let rise in refrigerator overnight. Stir down batter.

To shape 1 large brioche, cut off about 1 cup of the dough and set aside. Shape the remaining portion into a smooth, round ball. Place into well-greased large brioche tin. Make a deep indentation in the center of the ball of dough (your finger should touch the bottom of the pan). Shape the remaining dough into a teardrop with a smooth top. Insert the pointed end into the center of the indentation. Let rise until doubled. Preheat the oven to 350°F. Bake for 35 to 45 minutes, or until loaf sounds hollow when tapped. Cool on rack.

For smaller individual brioches, divide half the dough (return the second half of dough to refrigerator) into 16 parts (divide into quarters, then divide each of the quarters into 4 parts). Shape 12 of the parts into balls and place in greased muffin or brioche cups. Flatten balls and make deep indentations in the centers. Divide remaining parts into 3 parts each. Roll each into little tear-shaped balls and place pointed side down into the indentations of the larger buns. Repeat shaping procedure for second half of the dough. Cover and let rise in a warm place until doubled, about 45 minutes. Preheat oven at 350°F. Make glaze by beating egg white and 1 tablespoon sugar; then brush mixture over each brioche. Bake for 20 minutes or until golden. Cool on rack.

MAKES 24 BRIOCHES OR 1 LARGE LOAF

Apple-filled Brioche

1 recipe Whole Wheat Brioche (page 110)
2 lemons
¼ cup butter
3½ pounds Golden Delicious apples,
    cored, peeled, and thinly sliced

½ cup dark brown sugar
2 egg yolks
½ cup heavy cream
Powdered sugar
Whipped cream for serving

Prepare brioche dough and, while dough is rising, prepare filling. Grate lemon rind and squeeze juice; you should have ⅓ cup lemon juice. Melt butter in large skillet and add apples, brown sugar, lemon rind, and juice. Stir and cook, covered, for 4 to 5 minutes until apples begin to soften. Cook until moisture has evaporated. Cool to room temperature.

Punch down risen dough. Pat out in a large, lightly greased, rimmed pan about 13 × 18 inches, spreading dough out to corners and forming a 1-inch rim all around. Let rise for 30 minutes. Spread apple mixture evenly over top of dough. Preheat oven to 375°F. Bake for 15 minutes. Meanwhile, mix egg yolks and cream; after brioche has baked 15 minutes, remove from oven and spread the egg-cream mixture evenly over apples. Bake for 20 to 25 minutes more until edges are browned. Remove from pan and cool on rack. Sprinkle with powdered sugar. Serve with whipped cream.

MAKES 10 TO 12 SERVINGS

Golden Nut Stuffed Brioche

Brioche, the golden, egg-rich French bread in its traditional form has a topknot and is baked in a flared, fluted pan. I like to stuff the brioche with a delicious nut-based filling and serve it for a special holiday breakfast or brunch.

3 cups all-purpose flour
1 package (3 teaspoons) active dry yeast
¼ cup sugar
½ teaspoon salt
½ cup milk, scalded and cooled to
    about 130°F
3 large eggs, slightly beaten
½ cup butter, at room temperature

HONEY-NUT FILLING

3 cups ground pecans or walnuts
¾ cup undiluted evaporated milk
¾ cup sugar
⅓ cup honey
½ teaspoon vanilla

CINNAMON-ALMOND FILLING

12 ounces almond paste
2 egg whites
¾ cup ground almonds
2 teaspoons cinnamon
¼ teaspoon almond extract
1 egg beaten with 1 tablespoon milk, for
    brushing
½ cup sliced almonds, for topping

Combine 2 cups of the flour, the yeast, sugar, and salt in a food processor or in the bowl of an electric mixer with a dough hook. Add the milk and eggs, and process until the mixture is smooth. Add the remaining flour and the butter, and process until the dough is smooth and cleans the sides of the work bowl. Let the dough rest, covered, in the work bowl for 30 minutes.

Process again until the dough turns around the bowl about 25 times, or about 30 seconds. Let the dough rest, covered, in the work bowl for another 30 minutes. Meanwhile, prepare one of the fillings.

To make the honey-nut filling, combine the nuts, milk, and sugar in a 2-quart saucepan. Stir in the honey. Bring to a boil over medium-high heat, stirring constantly, and let boil for 1 minute. Remove from the heat, and add the vanilla. Cover and let cool to room temperature.

To make the cinnamon-almond filling, in a bowl, mix together the almond paste, egg whites, almonds, cinnamon, and almond extract. Form into a roughly shaped square and place between 2 sheets of plastic wrap. Roll out to make a 12-inch square and set aside.

Turn the yeast dough onto a lightly oiled surface. Pinch off about ½ cup of the dough, shape into a smooth ball, and reserve. Roll out the remaining dough to make a 12-inch square.

To fill with the honey-nut filling, spread the cooled filling evenly across the dough square.

To fill with the cinnamon-almond filling, peel the top sheet of plastic wrap from the almond paste mixture and flip the paste over onto the dough square. Peel off the plastic from the top.

For either filling, roll the square up as for a jelly roll; then bring the ends together to form a ring.

Place the ring of dough, seam side down, in a buttered 2-quart brioche pan (see Note). Shape the reserved dough into a teardrop shape and poke it, pointed side down, into the center of the dough ring. Cover and let rise until the dough reaches the top of the pan, 1 to 1½ hours. Brush with the beaten egg and milk mixture and sprinkle with the sliced almonds.

Preheat the oven to 350°F. Bake for 40 to 45 minutes or until golden and a wooden skewer inserted in the center comes out clean. If the brioche begins to brown too quickly, cover lightly with foil until the loaf tests done. Cool in the pan for 10 minutes; then turn out of the pan and finish cooling on a wire rack. Serve warm.

MAKES 1 LARGE FILLED BRIOCHE

Note: If you do not have a brioche pan, you can use a regular cake pan or a springform pan. Shape the bread, let rise, and bake as described. The brioche can also be baked in a tube pan such as an angel food pan or kugelhopf pan, but then do not reserve the ½ cup dough for the topknot. Fill and shape the entire batch of dough, eliminating the topknot step. Baking time will remain the same.

Basic Whole Wheat Refrigerator Dough

With this handy refrigerator dough, you can make a variety of coffee breads, baking just one part of the dough—or all of it if you wish; you may keep the dough refrigerated up to 4 days.

2 packages (5½ teaspoons) active
    dry yeast
½ cup warm water (105°F to 115°F)
½ cup milk, scalded and cooled to 105°F
    to 115°F
½ cup melted butter

½ cup light or dark brown sugar, tightly
    packed
3 eggs, slightly beaten
1 teaspoon salt
2 cups whole wheat flour
3 cups bread flour or unbleached all-
    purpose flour

In a large bowl, dissolve the yeast in the warm water; let stand 5 minutes until yeast foams. Stir in the milk, butter, brown sugar, eggs, salt, and whole wheat flour. Beat until smooth, using electric mixer or wooden spoon. Stir in bread flour to make a dough that is stiff, but too soft to knead. Cover and refrigerate at least 2 hours or up to 2 days. Use as directed in the following recipes.

MAKES ENOUGH FOR 2 COFFEE CAKES

Whole Wheat Cinnamon Refrigerator Rolls

This is a handy refrigerator dough recipe for making rolls. You may use all of the dough at once, as directed in the recipe, or just bake a portion of it. This is also good shaped into individual dinner rolls.

**1 recipe Basic Whole Wheat
   Refrigerator Dough**

FILLING
½ cup softened butter
**½ cup sugar mixed with 1 tablespoon
   cinnamon**

GLAZE
1 cup powdered sugar
2 to 3 tablespoons hot coffee

In a large bowl, dissolve the yeast in the warm water; let stand 5 minutes until yeast foams. Stir in the milk, butter, brown sugar, eggs, salt, and whole wheat flour. Beat until smooth using an electric mixer or wooden spoon. Stir in bread flour to make a dough that is stiff, but too soft to knead. Cover and refrigerate at least 2 hours or up to 2 days. Cut dough into 4 parts. Roll out, 1 part at a time, to make a 12-inch square. Spread with 2 tablespoons of the butter and sprinkle with 2 tablespoons of the cinnamon sugar. Roll up, jelly-roll fashion. Cut into 1-inch slices. Grease an 8-inch round pan. Place cut slices, evenly spaced, in the pan. Repeat for remaining portions of the dough. Let rise until doubled, about 1 hour and 15 minutes. Preheat the oven to 375ºF, and bake rolls for 15 to 20 minutes or until golden. While rolls bake, mix powdered sugar and coffee to make a smooth, thin glaze. Remove hot rolls from pan and cool on rack. While rolls are hot, drizzle with the glaze.

MAKES 4 DOZEN ROLLS

Streusel Wheat Coffee Cake

Whole grain coffee cakes take well to the usual coffee cake embellishments: streusel toppings, spices, apples, and nuts. This is a quick batter bread.

**1 recipe Basic Whole Wheat Refrigerator
   Dough**

CINNAMON STREUSEL TOPPING
½ cup sugar

¾ cup whole wheat flour
¼ cup softened butter
2 teaspoons cinnamon
¼ cup chopped pecans or walnuts

In a large bowl, dissolve the yeast for coffee cake in the warm water; let stand 5 minutes until yeast foams. Add the milk, butter, brown sugar, salt, cinnamon, and eggs; beat well. Beat in the whole wheat flour and all-purpose flour. With spoon or electric mixer, beat until very smooth and elastic. Cover and let rise in a warm place for 30 minutes. Beat down and spread in well-buttered 9 × 13-inch pan. Combine the ingredients for streusel topping, stirring until crumbly. Sprinkle over the top. Cover; let rise until doubled, 30 to 45 minutes. Preheat the oven to 350°F. Bake for 25 to 30 minutes or until golden. If desired, frost while warm with a vanilla glaze.

MAKES ONE 13 × 9-INCH COFFEE CAKE

For vanilla glaze

Blend 1 cup powdered sugar with 2 to 3 tablespoons hot coffee and ½ teaspoon vanilla extract to make a smooth glaze that you can drizzle over the coffee cake.

Wheat Farmer's Cinnamon Braid

Each strand of this bread, before braiding, is coated with cinnamon sugar; you then fold the braid and place the fold into a loaf pan. When baked, the loaf is attractive, and each slice has an interesting pattern of cinnamon sugar swirls and raisins. Serve it toasted for breakfast with softened cream cheese.

1 package (3 teaspoons) active dry yeast
1 cup warm water (105°F to 115°F)
¼ cup nonfat dry milk
⅓ cup instant potato flakes
¼ cup softened butter or margarine
1 teaspoon salt
1 egg

1 cup whole wheat flour
1½ to 2 cups unbleached all-purpose flour
½ cup dark raisins
¼ cup wheat germ
¼ cup sugar blended with 1 tablespoon cinnamon
Powdered sugar (optional)

In a large bowl, dissolve the yeast in the warm water; add the dry milk and let stand 5 minutes until yeast foams. Add the potato flakes, butter, salt, and egg; beat well. Stir in the whole wheat flour; beat well. Slowly add the all-purpose flour until dough is stiff. Let rest 15 minutes. Turn dough out onto a floured surface and knead until smooth and elastic, about 8 to 10 minutes. Wash bowl, oil it, and add dough to the bowl; turn over to oil the top of the dough. Cover and let rise in a warm place until doubled, about 1 hour. Turn out onto lightly oiled work surface. Knead in the raisins and wheat germ. Divide into 3 parts. Roll out each part to make a strand about 20 inches long. Roll each strand in sugar-cinnamon mixture. Braid the three strands together. Grease a 9 × 5-inch loaf pan. Fold braid into thirds lengthwise, and place into pan with what were the edges of the braid upward. Let rise in a warm place until doubled, about 45 minutes to 1 hour. Preheat the oven to 350°F. Bake for 35 to 40 minutes, until loaf sounds hollow when tapped. Remove from pan and cool on wire rack. Dust with powdered sugar if desired.

MAKES 1 LOAF

Wheat Germ Almond-filled Braid

Each strand in this braid is filled with toasted wheat germ and ground almonds, combined to give a wholesome whole grain flavor.

½ cup toasted wheat germ (with brown
    sugar and honey), or whole wheat
    flakes
½ cup blanched almonds
¼ cup light or dark brown sugar
1 egg white
1 tablespoon butter, at room temperature

½ teaspoon almond extract
½ recipe Basic Whole Wheat Refrigerator
    Dough

GLAZE
1 egg beaten with 1 tablespoon cream or
    milk
¼ cup sliced almonds

In food processor with metal blade in place, process the wheat germ, almonds, brown sugar, egg white, butter, and almond extract until a smooth paste forms. Divide dough into 3 equal parts. On lightly floured surface, roll out each portion to make an 18 × 3½-inch strip. Spoon ⅓ of the wheat germ mixture down the length of each strip. Bring edges together and pinch lightly to make a round strand. Place strips side by side, seam sides down, on a greased or parchment-covered 14 × 17-inch baking sheet. Starting from the center, braid the 3 strips, taking care not to stretch the dough. Pinch the ends together and tuck under. Cover with plastic wrap and let rise in a warm place until doubled, about 1 hour. Mix egg and cream for glaze and brush over top of braid. Sprinkle with sliced almonds. Preheat the oven to 350°F. Bake for 35 to 40 minutes or until golden.

MAKES ONE 16-INCH BRAID

Whole Wheat Honey Croissants

Wait till you taste these delectable treats! These are easier to make than the classic croissants, which require rolling in layers of butter, but they are remarkably good.

2 packages (5½ teaspoons) active dry yeast
1¼ cups warm water (105°F to 115°F)
½ cup nonfat dry milk
4 tablespoons honey
2 cups unbleached all-purpose flour

2 cups whole wheat flour, preferably stone-ground
2 teaspoons salt
1½ cups butter, cut into ½-inch pieces
1 egg, beaten with 1 tablespoon milk

In a small bowl, dissolve the yeast in the warm water; add milk and honey, and set aside until the yeast foams. In a large bowl, combine the all-purpose flour, whole wheat flour, and salt. Cut in butter until butter pieces are the size of kidney beans. Add yeast mixture to flour mixture and, with spatula, carefully fold mixtures together just until flour is moistened. Press dough into a ball. Wrap and refrigerate 4 to 24 hours. On a lightly floured surface, pound dough with the side of a rolling pin to flatten to about 8 inches square. Roll out to about 12 inches square. Fold in thirds. Pound with the side of a rolling pin again to double the width of the dough, and roll out to make a rectangle about 8 × 14 inches; fold in the opposite direction. At this point, the dough should have rather even edges. Roll out again and repeat the folding and rolling process 6 times. If necessary, refrigerate between "turns." Refrigerate dough for 30 minutes after last rolling. Divide in half. Place one part in the refrigerator and roll the second part out to 16 inches square. Cut into thirds, making 3 strips 16 inches long. Cut into triangles, making the cuts about 5 inches wide at the base; you will end up with 5 perfect triangles and two "halves." Piece the halves together to make the sixth triangle. Roll up each triangle, beginning with the 5-inch edge toward the tip. Cover baking sheets with parchment paper and arrange the rolls in a crescent shape, at least 3 inches apart, on prepared pans. Repeat to make 6 croissants from each strip. Repeat for second half of dough. Let rise until about doubled, 30 to 45 minutes when the kitchen is warm, 1 to 2 hours when it is cold. Preheat the oven to 450ºF. Brush croissants with egg/milk mixture and bake for 10 to 12 minutes or until golden. Remove from pans and cool on wire racks.

MAKES 36 CROISSANTS

Cinnamon Wheat Kugelhupf

This is a cinnamon and walnut-filled yeast-risen sweet bread that is baked in a fancy "kugelhupf" mold. Kugelhupf is also called "Turk's Head," so named when the Turks ruled Hungary.

2 packages (5½ teaspoons) active
    dry yeast
½ cup warm water (105°F to 115°F)
½ cup sugar
1 cup milk, scalded and cooled to 105°F
    to 115°F
4 egg yolks
¼ cup sour cream
½ teaspoon salt
2 cups whole wheat flour

2 to 2½ cups unbleached all-purpose flour
½ cup butter, melted and cooled
½ cup toasted wheat germ
Powdered sugar

FILLING
2 egg whites, stiffly beaten
1 cup sugar
½ pound walnuts, pulverized
½ tablespoon cinnamon

In a large bowl, dissolve the yeast in the warm water; add sugar, and set aside for 5 minutes until yeast foams. Add milk, egg yolks, sour cream, salt, and whole wheat flour; beat well. Beat in all-purpose flour to make a smooth, shiny batter, gradually adding the melted butter. Cover dough and set aside in a warm place for 1 hour or until dough doubles.

Meanwhile, prepare filling. Fold egg whites into the sugar; add the walnuts and cinnamon. Set aside. Turn dough out onto a lightly floured surface; knead until air bubbles are removed. Roll dough out to ½-inch thickness; sprinkle with wheat germ and spread with the walnut filling. Roll up like a jelly roll. Generously butter a 12-cup fancy tube mold. Put roll into the pan; pan should be about half full. Let rise until dough fills pan, 45 minutes to 1 hour. Preheat the oven to 325°F. Bake for 60 minutes, until golden. Invert on rack to cool. Sprinkle with powdered sugar.

MAKES 1 LARGE KUGELHUPF

State Fair Spiced Raisin Rolls

Just like grandma used to make and take to the fair! These raisin-studded swirls rise up so that the center pops out when you bake them close together in a pan.

1 package (3 teaspoons) active dry yeast
½ cup warm water (105°F to 115°F)
¼ cup light or dark brown sugar
½ cup milk, scalded and cooled to 105°F
    to 115°F
½ cup softened butter
1 egg
1 cup whole wheat flour

1 teaspoon salt
2 to 2½ cups unbleached all-purpose flour

FILLING
¼ cup softened butter
⅓ cup sugar
⅓ cup brown sugar
½ cup dark or light raisins
2 teaspoons cinnamon

In a large bowl, dissolve the yeast in the warm water; add 1 tablespoon of the brown sugar; stir and let stand 5 minutes until yeast foams. Add milk, butter, egg, whole wheat flour, remainder of brown sugar, and salt; beat well. Add the all-purpose flour gradually until dough is stiff; turn out onto a lightly floured surface and knead until smooth and satiny, about 5 minutes. Wash bowl, oil it, add dough to bowl; turn it over to oil the top of the dough, and cover. Let rise in a warm place until doubled, 1 to 1½ hours. Punch down and roll out to make a 12 × 18-inch rectangle. Generously butter a 9 × 13-inch baking pan. Spread dough with the softened butter for the filling. Combine sugars, raisins, and cinnamon, and sprinkle over dough. Roll up, starting with the 18-inch side. Cut into 1-inch slices. Place slices cut side down in pan. Cover and let rise 1 hour, or until light and doubled. Preheat the oven to 375ºF. Bake for 25 to 30 minutes. Frost if desired with your favorite powdered sugar icing or use the vanilla glaze of the Streusel Wheat Coffee Cake on page 115.

MAKES 18 ROLLS

Fruited Bath Buns

A classic from Bath, England. We once enjoyed the white flour version of these buns hot for breakfast with a pot of steaming tea. I have since learned to make them with whole wheat flour and enjoy them even more!

2 cups whole wheat flour

1 to 1½ cups bread flour or unbleached
   all-purpose flour

¼ cup light or dark brown sugar

¼ cup softened butter

1 package (3 teaspoons) active dry yeast

½ teaspoon salt

½ cup milk

1 egg, beaten

½ teaspoon almond extract

½ cup finely chopped mixed candied fruit

1 egg white

1 tablespoon cold milk

Sugar, preferably coarse pearl sugar or
   crushed sugar cubes

In a large bowl, measure 1 cup of the whole wheat flour, the brown sugar, butter, yeast, and salt. With electric mixer, mix until blended, about 1 minute. Heat milk in saucepan to 120ºF to 130ºF; blend egg and almond extract into milk. With mixer going, add milk to flour mixture and beat until smooth, about 3 minutes on high speed. Add the remaining whole wheat flour and the bread flour gradually until the dough becomes very stiff. When mixer can no longer handle the dough, stir with a spoon. Let rest 15 minutes. On a lightly floured surface, knead until smooth and satiny, about 5 minutes. Let rest 15 minutes; then knead the candied fruit into the dough. Shape into a ball and place in a lightly oiled bowl; turn to oil the top of the dough. Cover and refrigerate 4 to 24 hours, or let rise until doubled. Uncover dough and let stand at room temperature (if refrigerated) for 20 minutes. Divide into 12 equal parts. Shape each into a smooth ball and place on a greased or parchment-covered baking sheet; flatten dough with the palm of your hand. Beat egg white and cold milk together to make a glaze and brush top of each bun with it. Sprinkle with the sugar. Let rise about 30 minutes. Preheat the oven to 350ºF. Bake for 15 to 20 minutes, until golden. Remove from pan and cool on wire rack.

MAKES 12 BUNS

Butterhorns

Butterhorns are a "never-fail" favorite of many Scandinavian American cooks. A Norwegian friend gave me this recipe. As she says in her instructions, "Chust mix them as you do for any rolls and then roll them into rolls!"

2 packages (5½ teaspoons) active
   dry yeast

½ cup warm water (105°F to 115°F)

¼ cup sugar

1 teaspoon salt

1 cup milk, scalded and cooled to
   lukewarm

3 eggs

½ cup softened butter
5 to 6 cups unbleached all-purpose flour
About ½ cup softened butter

GLAZE
1 egg
3 tablespoons milk

In a large bowl, dissolve the yeast in the warm water. Add the sugar. Let stand 5 minutes until the yeast foams. Stir in the salt, milk, eggs, and butter. Mix in 5 cups of the flour, 1 cup at a time, beating after each addition until smooth. Cover and let rest 15 minutes. Turn out onto a lightly floured surface and knead until smooth and satiny. Dough should feel quite soft, and the softer the dough you can handle the lighter the rolls will be. Clean the bowl and oil it lightly. Add dough to the bowl, turning over to oil the top of the dough. Cover and let rise in a warm place until doubled, about 1 to 1½ hours.

Cover baking sheets with parchment paper or lightly grease them.

Lightly oil a work surface. Turn the risen dough out onto the surface and divide into 3 equal parts.

Roll 1 part out at a time to make a circle 12 to 14 inches in diameter. Rolling out yeast dough can be frustrating because it tends to shrink back. The trick is to roll it out, then give it a rest, roll out again and give it a rest, and in so doing you can roll it to the desired size.

Brush the circle of dough with softened butter; then cut into 8 equal wedges. Starting from the wide end, roll up toward the tip of the piece of dough; tug slightly at the wide ends of the piece to exaggerate the width. Place rolls on the prepared baking sheets, about 2 inches apart, placing the tip beneath the roll so it won't pop up as it rises and bakes.

Repeat with the remaining balls of dough. Let rise in a warm place until almost doubled. Preheat the oven to 375°F.

Beat the egg with the milk to make a glaze and brush rolls lightly with the mixture. Bake for 15 to 18 minutes or until golden.

The dough will seem very soft after rising, but resist the temptation to add more flour; instead, oil or butter your fingers to prevent stickiness. You may use a slight dusting of flour on the outside of the dough to keep it from sticking.

MAKES 2 DOZEN ROLLS

Herbed Oatmeal Butterhorns

A well-chosen bread can stand alone as the food served for tea or a simple brunch. Herbed and buttered, these fragrant crescent rolls are excellent with green pepper jelly and cream cheese as the only accompaniments.

2 packages (5½ teaspoons) active
    dry yeast
¼ cup warm water (105°F to 115°F)
½ cup sugar
1 cup milk, scalded and cooled to 105°F
    to 115°F
½ cup melted butter

1 teaspoon salt
4 eggs, beaten
1 cup rolled oats
3½ to 4 cups unbleached all-purpose
    flour
½ cup herb butter (recipe follows)

In a large bowl, dissolve the yeast in the warm water; add 1 tablespoon of the sugar and let stand 5 minutes until yeast foams. Stir in the remaining sugar, milk, butter, salt, eggs, and rolled oats and beat until blended. Slowly add the flour to make a smooth but still sticky dough. Cover and let rise until doubled, about 1 hour. Punch down, and divide dough into quarters. On a lightly oiled surface, roll out one piece at a time to make a circle 10 inches in diameter. Brush each circle with ¼ of the herb butter. Cut each circle into 8 pie-shaped wedges. Cover 4 baking sheets with parchment paper or lightly grease them. Roll wedges from wide side toward tips and shape into crescents; place them on the prepared baking sheets with the points under. Let rise until puffy, about 45 minutes. Preheat the oven of 375ºF, and bake rolls about 15 minutes or until golden.

MAKES 32 BUTTERHORNS

For herb butter

Blend ½ cup softened butter with 1 tablespoon mixed herbs (tarragon, chervil, parsley, basil).

Swedish Cinnamon Butterhorns

These are crescent-shaped rolls that are filled with cinnamon and butter.

1½ cups scalded milk
½ cup butter
3 eggs
½ cup sugar
½ teaspoon salt
1 package (3 teaspoons) active dry yeast
¼ cup warm water (105°F to 115°F)
6 cups all-purpose flour

FILLING
½ cup softened butter
1 cup sugar
1 tablespoon cinnamon

GLAZE
1 egg
2 tablespoons milk
Pearl sugar or crushed sugar cubes

In a large bowl, combine the milk and butter; stir until butter is melted. Beat in the eggs, sugar, and salt. In a small dish, dissolve yeast in the warm water; let stand 5 minutes. Add to the cooled milk mixture. Stir in flour, beating to make a smooth but thick batter. Cover and refrigerate 2 to 24 hours.

Divide the dough into 4 parts. On a floured surface, roll each part out to make a 12-inch circle. Spread with softened butter. Mix cinnamon and sugar together and sprinkle over the dough evenly. Cut each circle into 8 wedges. Roll up each wedge, starting from the wide end, to make a crescent-shaped roll.

Cover baking sheets with parchment paper or lightly grease them. Place rolls on the prepared baking sheets. Let rise about 45 minutes until puffy. Beat the egg and milk together, and brush rolls lightly with the mixture. Sprinkle with pearl sugar. Preheat the oven to 375°F. Bake for 13 to 15 minutes until golden.

MAKES 32 ROLLS

Graham Rusks

In Norway, these twice-baked breads, or "rusks," are served for breakfast or topped with cheese for lunch.

1 package (3 teaspoons) active dry yeast
2 cups warm water (110°F)
3 tablespoons vegetable shortening,
    melted

3 tablespoons sugar
1 teaspoon salt
2 cups graham flour or whole wheat flour
2 to 2½ cups all-purpose or bread flour

In a large bowl, stir yeast into the warm water; let stand 5 minutes. Stir in the short-ening, sugar, salt, and graham flour or whole wheat flour. Beat until smooth. Stir in enough all-purpose or bread flour to make a stiff dough. Turn out onto a lightly floured surface. Cover with a dry cloth; let stand 5 to 15 minutes. Wash and oil bowl; set aside. Knead the dough until smooth, about 10 minutes. Place in the oiled bowl, turning to oil all sides. Cover and let rise in a warm place until doubled, about 2 hours. Grease 2 large baking sheets; set aside. Punch down dough; turn out onto a lightly oiled surface. Cut dough in half; divide each half into 12 pieces. Shape each piece into a ball, 2½ inches in diameter. Arrange buns on prepared baking sheets, about 2 inches apart. Cover and let rise until doubled, about 45 minutes. Preheat the oven to 425°F. Bake buns for 12 to 15 minutes or until golden brown. Cool on racks. When buns are cooled, split horizontally, using 2 forks to pull buns apart. Reduce heat to 250°F. Place split buns on baking sheets, split side up; bake until completely dry, about 1 hour.

MAKES 48 RUSKS

Hot Cross Buns

These small yeast buns, freckled with currants or raisins, and sometimes fruit and nuts, are traditionally served on Good Friday. They are slashed with a cross just before baking and the cross is filled with icing after they've cooled. I usually make them ahead of time and freeze them unfrosted. Then on Easter morning, I warm them in the oven and frost them for breakfast or brunch.

3 cups unbleached all-purpose flour
2 packages (5½ teaspoons) active
    dry yeast
¼ cup sugar
½ teaspoon salt
½ teaspoon grated fresh lemon zest
¾ cup milk
¼ cup butter, cut into pieces
2 large eggs, beaten
½ cup raisins or currants

¼ cup chopped blanched almonds
2 tablespoons chopped mixed
    candied fruits

GLAZE
1 large egg, beaten with 1 tablespoon milk

ICING
1 cup powdered sugar
2 to 3 tablespoons cream or milk
½ teaspoon almond extract

Measure the flour, yeast, sugar, salt, and lemon zest into a large mixing bowl or into the work bowl of a food processor.

Heat milk to boiling in a small saucepan over medium-high heat. Remove from heat and add the butter. Stir until the butter is melted. Stir in the eggs. Add the liquid ingredients to the dry ingredients, and process or mix with an electric mixer until the dough is smooth but soft, about 2 minutes. Mix in the raisins, almonds, and candied fruits.

Cover with plastic wrap and let rise for 1 hour. Cover a baking sheet with parchment paper.

Turn the dough out onto an oiled surface. Dust the dough with flour and knead to release the air bubbles. Divide the dough into 16 equal parts. Shape each into a ball. Place the balls of dough, smooth side up, about 3 inches apart on the prepared baking sheet. Let rise in a warm place, lightly covered, until almost doubled, for 45 minutes to 1 hour.

Preheat the oven to 400°F. Brush the tops of the buns with the egg glaze. Slash a cross in the center of each bun with a sharp knife.

Bake for 10 to 12 minutes, until golden. While the buns bake, mix the icing ingredients in a small bowl. Place the icing into a pastry bag with a small tip. Slide the parchment onto the countertop to cool or transfer the rolls onto a wire rack to cool. Pipe the icing into the shape of a cross on top of each bun. Serve warm.

MAKES 16 BUNS

Giant Cinnamon Pecan Rolls

Big, fat yeast rolls never taste so good to me as in the fall, when mornings have a nip to them and the day is sunny, dry, and warm. With a food processor, the mixing is a snap, but you can do the mixing and kneading by hand, too.

DOUGH
2½ cups all-purpose flour
3 tablespoons sugar
½ teaspoon salt
1 package (3 teaspoons) active dry yeast

1 cup milk, scalded and cooled to very warm (about 130°F)
2 tablespoons butter, at room temperature

FILLING

2 tablespoons melted butter

¼ cup packed brown sugar

½ teaspoon cinnamon

½ cup chopped pecans

GLAZE

1 cup powdered sugar

2 tablespoons hot, strong coffee

In a food processor with the dough blade in place or in a large mixing bowl, combine the flour, sugar, salt, and yeast. Combine the milk and butter. Pour the milk mixture over the dry ingredients and mix or process until a dough forms.

Let the dough rest for 10 minutes. Grease 6 large muffin cups or one 9-inch round cake pan. Turn out onto a floured surface and roll out to make a 13 × 8-inch rectangle. Fill the dough by spreading it with the melted butter. Sprinkle with the brown sugar, then the cinnamon and pecans. Roll up from the short side.

Cut the roll into 6 equal-size slices. Place the slices, cut side down, into the muffin cups. Or place the rolls, evenly spaced, into the prepared round pan. Cover and let rise in a warm place until doubled, about 25 to 35 minutes.

Preheat the oven to 375ºF. Bake for 20 to 30 minutes or until light brown and a skewer inserted into the center of a roll comes out clean. Remove from the cups or baking pan and cool on a wire rack.

To make the glaze, mix the powdered sugar and coffee together in a small bowl, and drizzle over the warm rolls. Serve warm.

MAKES 6 LARGE ROLLS

Danish Poppyseed Rolls

The Danes enjoy these rolls freshly baked for breakfast.

1 package (3 teaspoons) active dry yeast

¼ cup warm water (105°F to 115°F)

1 tablespoon sugar

1 cup milk, scalded and cooled to
    lukewarm

1 egg

½ teaspoon salt

1 cup butter, at room temperature

4 cups all-purpose flour

GLAZE AND TOPPING

1 egg white

1 tablespoon water

2 tablespoons poppyseeds

In a small bowl, dissolve the yeast in the warm water. Add the sugar, milk, egg, and salt to the yeast. Let stand 15 to 20 minutes until frothy.

In a large bowl, rub ½ cup of the butter into the flour with your fingers until the mixture resembles coarse crumbs. Add the yeast mixture and turn out onto a lightly floured surface. Knead until smooth and elastic, about 5 minutes. Clean the bowl and lightly oil it. Place dough into the bowl, turn over to oil the top, and let rise for 20 to 30 minutes.

Cover a baking sheet with parchment paper or grease it lightly.

On a lightly floured surface, roll the dough out to make a 16-inch square. Spread the remaining butter over half the dough to within ½ inch of the edge. Fold the unbuttered half over onto the buttered half of the dough, enclosing the butter, and seal the edges. Fold the dough again lengthwise and seal the edges to make a long roll 3 to 4 inches wide; it should stretch itself out to about 20 inches.

Place the dough on the prepared baking sheet. Mix the egg white and water to make a glaze, and brush the top of the roll with the glaze. Sprinkle with poppyseeds. Cut into 14 to 16 triangles. Separate the triangles slightly. Let rise until almost doubled, 30 to 45 minutes.

Preheat the oven to 400ºF. Bake for 15 minutes or until golden.

MAKES 14 TO 16 ROLLS

Healthy Rusks

Scandinavians in general love to keep rusks or "twice-baked breads" on hand. Rusks are a perfect base for cheese at breakfast; they are equally good for picnics or lunches, and in the summertime they keep well in a tin at a summer cottage. Vacation at the lake is not the time for baking! Rusks are made ahead at home or purchased in the wonderful home-style bakeries found all over Finland, as well as Sweden, Norway, Denmark, and Iceland.

2 packages (5½ teaspoons) active
   dry yeast
½ cup warm water (105°F to 115°F)
2 tablespoons brown sugar
1½ teaspoons salt
½ teaspoon anise seed

1½ cups milk, scalded and cooled to
   lukewarm
½ cup dark rye flour
¾ cup whole wheat flour
4 to 4½ cups bread flour or unbleached
   all-purpose flour
¼ cup softened butter

In a large bowl, dissolve the yeast in the warm water. Add the brown sugar and let stand 5 minutes until yeast foams. Stir in the salt, anise seed, milk, rye and whole wheat flour, and beat until smooth.

Add the bread flour or all-purpose flour a cup at a time, beating between additions until the dough is stiff and will not absorb more flour. Let stand, covered, 15 minutes.

Turn dough out onto a floured surface. Knead, adding flour to prevent stickiness, until dough is smooth and satiny, about 10 minutes. Knead in the softened butter.

Wash bowl and oil it. Add dough to the bowl and turn over to oil the top of the dough. Cover and let rise in a warm place until doubled, about 1 hour.

Punch dough down and turn out onto an oiled surface. Cut the dough into quarters. Cut each quarter into quarters; then cut each piece of dough in half to make 32 pieces. Shape each into a small round roll. Place on a floured baking sheet. Cover with a towel and let rise until doubled, about 45 minutes.

Preheat the oven to 425ºF. Bake rolls for 15 minutes until golden. Cool. Lower oven heat to 300ºF. With 2 forks, split the rolls into halves horizontally. Place on baking sheet with cut side up. Bake until golden and dried, about 30 minutes. Remove from oven and cool on racks. Store in an airtight container.

MAKES 64 RUSKS

Norwegian Wheat Rusks

Here is another classic twice-baked bread of Scandinavia, a summertime favorite to have on hand when it is too warm to think of baking. Rusks keep well in airtight containers and are eaten as a substitute for freshly baked bread.

1 package (3 teaspoons) active dry yeast
¼ cup warm water (105°F to 115°F)
3 tablespoons sugar
2 teaspoons salt

3 tablespoons melted butter
2 cups warm water (105°F to 115°F)
4½ to 5 cups whole wheat or graham flour

In a large bowl, dissolve the yeast in the ¼ cup warm water; add the sugar. Let stand 5 minutes until yeast foams. Stir in the salt, butter, and 2 cups warm water; add 2 cups of the flour. Cover and let rise until doubled, about 1 hour. Stirring batter, add more flour a cup at a time until the dough is stiff and will not easily absorb more flour. Cover and let stand 15 minutes. Turn out onto a lightly floured surface and knead until dough is no longer sticky (a 100% whole wheat dough will be "tacky," not sticky).

Wash bowl, oil it lightly, and add dough to the bowl. Turn over to oil the top of the dough. Cover and let rise again until doubled.

Meanwhile, cover baking sheets with parchment paper or lightly grease them. Turn dough out onto a lightly oiled work surface. Knead lightly to press out air bubbles, and divide in half. Divide each half into quarters, then again into quarters, making a total of 32 pieces of dough. Shape into smooth round rolls. Place rolls on prepared baking sheets. Cover with a towel and let rise in a warm place until almost doubled.

Preheat the oven to 425°F. Bake for 12 to 15 minutes. Remove from oven, cool on racks, and with 2 forks, split each roll horizontally into 2 parts. Lower oven heat to 250°F. Place on baking sheets again and bake for about 1 hour or until dry and crisp.

MAKES 64 RUSKS

Karelian Water Rings

These water-raised rolls resemble bagels. I remember women of my grand-mother's era talking about water rolls, but for some reason it wasn't until we were entertained by a Karelian family that I was reminded of them. We enjoyed them every morning for breakfast, freshly baked and split, with butter and jam.

2 packages (5½ teaspoons) active
   dry yeast
1¼ cups warm water (105°F to 115°F)
1 teaspoon salt

4 tablespoons melted butter
3 to 3½ cups bread or unbleached all-
   purpose flour

FOR RAISING
Boiling water

2 tablespoons salt
1 teaspoon baking soda

In a large bowl, dissolve the yeast in the warm water. Let stand 5 minutes. Add the salt, butter, and half the flour, beating until smooth. Blend in the remaining flour until the dough is stiff. Let rest 15 minutes, covered. Turn dough out onto a floured surface and knead until smooth and satiny, 5 to 10 minutes. Clean the bowl, lightly oil it, and add dough to the bowl. Turn over to oil the top of the dough. Cover and let rise in a warm place until doubled, about 1 hour. (Dough may also rise in a cool kitchen overnight.)

Turn dough onto an oiled surface. Divide into 16 parts. Shape each part into a strand 6 to 8 inches long. Turn into a ring and pinch ends together. Place on a sheet of lightly oiled waxed paper and let rise for 30 minutes.

Preheat the oven to 400°F. Cover a baking sheet with parchment paper and lightly spray with nonstick spray. Or, grease and flour a baking sheet.

Bring a wide pan (I use a 14-inch deep-frying pan) half-full of water to a boil; add the salt and soda. Lower the rings one at a time into the water and cook 30 seconds. Remove from the water with a pancake turner and place on prepared baking sheets.

Bake for 15 to 20 minutes until golden.

MAKES 16 ROLLS

Norwegian Coffee Buns

These simple buns are served fresh with morning coffee.

2 packages (5½ teaspoons) active
    dry yeast
½ cup warm water (105°F to 115°F)
⅓ cup sugar
1 teaspoon salt
½ cup melted butter
1 teaspoon pulverized cardamom seeds
2 cups milk, scalded and cooled to
    lukewarm
6 to 6½ cups all-purpose flour

GLAZE
1 slightly beaten egg
2 tablespoons milk
Pearl sugar, plain sugar, or crushed sugar
    cubes for topping

In a large bowl, dissolve the yeast in the warm water. Add a pinch of the sugar and let stand 5 minutes until yeast foams. Stir in the remaining sugar, salt, butter, cardamom, and milk.

Add half the flour and beat until smooth and satiny. Add the remaining flour slowly, stirring until mixture will not absorb more flour. Let stand 15 minutes.

Turn dough out onto a lightly floured surface and knead until smooth and satiny, 5 to 10 minutes. Wash bowl, oil it, and place dough in bowl, turning to oil the top of the dough. Cover and let rise until doubled, about 1 hour.

Turn dough out onto a lightly oiled surface. Divide into 24 parts. Shape into smooth balls.

Cover baking sheets with parchment paper or lightly grease them. Place dough on baking sheets and let rise until almost doubled, about 45 minutes. Preheat the oven to 375°F.

Mix egg and milk together, and brush rolls with the mixture. Sprinkle with the sugar. Bake for 15 minutes or until golden.

MAKES 24 ROLLS

Danish Currant Buns

These buns are quick to make, require just one short rising, and are very rich and buttery.

1 package (3 teaspoons) active dry yeast
¼ cup warm water (105°F to 115°F)
¼ cup milk
2 tablespoons sugar
1 egg
½ cup butter, at room temperature
2 cups unbleached all-purpose flour
½ cup currants

GLAZE
1 egg, slightly beaten
2 tablespoons milk

ICING
½ cup powdered sugar
2 to 3 teaspoons hot water or coffee
½ teaspoon almond extract

In a large bowl, dissolve the yeast in the warm water. Let stand 5 minutes. Add the milk, sugar, egg, and butter. Mix in the flour and currants. Beat well by hand. The dough will feel smooth and rich. Turn it out onto a floured surface and cut dough into quarters. Shape each quarter into a ball and cut again into quarters to make 16 pieces in all. Shape each piece into a smooth round bun.

Cover baking sheet with parchment paper or lightly grease it. Place buns on the baking sheet with the smooth side up and press with the palm of your hand to flatten slightly.

Mix egg and milk and brush buns with this glaze. Let rise for about 20 minutes until puffy but not doubled.

Preheat the oven to 375ºF. Bake for 13 to 15 minutes or until golden. To make the icing, mix the powdered sugar, water or coffee, and almond extract. Drizzle this icing over hot baked buns.

MAKES 16 BUNS

Danish Almond Cinnamon Rolls

Danish bakers love to roll butter into any dough to make it extra rich, extra good, extra light.

2 packages (5½ teaspoons) active
    dry yeast
½ cup warm water (105°F to 115°F)
¼ teaspoon salt
2 tablespoons sugar
2 tablespoons butter
¾ cup scalded milk
2 eggs
¼ teaspoon nutmeg
3½ cups all-purpose flour

½ cup butter, at room temperature

FILLING
4 tablespoons sugar
2 teaspoons cinnamon
¼ cup finely ground almonds

ICING
1 cup powdered sugar
2 to 3 teaspoons strong hot coffee

In a large bowl, dissolve the yeast in the warm water. Let stand 5 minutes. In a separate bowl, add the salt, sugar, and 2 tablespoons butter to the scalded milk; cool to lukewarm.

Add the milk mixture to the yeast mixture; beat in the eggs and nutmeg. Mix in the flour, beating until the dough is satiny and smooth and rather soft. Scrape down sides of the bowl. Let rise until doubled, about 1 hour.

Dust dough with additional flour. Scrape down sides of bowl. Rub work surface with oil and turn dough out onto it. Dust lightly with flour if necessary to prevent stickiness on the surface of the dough. Pat out to make a rectangle 10 by 12 inches.

Spread half of the ½ cup butter along one long half of the dough. Fold unbuttered side over the dough. Press edges together. Transfer onto an oiled baking sheet and chill for 1 hour.

Without removing the dough from the baking sheet, pat out to 10 by 16 inches. Spread the center third with the remaining butter. Fold 1 side of dough over the buttered center; then fold the other side over to make 3 thicknesses of dough. You should end up with close to a square shape. Chill 1 hour longer.

On a lightly floured surface, roll dough out to make a 16-inch square. Combine the 4 tablespoons sugar with the cinnamon and ground almonds. Sprinkle over the dough. Roll up as for a jelly roll. Cut into 24 slices.

Lightly grease 24 muffin cups or line with paper cupcake liners. Place 1 slice of dough with cut side up into each. Let rise until puffy, about 45 minutes.

Preheat the oven to 375°F. Bake for 15 to 20 minutes until golden. Mix the powdered sugar with the coffee and drizzle this icing on the hot rolls.

MAKES 24 ROLLS

....

Icelandic Almond Rolls

....

Icelandics love their morning coffee and far prefer yeast rolls to other sweets. These sweet yeast rolls are filled with almond paste and cinnamon.

2 packages (5½ teaspoons) active
    dry yeast
½ cup warm water (105°F to 115°F)
1½ cups rich milk, scalded and cooled to
    lukewarm
½ cup softened butter
½ cup sugar
1 teaspoon salt
2 eggs
6 to 6½ cups unbleached all-purpose
    flour

FILLING
1 cup almond paste
1 egg
2 tablespoons sugar
4 tablespoons butter
1 teaspoon vanilla

GLAZE AND DECORATION
1 cup powdered sugar
2 to 3 tablespoons cream
1 teaspoon almond extract
1 cup toasted chopped almonds*

In a large bowl, dissolve the yeast in the warm water. Let stand 5 minutes. Stir in the milk, butter, sugar, salt, and eggs. Add the flour a cup at a time, beating well, until mixture will not readily absorb more flour. Cover and let dough stand 15 minutes. Turn out onto a lightly floured surface. Knead, adding just enough flour to keep the dough from sticking, until smooth and satiny, about 10 minutes. Wash bowl, lightly oil it, and turn dough into the bowl; turn dough over to oil the top. Cover and let rise until doubled.

While the dough rises, prepare the almond filling. In food processor or bowl, blend the almond paste with the egg, sugar, butter, and vanilla until mixture is smooth and spreadable.

Line 30 muffin cups with paper cupcake liners.

Roll out the risen dough to make a rectangle about 24 inches long by 14 inches wide. Spread the almond filling to within 1 inch of the edge. Roll up as for a jelly roll. Cut into 1-inch pieces. Place in paper-lined muffin cups with cut sides up.

Let rise in a warm place until about doubled.

Preheat the oven to 400°F. Bake for 10 minutes or until golden. Combine the powdered sugar, cream, and almond extract to make a glaze, brush the hot rolls with the glaze, and sprinkle with toasted chopped almonds.

MAKES 30 ROLLS

* To toast the chopped almonds, bake in a 300°F oven for 5 to 10 minutes.

....

Finnish Sunday Rolls

....

Traditionally, these are baked on Saturday so they will be fresh for Sunday morning's coffee. Rolls left from the previous week's baking are split and baked into rusks, which are then served during the week as "dunkers."

1 package (3 teaspoons) active dry yeast
¼ cup warm water (105°F to 115°F)
1 cup milk, scalded and cooled to
    lukewarm
1 cup sugar
1 teaspoon salt
2 eggs
¾ cup softened butter

5½ to 6 cups unbleached all-purpose flour

GLAZE AND DECORATION
1 egg, beaten
½ cup sliced almonds
Pearl sugar or crushed sugar cubes

In a large bowl, dissolve the yeast in the warm water. Let stand 5 minutes. Add the milk, sugar, salt, and eggs. Add the butter and 2 cups of the flour, and beat until batter is satiny and smooth. Slowly stir in additional flour until the dough is stiff and does not absorb more flour. Cover and let rest 15 minutes.

Turn dough out onto a lightly floured surface. Knead, adding flour to prevent stickiness, for 10 minutes or until smooth and satiny. Wash bowl, oil it, and add dough to the bowl. Turn over to oil the top of the dough. Cover and let rise in a warm place until doubled, about 1 hour.

Turn dough out onto a lightly oiled work surface and cut into 36 equal portions. Shape each into a ball. Cover baking sheet with parchment paper or lightly oil it. Place shaped rolls onto the baking sheet with the smooth side up. With the palm of your hand flatten slightly. Let rise until puffy.

Preheat the oven to 400ºF. Brush risen rolls with beaten egg and sprinkle with sliced almonds and sugar. Bake for 10 to 12 minutes until golden. Do not overbake. Remove from baking sheet and cool on racks.

MAKES 3 DOZEN ROLLS

Cinnamon Ears

These coffee rolls are a favorite in Finland. They are made of a simple sweet yeast dough filled with cinnamon and sugar. The refrigerated dough is easy to handle.

2 packages (5½ teaspoons) active dry yeast
1 cup warm water (105°F to 115°F)
½ cup melted butter
½ cup sugar
3 eggs, slightly beaten
½ teaspoon salt
1 teaspoon ground cardamom (optional)
4½ to 5 cups all-purpose flour

FILLING
½ cup soft butter
½ cup sugar
1 tablespoon cinnamon

GLAZE
1 egg, slightly beaten
2 tablespoons milk
Pearl sugar or crushed sugar cubes

In a large bowl, dissolve the yeast in the warm water and let stand 5 minutes. Stir in the melted butter, sugar, eggs, salt, cardamom, and 4½ cups flour until dough is smooth. Cover and refrigerate 2 to 24 hours.

Divide dough into 2 parts. Turn out onto a lightly floured surface, and roll out each part to make a rectangle about 12 inches by 24 inches. Spread each piece of dough with half the butter and sprinkle with half the sugar and cinnamon. Roll up, starting from the 24-inch side. Cut each roll diagonally into 12 pieces. Each piece will be about ½ inch on one side and 3 inches thick on the other. With two thumbs, press down the middle of the side of each roll. In so doing, the 2 cut edges will be forced upward. The rolls will resemble 2 "ears."

Cover 2 baking sheets with parchment paper or lightly grease them. Place cinnamon ears on prepared baking sheets. Let rise until puffy. Combine the egg and milk to make a glaze. Brush rolls with the glaze and sprinkle with the pearl sugar.

Preheat the oven to 400°F. Bake for 8 to 10 minutes or just until golden.

MAKES 24 ROLLS

Saint Lucia Wreath and Buns

1 package (3 teaspoons) active dry yeast
¼ cup warm water (105°F to 115°F)
¾ cup milk
½ cup butter
1 teaspoon saffron threads
½ cup sugar
¼ teaspoon salt
½ cup chopped raisins
2 eggs
3½ to 4 cups flour
1 egg, beaten

In a large bowl, dissolve the yeast in the warm water. Scald the milk and add the butter to it; cool until the butter is melted and the mixture is lukewarm.

Preheat the oven to 250°F. Lay the saffron threads on a piece of foil and place in the oven until toasted, about 5 minutes. Pulverize the toasted saffron with 1 teaspoon of the sugar, using a mortar and pestle or with the back of a spoon in a cup. Add 1 tablespoon of the milk and butter mixture.

Add the saffron mixture, milk and butter mixture, sugar, salt, raisins, and eggs to the yeast. Beat until blended. Stir in half the flour and beat until smooth and satiny. Add the remaining flour gradually to make a stiff dough. Let stand for 15 minutes.

Turn the dough out onto a lightly floured surface. Knead for 10 minutes or until the dough is smooth and satiny. Place the dough in a lightly oiled bowl. Turn the dough over to oil the top. Cover and let rise in a warm place until doubled, about 1 hour.

Saint Lucia Braided Wreath

Punch the dough down and divide into 3 parts. Shape each part into a ropelike strand about 36 inches long. Braid the strands by aligning them vertically and alternately crossing each outer strand over the center strand. Shape the braid into a circle and place on a greased or parchment-covered baking sheet. Pinch the ends together where they meet to seal the strands and to conceal the beginning and end of the braid. Brush with the beaten egg. Let rise for about 45 minutes or just until puffy. Preheat the oven to 375ºF. Bake for 20 to 25 minutes, until lightly browned, or until a wooden skewer inserted into the center of the dough comes out clean and dry. Cool on a rack.

MAKES 1 LARGE WREATH

Saint Lucia Buns

Cover 2 baking sheets with parchment paper.

Punch the dough down and divide it into 32 parts. Shape each part into a rope about 8 inches long. Place 2 ropes side by side so they are parallel and touching each other. Curl all 4 ends toward the center to form a square with rounded corners. Place the buns on the parchment-covered baking sheets. Let rise until puffy, about 30 minutes. Brush with the beaten egg. Preheat the oven to 450ºF, and bake for about 10 minutes, until golden. Cool on a rack.

MAKES 16 BUNS

Honey Molasses Wheat Bread

This is honestly a quick bread—the recipe goes together in just a couple of minutes. If you have any left, cut it into slices and toast it for breakfast.

2 cups whole wheat flour
½ cup bread flour or unbleached all-
    purpose flour

1 teaspoon baking powder
1 teaspoon baking soda
½ teaspoon salt

1½ cups buttermilk

¼ cup vegetable oil

¼ cup honey

¼ cup light or dark molasses

In a large bowl, combine all the ingredients, adding them in the order given. Stir 75 strokes until dry ingredients are moistened. Pour into a greased 9 × 5-inch loaf pan. Preheat the oven to 350ºF. Bake for 40 to 50 minutes or until a skewer or toothpick inserted in the center comes out clean. Serve with butter or cream cheese.

MAKES 1 LOAF

Fig Banana Wheat Bread

The addition of dried figs and the use of whole wheat flour make this banana bread exceptional.

1 cup sugar

½ cup butter, at room temperature

2 eggs

1½ cups (3 to 4 medium) mashed ripe bananas

1 tablespoon fresh lemon juice

2 cups whole wheat flour

2 teaspoons baking powder

1 teaspoon baking soda

½ teaspoon salt

1 cup chopped dried figs

In a large bowl, cream the sugar and butter until blended and smooth; add the eggs and beat until light; stir in bananas and lemon juice. In a separate bowl, stir the flour, baking powder, soda, and salt together. Add to creamed mixture. Stir in figs.

Grease a 9 × 5-inch loaf pan or 4 small, 5½ × 3-inch loaf pans. Turn mixture into pans. Preheat the oven to 350ºF. Bake large loaf for about 1 hour or until toothpick inserted in the center comes out clean; bake smaller loaves for 30 minutes. Remove from pan or pans and cool on rack.

MAKES 1 LARGE LOAF OR 4 SMALL LOAVES

Rice Flour Banana Bread

Use brown or white rice flour in this bread. It is a good bread for people who cannot tolerate wheat flour or gluten.

⅓ cup softened butter
⅔ cup sugar
2 eggs
3 tablespoons buttermilk
1 teaspoon lemon extract
2 cups brown or white rice flour

1 teaspoon baking powder
½ teaspoon baking soda
½ teaspoon salt
1 cup mashed ripe bananas
1 cup toasted flaked coconut

In a large bowl, cream the butter and sugar; beat in the eggs, 1 at a time. Stir in the buttermilk and lemon extract. In a separate bowl, stir the rice flour, baking powder, soda, and salt together and add to the butter mixture along with the bananas; beat until well blended. Fold in the coconut. Turn into 2 greased 5½ × 3-inch loaf pans. Preheat the oven to 350ºF. Bake for 50 to 55 minutes or until a toothpick inserted in the center comes out clean. Remove from the pans and cool on wire racks.

MAKES 2 SMALL LOAVES

Apricot Almond Pistachio Bread

The day I found a two-pound jar of shelled pistachios at our local wholesale market, I was so excited that I came home and created this bread immediately. The pistachios, almonds, and apricots make a pretty mosaic in each slice of this light nut bread.

1 cup dried apricots, chopped
½ cup brandy
¼ cup butter, at room temperature
½ cup sugar
1 egg
1¾ cups all-purpose flour
2 teaspoons baking powder

¼ teaspoon baking soda
¼ teaspoon salt
¼ cup milk
¼ cup almonds, chopped
¼ cup shelled pistachios, coarsely
    chopped

In a small bowl, combine the apricots and brandy. Cover and let stand for 4 hours.

Preheat the oven to 350ºF. Butter and flour two 5¾ × 3½-inch pans or one 8½ × 4½-inch loaf pan.

In a large bowl, cream together the butter and sugar. Blend in the egg and beat until light. In a small bowl, mix the flour, baking powder, soda, and salt. Add to the creamed mixture along with the milk and apricot/brandy mixture. Mix in the almonds and pistachios. Spoon into the prepared pan or pans.

Bake for 40 to 45 minutes for the small loaves, or 55 to 60 minutes for the large loaf, or until a wooden skewer inserted in the center of the loaf comes out clean. Remove the breads from the pans and cool on wire racks. Serve warm or cool. To mellow the bread, wrap the cooled loaf in clear plastic wrap and store in a cool place for 2 days. To keep longer, wrap in foil, label, and freeze.

MAKES 1 LARGE OR 2 SMALL LOAVES

Orange Pecan Bread

So delicious and so very quick! The aroma of orange peel wafts out of this bread when it's hot. Feel free to substitute 2 egg whites for the whole egg and use skim milk instead of whole milk.

¾ cup sugar	2 cups all-purpose flour
¼ cup vegetable oil	½ cup whole wheat flour
1 egg	1 tablespoon baking powder
1¼ cups milk	3 tablespoons grated orange peel
1 teaspoon salt	1 cup chopped pecans

Preheat the oven to 350ºF. Grease one 9½ × 5½-inch loaf pan or two 8½ × 4½-inch loaf pans.

Measure all of the ingredients into a large bowl. Beat for 30 seconds. Pour into the pan or pans. Bake 55 to 65 minutes for the large loaf, or 55 to 60 minutes for the medium-sized loaves, or until they test done. Cool in the pan for 5 minutes; then remove from the pan and finish cooling on a rack. Cool completely before slicing.

MAKES 1 LARGE OR 2 MEDIUM LOAVES

Sour Cream Orange Filbert Bread

Toasting the nuts intensifies their flavor. Spread them on a baking sheet in a single layer and place in a 350ºF oven for 5 minutes. Stir once, or until the nuts are toasted; cool. The skins will be loose, so rub the nuts in a terry towel to remove most of them. Not all of the skins will come off, but that's okay; they will add a nice brown fleck to the bread.

2 tablespoons freshly grated orange rind	**2 cups all-purpose flour**
2 tablespoons melted butter	**2 teaspoons baking powder**
¼ teaspoon salt	**1 teaspoon baking soda**
½ cup sugar	**1½ cups sour cream**
2 eggs	**1 cup chopped, toasted filberts or pecans**

Preheat the oven to 350°F. Grease one 9½ × 5½-inch loaf pan or three 5¾ × 3½-inch loaf pans.

In a large bowl, cream together the orange rind, butter, salt, and sugar until blended. Add the eggs and beat until light. In another bowl, stir together the flour, baking powder, and soda. Blend the dry ingredients into the creamed mixture alternately with the sour cream; mix just until blended. Stir in the nuts.

Spoon the mixture into the prepared pan or pans. Bake 50 to 60 minutes for the large loaf or 35 to 45 minutes for the smaller loaves, or until they test done.

Remove from the oven and cool for 5 minutes in the pan; then turn out onto a rack to finish cooling.

MAKES 1 LARGE OR 3 SMALL LOAVES

Pumpkin Pecan Tea Bread

I've always loved the taste of pumpkin. This bread has a nice, even texture and is moist and spicy. If you don't have pumpkin pie spice, you can use a combination of 2 teaspoons cinnamon, ½ teaspoon nutmeg, and ¼ teaspoon each of ground ginger and ground cloves.

⅔ cup butter, at room temperature	**3½ cups all-purpose flour**
1¾ cups sugar	**1 tablespoon pumpkin pie spice**
4 eggs	**3 teaspoons baking powder**
2 cups (one 15- to 16-ounce can) cooked pumpkin puree	**½ teaspoon baking soda**
	1 teaspoon salt
⅔ cup milk	**1½ cups chopped pecans**

Preheat the oven to 350ºF. Grease and lightly flour two 9½ × 5½-inch loaf pans or six 5¾ × 3½-inch loaf pans.

In a large bowl, cream the butter and sugar until smooth; add the eggs and beat until light. Blend in the pumpkin and milk. In another bowl, combine the flour, pumpkin pie spice, baking powder, soda, salt, and pecans. Add the dry ingredients to the pumpkin mixture and stir just until the flour is moistened. Turn into the prepared pans and bake 1 hour to 1 hour and 15 minutes for the large loaves, or 50 minutes to 1 hour for the smaller loaves, or until they test done. Cool 5 minutes in the pans; then turn out onto racks to finish cooling.

MAKES 2 LARGE OR 6 SMALL LOAVES

Cranberry Raisin Bread

This moist, sweet-tart, and easy-to-make bread is perfect for holiday brunches, bazaars, and bake sales. It's great with a fruit-flavored cream cheese. It slices best the next day.

2 cups all-purpose flour
1 cup sugar
1½ teaspoons baking powder
¼ teaspoon salt
1 teaspoon grated orange peel
¼ cup melted butter

1 egg, slightly beaten
¾ cup orange juice
1½ cups raisins, golden or dark
1 cup fresh or frozen cranberries, chopped
½ cup chopped pecans

Preheat the oven to 350ºF. Grease one 9½ × 5½-inch loaf pan or three 5¾ × 3½-inch loaf pans.

Measure all of the ingredients into a large bowl in the order listed. Stir just until moistened. Turn into the prepared pan or pans. Bake 35 to 45 minutes for small loaves or 1 hour for the large loaf, or until they test done. Turn out of the pan and cool on a rack.

MAKES 1 LARGE OR 3 SMALL LOAVES

Cinnamon Pear Tea Bread

This bread is moist and aromatic with cinnamon. Make it when pears are in season and at their tastiest.

¼ cup butter, at room temperature
½ cup sugar
1 egg
½ teaspoon vanilla
1 cup all-purpose flour
½ teaspoon baking powder
½ teaspoon baking soda
½ teaspoon cinnamon
¼ teaspoon salt

½ cup sour cream
1 large pear, peeled and diced into ½-inch
   cubes (about 1½ cups)

NUT TOPPING
2 tablespoons butter or margarine, at
   room temperature
¾ teaspoon cinnamon
½ cup light brown sugar, packed
½ cup chopped walnuts

Preheat the oven to 350°F. Grease and flour one 9½ × 5½-inch loaf pan or three 5¾ × 3½-inch loaf pans.

In a large bowl, cream the butter and sugar together until blended. Add the egg and vanilla, and beat until light. In a small bowl, combine the flour, baking powder, soda, cinnamon, and salt. Add to the creamed mixture alternately with the sour cream, mixing just to blend after each addition. Stir in the diced pear. Turn into the prepared pan or pans.

In a small bowl, make the nut topping. Blend the butter, cinnamon, brown sugar, and nuts until well combined and crumbly. Sprinkle over the dough in the pan. Bake for 40 to 45 minutes for the small loaves or 50 to 55 minutes for the large loaf, or until they test done. Cool in the pan for 10 minutes; then turn out onto a rack and finish cooling.

MAKES 1 LARGE OR 3 SMALL LOAVES

Cheddar Apple Bread

This bread is delicious fresh from the oven, but try using it in French toast for a special treat.

½ cup butter, at room temperature
¾ cup sugar

2 eggs
1¾ cups all-purpose flour

1 teaspoon baking powder
½ teaspoon baking soda
½ teaspoon salt
½ teaspoon cinnamon
½ teaspoon freshly ground nutmeg

1 cup chopped tart apple (1 medium, peeled and cored)
½ cup shredded sharp cheddar cheese
⅓ cup chopped pecans

Preheat the oven to 350°F. Grease and flour one 9½ × 5½-inch loaf pan or three 5¾ × 3½-inch loaf pans.

In a large bowl, cream the butter and sugar; add the eggs and beat until light. In a separate bowl, stir the flour, baking powder, soda, salt, cinnamon, and nutmeg together. Add to the creamed mixture along with the apple. Fold in the cheese and pecans. Turn into the prepared pan or pans. Bake 1 hour for a large loaf, 40 to 45 minutes for small loaves, or until they test done. Cool in the pan for 5 minutes; then turn out onto a rack to finish cooling.

MAKES 1 LARGE OR 3 SMALL LOAVES

Zucchini Walnut Bread

In a quick bread, zucchini adds a pretty, confetti-like fleck as well as moistness and flavor.

1½ cups all-purpose flour
1½ teaspoons cinnamon
½ teaspoon salt
1 teaspoon baking powder
½ teaspoon baking soda
2 eggs, beaten

1 cup sugar
1½ teaspoons vanilla
½ cup vegetable oil
1½ cups shredded zucchini
½ cup chopped black walnuts

Preheat the oven to 350°F. Grease a 9½ × 5½-inch loaf pan or three 5¾ × 3½-inch loaf pans.

In a medium bowl, stir together the flour, cinnamon, salt, baking powder, and soda. In another bowl, beat the eggs with the sugar, vanilla, and vegetable oil until thick. Fold the dry ingredients into the beaten mixture until well blended. Stir in the zucchini and the nuts. Pour into the prepared loaf pan or pans, and bake 1 hour for the large loaf or 40 to 45 minutes for the small loaves, or until they test done. Remove from the pan and cool on a rack.

MAKES 1 LARGE OR 3 SMALL LOAVES

Date Nut Cranberry Bread

Keep a loaf of this bread on hand in the freezer—it makes great, unusual turkey sandwiches. Just spread with cream cheese, top with thinly sliced plain or smoked turkey breast, and garnish with a dab of cranberry sauce.

2 cups all-purpose flour
2 teaspoons baking powder
½ teaspoon baking soda
¼ teaspoon salt
4 tablespoons butter
¾ cup sugar
1 cup chopped walnuts
1 tablespoon grated orange rind

1 egg
⅔ cup orange juice
1 cup fresh raw cranberries, chopped
1 cup chopped dates

GLAZE
1 tablespoon milk
1 tablespoon sugar

Preheat the oven to 350ºF. Grease and flour a 9½ × 5½-inch loaf pan or three 5¾ × 3½-inch loaf pans.

In a large bowl, stir the flour, baking powder, soda, and salt together. With a fork or pastry blender, cut in the butter until the mixture is crumbly. Stir in the sugar, walnuts, and orange rind. In a small bowl, whisk the egg and orange juice together and stir into the dry ingredients just until blended; the mixture will be lumpy. Blend in the cranberries and dates. Spoon into the prepared pan or pans.

To glaze, smooth the top of the loaf or loaves and brush with the milk; then sprinkle with the sugar. Bake 45 to 55 minutes for small loaves or 1 hour to 1 hour 15 minutes for the large loaf, or until they test done. Remove from the oven and cool in the pan for 10 minutes. Turn out onto a rack to finish cooling.

MAKES 1 LARGE OR 3 SMALL LOAVES

Carrot Walnut Bread

This bread falls somewhere between golden and dark and rich. It is especially good toasted with a slice of Monterey Jack cheese.

2 cups all-purpose flour
1 cup chopped walnuts
½ cup granulated sugar

½ cup brown sugar, packed
3 teaspoons baking powder
1 teaspoon cinnamon

½ teaspoon salt
2 cups finely shredded fresh carrots
½ cup milk

⅓ cup vegetable oil
1 egg

Preheat the oven to 350ºF. Grease and flour one 9½ × 5½-inch loaf pan or three 5¾ × 3½-inch loaf pans.

In a large bowl, combine the flour, nuts, sugars, baking powder, cinnamon, and salt until well blended. Stir in the remaining ingredients just until moistened. Spoon into pan or pans. Bake 50 to 60 minutes for a large loaf, 35 to 45 minutes for small loaves, or until they test done. Cool in the pan for 10 minutes; then turn out onto a rack to finish cooling.

MAKES 1 LARGE OR 3 SMALL LOAVES

Granola Chocolate Cherry Bread

This pretty, festive-looking bread is sure to please chocolate lovers.

1⅓ cups all-purpose flour
⅓ cup sugar
1 teaspoon baking soda
½ teaspoon salt
1 cup buttermilk
⅓ cup vegetable oil

1 teaspoon vanilla
1 egg
1 cup granola breakfast cereal
½ cup chopped almonds
½ cup semisweet mini chocolate chips
¾ cup chopped candied cherries

Preheat the oven to 350ºF. Grease and flour an 8½ × 4½-inch loaf pan.

In a medium bowl, stir together the flour, sugar, baking soda, and salt. In a large mixing bowl, blend the buttermilk, oil, vanilla, and egg. Stir in the dry ingredients just until blended. Fold in the granola, almonds, chocolate chips, and cherries. Spoon into the prepared pan. Bake for 55 to 60 minutes, or until the bread tests done. Let cool in the pan for 10 minutes, remove, and finish cooling on a rack.

MAKES 1 MEDIUM LOAF

Fruited Apple Loaf

This is terrific for the holidays, a cross between a nut bread and an aged fruitcake, but less dense. Keep the loaves wrapped and refrigerated up to a month. Cut in thin slices and spread with fruit-flavored cream cheese.

1 cup light or dark brown sugar, packed
½ cup vegetable oil
2 tablespoons sherry
2 eggs
1 teaspoon vanilla
1 cup light or dark raisins
1 cup coarsely chopped mixed candied
    fruits
1 cup chopped walnuts or pecans

1 cup pitted chopped dates
1½ cups chopped tart apple (about 3
    small, peeled and cored)
2 teaspoons baking soda
2 cups all-purpose flour
½ teaspoon salt
½ teaspoon cinnamon
¼ teaspoon freshly ground nutmeg

Preheat the oven to 350°F. Grease and flour one 9½ × 5½-inch loaf pan or three 5¾ × 3½-inch loaf pans.

In a large bowl, combine the brown sugar, oil, sherry, eggs, vanilla, raisins, fruits, nuts, and dates. In a small bowl, stir the apples and baking soda together and add to the fruit-nut mixture. In another bowl, stir the flour, salt, cinnamon, and nutmeg together; then blend the dry mixture into the fruit mixture.

Spoon into the prepared pan or pans, and bake 1 hour and 25 minutes for the large loaf or 50 to 60 minutes for the smaller loaves, or until they test done. Cool 5 minutes in the pan; then turn out onto a rack to finish cooling.

MAKES 1 LARGE OR 3 SMALL LOAVES

Whole Wheat Walnut Banana Bread

When bananas turn black, I often whirl them in the blender, pack 1-cup batches in heavy-duty plastic bags, and freeze. They work well in banana breads like this one. Simply set the bag of frozen fruit in a bowl of warm water to thaw.

½ cup butter, at room temperature

1 cup sugar

2 eggs

1 cup mashed ripe bananas (about 3 medium)

1 cup all-purpose flour

1 cup whole wheat flour

1 teaspoon baking powder

½ teaspoon baking soda

½ teaspoon salt

½ cup chopped walnuts

Preheat the oven to 350°F. Grease and flour one 9½ × 5½-inch loaf pan or three 5¾ × 3½-inch loaf pans.

In a large bowl, cream the butter and sugar until well blended. Beat in the eggs and mashed banana. In a small bowl, combine the flours, baking powder, soda, and salt and blend into the creamed mixture. Stir in the nuts. Turn into the prepared pan or pans. Bake 1 hour and 10 minutes for the large loaf or 45 to 55 minutes for the smaller loaves, or until they test done. Cool in the pan 5 minutes; then remove to a rack and finish cooling.

MAKES 1 LARGE OR 3 SMALL LOAVES

Yogurt Nut Brown Bread

It's compact, dark, grainy, and rich-tasting—yet there's no fat or egg in this loaf!

1 cup stone-ground rye flour

1 cup whole wheat flour

½ cup all-purpose flour

2 teaspoons baking soda

1 teaspoon salt

2 cups plain yogurt

⅓ cup light molasses

½ cup chopped walnuts

Preheat the oven to 350°F. Grease one 9½ × 5½-inch loaf pan or three 5¾ × 3½-inch loaf pans.

In a large bowl, stir together the flours, baking soda, and salt. In another bowl, stir together the yogurt and molasses. Blend the yogurt mixture into the dry ingredients and stir in the walnuts just until all the ingredients are moistened. Spoon into the prepared pan or pans. Bake 1 hour for the large loaf or 35 to 45 minutes for the smaller loaves, or until they test done. Remove from the oven, let cool in the pan for 10 minutes, then turn onto a rack to finish cooling.

MAKES 1 LARGE OR 3 SMALL LOAVES

Hot Raisin Bread

Here's another quick-to-mix—and bake—bread. It's best hot out of the oven and just right for afternoon tea or morning coffee.

2 cups all-purpose flour
2 teaspoons baking powder
¼ teaspoon salt
¼ cup vegetable oil
¾ cup milk

⅓ cup golden or dark raisins
2 tablespoons sugar
2 tablespoons butter, melted or soft
¼ cup cinnamon sugar (¼ cup sugar plus
 ½ teaspoon cinnamon)

Preheat the oven to 450°F. Grease a baking sheet or cover with parchment paper.

In a mixing bowl, combine the flour, baking powder, salt, oil, milk, raisins, and sugar, and mix into a soft dough. Transfer it to the baking sheet and, with floured hands, pat the dough into an 8-inch square, about ½-inch thick. Spread with the butter and sprinkle with the cinnamon sugar. Bake for 10 to 12 minutes, or until just golden. Cut into squares and serve hot.

MAKES ONE 8-INCH SQUARE LOAF

Blueberry Gingerbread

Not just for breakfast—this makes a delightful old-fashioned dessert when topped with softly whipped cream.

½ cup vegetable oil
1 cup plus 2 tablespoons sugar
1 egg
½ cup light molasses
1 cup fresh (or frozen, thawed) blueberries
2 cups all-purpose flour

1 teaspoon baking soda
1 teaspoon cinnamon
½ teaspoon ground ginger
½ teaspoon ground nutmeg
½ teaspoon salt
1 cup buttermilk

Preheat the oven to 350°F. Grease a 9-inch square cake pan.

In a large bowl, beat the oil, sugar, and egg until light. Add the molasses and beat until thick. In a small bowl, toss the blueberries with 2 tablespoons of the flour until well coated. Mix the remaining flour with the dry ingredients. Add the flour mixture and the buttermilk alternately to the creamed mixture, and blend until smooth. Fold in the blueberries. Turn into the prepared pan. Bake for 45 to 50 minutes, or until it tests done. Serve warm.

MAKES ONE 9-INCH SQUARE CAKE

Cornmeal Spoon Bread

This is called spoon bread *because it is spooned from the pan. Often served for breakfast, it is delicious with butter and maple syrup. Some like it with the main course at dinner in place of bread or potatoes. In Virginia, it is a tradition to serve spoon bread with fried tomatoes.*

1 cup boiling water
½ cup cornmeal
½ cup milk
½ cup all-purpose flour

1½ teaspoons baking powder
½ teaspoon salt
1 tablespoon butter, softened or melted
4 eggs, separated

Preheat the oven to 400ºF. Grease a 1-quart casserole or soufflé dish. Pour boiling water over cornmeal in a medium-sized bowl. Beat in the milk. In a small bowl, combine the flour, baking powder, and salt. Stir into the cornmeal mixture along with the butter and egg yolks. In a large bowl, beat egg whites until stiff; fold into cornmeal mixture. Turn into greased dish. Bake just until puffed and golden, 25 to 30 minutes; do not overbake. Serve immediately.

MAKES 4 TO 6 SERVINGS

Early American Spoon Bread

Spoonbread is so named because you spoon it to serve.

2 cups milk
2 tablespoons butter
1 teaspoon sugar
½ teaspoon salt

⅔ cup yellow cornmeal
4 eggs, separated
Melted butter

Preheat the oven to 350ºF. Butter a deep 1½-quart casserole or soufflé dish. In a medium saucepan, combine milk, 2 tablespoons butter, sugar, salt, and cornmeal. Bring to a boil, stirring constantly. Cook and stir until thick and smooth. Quickly stir in egg yolks until blended; set aside. In a medium bowl, beat egg whites until soft peaks form. Fold egg whites into the cornmeal mixture. Turn into the buttered casserole. Bake 30 to 35 minutes or until puffy and set. Serve immediately with melted butter to pour over individual servings.

MAKES 6 SERVINGS

Johnny Cake

Johnnycake, the cornmeal bread that colonists first called journey cake, *is one that seems to originate from a large area of the eastern part of our country. Some say the first name originated from trips into the wilderness during which corn bread was cooked by campfires along the way. In Rhode Island, it is spelled without the "h" and it is made with white cornmeal. The first colonists learned from the Native Americans to make the cakes and called them* Shawnee cakes. *They're also known as* hoe cakes, ash cakes, *and* corn pone. *Each is cooked in a different way and each has its own special quality. The best cakes are made from the hard variety of corn, which grows in the North. Many Southern corn breads call for "dent" corn so named for the dents in the dry kernel.*

1 cup stone-ground cornmeal	1 tablespoon melted butter
1 teaspoon sugar	Cooking spray
¼ teaspoon salt	Butter
1¼ cups boiling water	Maple syrup

In a medium bowl, combine the cornmeal, sugar, and salt. Add the boiling water and melted butter; stir until smooth. Place a 10-inch skillet over medium-high heat. Coat pan with vegetable cooking spray. Drop batter by tablespoonfuls onto hot skillet, making a few cakes at a time. Cook until crisp and browned on 1 side. Turn and cook until the other side is golden. Repeat with remaining batter, spraying skillet with more cooking spray as required. Serve hot with butter and maple syrup.

MAKES ABOUT 24 CAKES

Dark Fruit Nut Loaf

This bread is a country favorite. The variations provide a way to use up over-ripe bananas and also give you a quick date nut loaf to put out for holiday entertaining.

⅔ cup sugar

⅓ cup softened butter or vegetable shortening

2 eggs

3 tablespoons buttermilk

1 cup freshly grated apple

2 cups all-purpose flour

1 teaspoon baking powder

½ teaspoon baking soda

½ teaspoon salt

1 cup chopped walnuts or pecans

Preheat the oven to 350ºF. Grease a 9 × 5-inch loaf pan. In a large bowl, beat sugar, butter or shortening, and eggs until smooth and light. Stir in the buttermilk and grated apple. Combine the flour, baking powder, soda, and salt into a medium-sized bowl. Stir into the egg mixture just until ingredients are blended; do not overmix. Fold in the nuts. Pour into prepared pan. Bake for 50 to 60 minutes or until a wooden skewer inserted in the center comes out clean. Remove from pan; cool on a rack.

MAKES 1 LOAF

Banana Nut Bread

Substitute 1 cup mashed bananas for grated apple. Bake as above.

Date Nut Bread

Substitute ½ cup packed brown sugar for ⅔ cup granulated sugar. Use 1 egg. Omit buttermilk and grated apple. Pour 1 cup boiling water over 1 cup chopped dates; let cool. Add to batter in place of apple. Bake as above.

Orange Date Loaf

Omit buttermilk and grated apple. Add grated peel of 1 orange. Measure juice from the orange. Add water to equal 1 cup. Add to batter in place of apple. Add 1 cup chopped dates. Bake as above.

Hardtack

Hardtack—also called crispbread—is a staple throughout Scandinavia, and there are many excellent varieties both homemade and store bought. This one is a quick oatmeal crispbread. Grind the rolled oats for this recipe in a food processor fitted with a steel blade or in a blender.

¾ cup melted butter
1½ cups buttermilk
3 cups flour

3 cups finely ground rolled oats
1 teaspoon baking soda
1 teaspoon salt

Preheat the oven to 375°F. Lightly grease four 11 × 17-inch cookie sheets.

In a large bowl, stir together the melted butter and the buttermilk. Add the remaining ingredients to make a stiff, sticky dough. Let it stand for 10 minutes (the dough will become less sticky). Divide into 4 parts and place 1 part on each cookie sheet. Using either a regular rolling pin or one made especially for hardtack, roll the dough out to the edges of the cookie sheets (it will be very thin). Trim the edges and score the dough into 2 × 4-inch pieces. If you are using a plain rolling pin, pierce the dough all over with a fork. If you are using a hobnailed hardtack rolling pin, you do not need to pierce the dough. Bake for 20 to 25 minutes, until golden and crisp.

MAKES APPROXIMATELY 112 CRACKERS

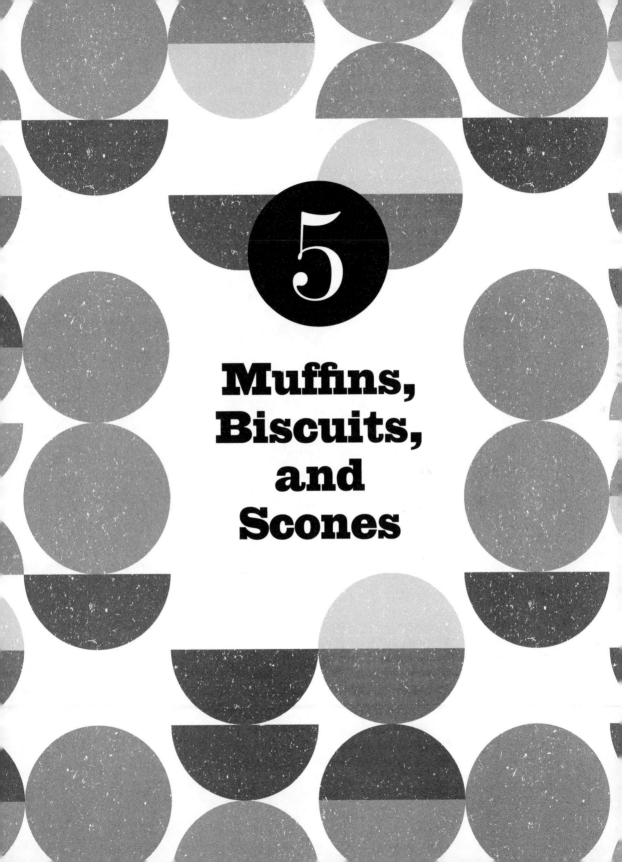

5

Muffins,
Biscuits,
and
Scones

A PERFECT MUFFIN HAS A ROUNDED TOP, is tender, and is evenly textured with a golden brown crust, which may be pebbly or slightly rough. Imperfect muffins have peaked tops with tunnels or holes inside and are tough.

The secret to making good muffins is simple—be sure not to overmix. The simplest way to handle the mixing is to combine all of the dry ingredients first, then add special ingredients, such as nuts or fruits, if used. Mix the liquid ingredients separately and then add them to the dry ingredients; mix only until the dry ingredients are moistened—fifteen to twenty strokes, using a spoon or rubber spatula to gently fold or stir the ingredients together. The batter will look lumpy and rough, but the lumps will disappear when the muffins bake. The consistency of the batter will vary, depending on the individual flours and liquids used in the recipe. Scoop or spoon the batter gently into the muffin pans for baking. Be careful not to mix the batter during this process.

Always preheat the oven before baking. Muffins are usually baked at 350°F to 400°F. Average muffins bake in 20 to 25 minutes. Miniature muffins take five to eight minutes less; giant-size muffins, five minutes more.

There are many textures that are acceptable for muffins, and that depends on the ingredients used. Muffins can be dense or light, moist or cake-like. Some are sweet and others are savory.

Wheat Germ English Muffins

These grainy and flavorful muffins are great split and toasted, served with jam and cream cheese. Or use them as a base for poached eggs, creamed seafood or chicken, or just melted cheese.

1 package (3 teaspoons) active dry yeast
½ cup warm water (105°F to 115°F)
½ cup milk
½ cup cold water
1 tablespoon honey
2 cups whole wheat flour

1 to 1¼ cups unbleached all-purpose flour
½ cup wheat germ
1 teaspoon salt
½ teaspoon baking soda
Yellow cornmeal, preferably stone-ground

In a large bowl, dissolve the yeast in the warm water; set aside for 5 minutes or until yeast foams. Scald milk and add cold water; pour into bowl, add honey, and cool to lukewarm. Add to yeast mixture along with whole wheat flour. Cover and let stand in warm place until doubled, about 1 hour. Stir down. Stir in 1 cup of the all-purpose flour, wheat germ, salt, and soda to make a stiff mixture. Turn out onto a lightly floured surface and knead until dough is smooth and springy, about 10 minutes. Wash bowl, lightly grease it, add dough, and turn over. Cover and let rise for 30 minutes or until mixture has not quite doubled. Grease 12 English muffin rings (tuna cans with both ends removed are ideal). Roll dough out to ⅓-inch thickness. Cut into circles using the rings and leave dough inside the can. Transfer to a flat surface, and let rise until doubled, about 1 hour. Dust both sides with cornmeal. Heat an ungreased griddle to 350ºF. Toast muffins on both sides until browned, about 6 to 8 minutes per side, removing ring after first side is browned. Let muffins cool on rack. Separate halves with fork. Wrap and refrigerate. Toast before serving.

MAKES 12 STANDARD MUFFINS

Cornmeal Oat English Muffins

These English muffins are really easy to make—basically a no-knead bread. The dough is ready for cutting out, rising, and baking after just a good beating with a spoon.

2 packages (5½ teaspoons) active
   dry yeast
2 cups warm water (105°F to 115°F)
½ cup butter
1 tablespoon sugar
2 teaspoons salt

½ cup yellow cornmeal
1 cup rolled oats, quick or old-fashioned
5 to 5½ cups bread flour or unbleached
   all-purpose flour
Cornmeal for dusting baking sheets

In a large bowl, dissolve the yeast in the water; let stand 5 minutes until yeast foams. Add butter, sugar, salt, cornmeal, oats, and 1 cup of the bread flour; beat until smooth. Gradually add remaining flour to make a stiff dough, beating well after each addition. On a floured surface, roll out to ¼- to ⅜-inch thickness. Cut into rounds with floured 4-inch cutter. Place on ungreased baking sheets sprinkled with cornmeal. Sprinkle with additional cornmeal. Let rise in warm place for 30 minutes or until light. With pancake turner, remove muffins from baking sheets and gently ease onto a preheated griddle, about 360ºF. Bake for 7 minutes on each side until light golden brown. Cool. Split, toast, and butter. Serve hot with marmalade or jelly.

MAKES ABOUT 18 MUFFINS

Carrot Spice Muffins

Glorious on a sunny morning in May, these fast and easy-to-make muffins are chock-full of flavor. I always think muffins are more interesting when they're made into either the giant size or the miniatures rather than the standard size. This recipe can go either way. Tiny muffins bake quickly and have lots of browned edges that appeal to the "crunchers" in the crowd, but you have to be careful not to overbake them or they can be dry. Giant muffins take a bit longer to bake but are satisfyingly moist and crumbly.

2 cups all-purpose flour
¾ cup sugar
2 teaspoons baking powder
½ teaspoon baking soda
½ teaspoon salt
1 teaspoon cinnamon
1 teaspoon freshly ground nutmeg
2 cups shredded fresh carrot

1 tart apple (such as Granny Smith), peeled, cored, and shredded
½ cup golden raisins
½ cup chopped pecans
3 large eggs, beaten
½ cup corn oil
2 teaspoons vanilla

Preheat the oven to 350°F. Grease 12 regular muffin cups, 36 miniature muffin cups, or 6 giant muffin cups, or line them with paper baking cups.

In a large mixing bowl, combine the flour, sugar, baking powder, soda, salt, cinnamon, nutmeg, carrot, apple, raisins, and pecans until all ingredients are well mixed. In another bowl, combine the eggs, oil, and vanilla. Stir into the flour mixture only until blended. Fill the prepared muffin cups three-quarters full with the batter.

Bake until a wooden skewer inserted in the center of the muffins comes out clean. For regular muffins, bake 20 to 25 minutes; for miniature muffins, bake 15 to 20 minutes; for giant muffins, bake 25 to 30 minutes. Remove from pans and serve warm or cool on a wire rack.

MAKES 12 REGULAR MUFFINS, 6 GIANT MUFFINS, OR 36 MINIATURE MUFFINS

Giant Whole Wheat Pumpkin Muffins

These hearty whole-grain muffins are quick to make and great served with a hearty stew on a chilly autumn day.

2 cups whole wheat flour
²⁄₃ cup all-purpose flour
²⁄₃ cup brown sugar, packed
2 teaspoons baking powder
1 teaspoon baking soda

1 teaspoon pumpkin pie spice
1½ cups buttermilk
1 cup puréed or canned pumpkin
¾ cup raisins

Preheat the oven to 350ºF. Lightly grease 6 large, 4-inch muffin cups. In a large bowl, stir together the whole wheat flour, all-purpose flour, brown sugar, baking powder, soda, and pumpkin pie spice.

In a medium-sized bowl, stir together the buttermilk and pumpkin. Add to the dry ingredients, mixing just until the flour mixture is moistened. Fold in the raisins. Spoon the mixture into the prepared muffin cups. Bake for 35 to 40 minutes or until a toothpick inserted in the center comes out clean. Remove from pans and cool on a wire rack.

MAKES 6 GIANT MUFFINS

Spiced Sweet Potato Muffins with Walnut Streusel

This is adapted from Eric Copage's book Kwanzaa, *which offers a vivid and detailed description of this African American holiday. Kwanzaa is a non-religious holiday designed to celebrate the African heritage of black Americans. It's celebrated from the day after Christmas to New Year's. There are no specified foods for this holiday, but most of the foods reflect a Southern (as in these muffins, which are made with sweet potatoes), Caribbean, Creole, or African theme. These are delicious, spicy, and soft-textured muffins with a crunchy topping.*

1 sweet potato or yam
½ cup milk
2 large eggs, beaten
¼ cup melted butter
2 cups all-purpose flour
½ cup sugar
1 tablespoon baking powder
1 teaspoon freshly ground nutmeg

1 teaspoon freshly ground cardamom
½ teaspoon salt

WALNUT STREUSEL
2 tablespoons coarsely chopped walnuts
2 tablespoons brown sugar, packed
2 tablespoons all-purpose flour
¼ teaspoon cinnamon
1 tablespoon butter, at room temperature

Preheat the oven to 400°F. Butter 12 muffin cups or line with paper liners.

Peel and cube the sweet potato. Place into a saucepan, add water to cover, and cook over medium heat until just tender, about 20 minutes. Drain, cool, and mash in a mixing bowl. You should have about 1 cup mashed potato.

Stir together the sweet potato and milk. Beat in the eggs and butter. In another bowl, mix the flour, sugar, baking powder, nutmeg, cardamom, and salt. Stir the dry ingredients into the potato mixture just until blended.

Make the streusel in a small bowl. Stir the walnuts, brown sugar, flour, and cinnamon together. Add the butter; mix until crumbly. Spoon the batter into the muffin cups, filling them 2/3 full. Sprinkle with the streusel mixture and gently pat it.

Bake for 20 to 25 minutes. Remove from the cups and cool on a wire rack.

MAKES 12 MUFFINS

Cornmeal Pineapple Muffins

Crushed pineapple in the batter and a surprise pocket of pineapple pre-serves in the center make these muffins moist and flavorful.

1½ cups all-purpose flour
1 cup yellow cornmeal
1 tablespoon sugar
4 teaspoons baking powder
½ teaspoon salt
2 eggs, lightly beaten

1¼ cups milk
4 tablespoons melted butter
½ cup well-drained canned crushed
    pineapple
6 tablespoons pineapple jam or preserves

Preheat the oven to 400ºF. Lightly grease 12 regular-sized muffin cups or 36 minia-ture cups, or coat with nonstick spray.

In a large bowl, thoroughly mix the flour, cornmeal, sugar, baking powder, and salt. In a small bowl, whisk together the eggs, milk, butter, and pineapple. Add the liquid ingredients to the dry ingredients and stir just until the dry ingredients are moist-ened, about 20 strokes.

Spoon 2 tablespoons of the batter into each regular-sized muffin cup, or 2 teaspoons of the batter into each miniature cup. Drop ½ teaspoon of the pineapple jam or pre-serves into the center of each larger muffin, or a tiny bit into the mini-muffins. Divide the remaining batter evenly among the muffin cups to cover the preserves. Bake for 15 to 20 minutes for regular-sized muffins, or 10 to 15 minutes for miniature muffins, or until a wooden skewer inserted in a muffin slightly off center comes out clean. Let the muffins cool in the tin for about 3 minutes, remove, and cool on a rack or transfer to a basket to serve warm.

MAKES 12 REGULAR-SIZED MUFFINS OR 36 MINI-MUFFINS

Dried Cranberry Raisin Grain Muffins

Tart dried cranberries look like crimson raisins and can be found bulk packaged in the produce department of the supermarket, or at specialty or health food stores.

1 cup all-purpose flour	2 teaspoons cinnamon
¾ cup whole wheat flour	½ cup dried cranberries
1 cup uncooked old-fashioned rolled oats	½ cup dark or golden raisins
½ cup brown sugar, packed	1 cup milk
½ cup dry Grape-Nuts cereal	3 tablespoons melted butter
4 teaspoons baking powder	2 eggs, lightly beaten, or 3 egg whites,
½ teaspoon salt	lightly beaten

Preheat the oven to 400ºF. Lightly grease 12 regular-sized muffin cups, or coat with nonstick spray.

In a large bowl, mix the flours, rolled oats, brown sugar, Grape-Nuts, baking powder, salt, cinnamon, dried cranberries, and raisins. Make a well in the center of the dry ingredients and add the milk, butter, and eggs or egg whites. Stir the mixture just until blended, about 20 strokes.

Spoon the batter into the muffin cups, dividing the batter evenly. Bake for 17 to 20 minutes, or until the muffins are lightly browned and a wooden skewer inserted into the center of a muffin comes out clean. Cool 1 minute; then remove from the muffin tin and transfer to a wire rack to cool or to a basket to serve warm.

MAKES 12 MUFFINS

Glorious Morning Muffins

Replacing most of the oil with applesauce makes an equally tasty muffin.

1 cup all-purpose flour
¾ cup whole wheat flour
¼ cup dry Grape-Nuts cereal
¾ cup brown sugar, packed
2 teaspoons baking powder
1 teaspoon baking soda
½ teaspoon salt
1 tablespoon cinnamon
2 cups grated peeled carrots

1 apple, such as Granny Smith, peeled, cored, and chopped
1 cup raisins
1 egg, lightly beaten
2 egg whites, lightly beaten
½ cup unsweetened applesauce
¼ cup safflower or corn oil
1 tablespoon vanilla
1 tablespoon finely chopped walnuts
1 tablespoon wheat germ

Preheat the oven to 400ºF. Lightly grease 12 regular-sized muffin cups, or coat with nonstick spray.

In a large bowl, mix the flours, Grape-Nuts, brown sugar, baking powder, soda, salt, cinnamon, carrots, apple, and raisins. Make a well in the center of the dry ingredients and add the egg, egg whites, applesauce, oil, and vanilla. Stir just until blended, about 20 strokes.

Spoon the batter into the muffin cups, dividing the batter evenly. Sprinkle with the nuts and wheat germ. Bake for 17 to 20 minutes, or until the muffins are lightly browned and a wooden skewer inserted in the center of a muffin comes out clean. Cool 1 minute; then remove from the muffin tin and transfer to a wire rack to cool or to a basket to serve warm.

MAKES 12 MUFFINS

Apple Cheddar Muffins

I've always loved the flavor of apple pie served with cheddar cheese, so I put these two ingredients together in a muffin.

1½ cups all-purpose flour
½ cup whole wheat flour
½ cup sugar
3 teaspoons baking powder
¼ teaspoon salt
½ teaspoon cinnamon

1½ cups tart apples, such as Granny
    Smith, peeled and chopped
1 cup shredded cheddar cheese
1 cup milk
2 tablespoons melted butter
1 egg, lightly beaten

Preheat the oven to 400°F. Lightly grease 12 regular-sized muffin cups, or coat with nonstick spray.

In a large bowl, mix the flours, sugar, baking powder, salt, and cinnamon. Add the chopped apples and the cheese and mix gently until the apple and cheese are evenly distributed in the flour mixture. In a small bowl, stir together the milk, melted butter, and egg. Stir the liquid ingredients into the dry ingredients just until blended, about 20 to 25 strokes.

Spoon the batter into the muffin cups, dividing the batter evenly. Bake for 20 to 25 minutes, or until the muffins are lightly browned and a wooden skewer inserted in the center of a muffin comes out clean. Cool 1 minute; then remove from the muffin tin and transfer to a wire rack to cool or to a basket to serve warm.

MAKES 12 MUFFINS

Hazelnut Pear Muffins

To make the most of the flavor and texture of filberts (hazelnuts), I use them as a topping for these muffins. To further enhance the flavor, I use hazelnut oil, which I buy in my favorite gourmet shop.

2 cups all-purpose flour
¼ cup whole wheat flour
3 teaspoons baking powder
½ teaspoon salt

1 teaspoon grated lemon zest
1 large ripe pear, peeled, seeded, and diced
¾ cup milk
4 tablespoons hazelnut or corn oil
⅓ cup honey

2 egg whites, lightly beaten

2 tablespoons chopped hazelnuts (filberts)

Preheat the oven to 400ºF. Lightly grease 12 regular-sized muffin cups, or coat with nonstick spray.

In a large bowl, mix the flours, baking powder, salt, and lemon zest. Fold in the diced pear until the pear pieces are coated. In a small bowl, beat the milk, oil, honey, and egg whites together. Stir the liquid ingredients into the dry ingredients just until blended, about 20 strokes.

Spoon the batter into the muffin cups, dividing the batter evenly. Sprinkle the tops of the muffins with the hazelnuts. Lightly press the nuts into the batter. Bake for 20 to 25 minutes, or until the muffins are lightly browned and a wooden skewer inserted in the center of a muffin comes out clean. Cool 1 minute; then remove from the muffin tin and transfer to a wire rack to cool or to a basket to serve warm.

MAKES 12 MUFFINS

Hot Cross Muffins

These are a muffin version of the classic hot cross buns that are traditionally served on Good Friday.

½ cup dark or golden raisins
2 cups sifted cake flour
½ cup sugar
2 teaspoons baking powder
½ teaspoon baking soda
¼ teaspoon salt
3 tablespoons melted butter

2 eggs, lightly beaten
1 cup nonfat plain yogurt
1 teaspoon grated orange zest

FROSTING
½ cup powdered sugar
½ teaspoon vanilla
1 to 2 tablespoons milk

In a small bowl, add hot water to cover the raisins. Let stand for 1 minute; then drain well. Preheat the oven to 400ºF. Lightly grease 12 regular-sized muffin cups, or coat with nonstick spray.

In a large bowl, stir the flour, sugar, baking powder, soda, salt, and raisins together. In a small bowl, mix the butter, eggs, yogurt, and orange zest together. Stir the liquid ingredients into the dry ingredients just until the dry ingredients are moistened.

Spoon the batter into the muffin cups, dividing the batter evenly. Bake for 18 to 20 minutes, until golden or a wooden skewer inserted in the center of a muffin comes out clean. Cool 1 minute; then remove from the muffin tin and transfer to a wire rack to cool.

To make the frosting, in a small bowl stir together the powdered sugar, vanilla, and enough milk to make a smooth frosting. Drizzle the frosting onto each muffin to make a cross.

MAKES 12 MUFFINS

Oat Cranberry Muffins

Cranberries provide a tart bite to these delicious muffins, which are perfect for an autumn breakfast or brunch. If you use frozen cranberries, you can add them to the batter without defrosting them, but expect the muffins to take up to 5 minutes longer to bake.

¾ cup all-purpose flour
¾ cup whole wheat flour
1 cup old-fashioned uncooked rolled oats
½ cup brown sugar, packed
3 teaspoons baking powder
½ teaspoon salt

1 teaspoon cinnamon
1 cup fresh or frozen whole cranberries
1 cup milk
3 tablespoons melted butter
1 egg, lightly beaten

Preheat the oven to 400°F. Lightly grease 12 regular-sized muffin cups, or coat with nonstick spray.

In a large bowl, mix the flours, rolled oats, brown sugar, baking powder, salt, cinnamon, and cranberries. In a small bowl, beat the milk, butter, and egg together. Stir the liquid ingredients into the dry ingredients just until blended, about 20 strokes.

Spoon the batter into the muffin cups, dividing the batter evenly. Bake for 20 to 25 minutes, or until the muffins are lightly browned and a wooden skewer inserted in the center of a muffin comes out clean. Cool 1 minute; then remove from the muffin tin and transfer to a wire rack to cool or to a basket to serve warm.

MAKES 12 MUFFINS

Oat Whole Wheat Banana Muffins

Low in fat and high in fiber, these muffins are almost a whole breakfast in themselves.

1½ cups uncooked quick rolled oats
1½ cups whole wheat flour
⅓ cup brown sugar, packed
3 teaspoons baking powder
½ teaspoon cinnamon
¼ teaspoon ground ginger

¼ teaspoon salt
1 cup fresh or dried blueberries (optional)
1 cup milk
½ cup (1 medium) mashed ripe banana
1 tablespoon walnut or corn oil
1 egg, beaten

Preheat the oven to 400°F. Lightly grease 12 regular-sized muffin cups, or coat with nonstick spray.

In a large bowl, thoroughly mix the rolled oats with the whole wheat flour, brown sugar, baking powder, cinnamon, ginger, and salt. Add the blueberries, if using, and stir gently until the berries are evenly distributed in the mixture. In a small bowl, stir together the milk, banana, oil, and egg until blended. Add the liquid ingredients to the dry ingredients and stir just until the dry ingredients are moistened, about 20 strokes.

Spoon the batter into the muffin cups, dividing the batter evenly. Bake for 15 to 20 minutes, or until a wooden skewer inserted in the center of a muffin comes out clean. Cool 3 minutes; then remove from the muffin tin and transfer to a wire rack to cool or to a basket to serve warm.

MAKES 12 MUFFINS

Orange and Prune Muffins

A bit of sugar sprinkled on top of these muffins before baking gives them a crunchy top. Break open a hot-from-the-oven muffin and catch the aroma of orange. Serve them with a fruit-flavored cream cheese.

2 cups all-purpose flour
½ cup plus 1 tablespoon sugar
3 teaspoons baking powder
½ teaspoon salt
2 teaspoons grated orange zest

1 cup chopped prunes
4 tablespoons melted butter, or 4
    tablespoons vegetable oil
1 egg, lightly beaten
1 cup milk

Preheat the oven to 400ºF. Lightly grease 12 regular-sized muffin cups, or coat with nonstick spray.

In a large bowl, stir the flour, ½ cup sugar, baking powder, salt, orange zest, and prunes together. In a small bowl, mix the butter or oil, egg, and milk until blended. Stir the liquid ingredients into the dry ingredients just until the dry ingredients are moistened, about 20 strokes.

Spoon the batter into the muffin cups, dividing the batter evenly. Sprinkle the tops of the muffins with the remaining 1 tablespoon sugar. Bake for 20 to 25 minutes, until the muffins are light golden brown or until a wooden skewer inserted in the center of a muffin comes out clean. Remove the muffins from the tin and place them in a basket to serve warm.

MAKES 12 MUFFINS

Colonial Brown Bread Muffins

This batter can also be baked in a 9 × 5-inch loaf pan for 1 hour until it is done. Very quick and easy!

2 cups buttermilk

2 cups whole wheat flour

⅔ cup all-purpose flour

1 cup brown sugar, packed

2 teaspoons baking soda

1 teaspoon pumpkin pie spice

½ teaspoon salt

¾ cup light or dark raisins

Preheat the oven to 350ºF. Grease 12 large muffin cups or line with cupcake liners. In a large bowl, combine all ingredients until blended. Fill prepared muffin cups ⅔ full. Bake for 25 to 30 minutes or until a wooden pick inserted in center of a muffin comes out clean.

MAKES 12 MUFFINS

Crumb-topped Apple Spice Muffins

Just perfect for a morning coffee meeting, these are so moist and flavorful that they surprise even the most skeptical judges of low-fat baking.

2 cups all-purpose flour
2 teaspoons baking powder
½ teaspoon baking soda
¼ teaspoon salt
1 teaspoon cinnamon
¼ teaspoon ground nutmeg
1 egg, lightly beaten
½ cup brown sugar, packed

4 tablespoons melted butter
1 cup plain nonfat yogurt, stirred
1 cup tart apples, such as Granny Smith,
    peeled and chopped

TOPPING
¼ cup brown sugar, packed
¼ cup all-purpose flour
2 tablespoons melted butter

Preheat the oven to 400°F. Lightly grease or coat with nonstick spray 12 standard muffin cups, or line with paper baking cups and spray lightly.

In a small bowl, dust the apples with 1 tablespoon of the flour. In a large bowl, combine the remaining flour, baking powder, soda, salt, cinnamon, and nutmeg until well mixed. In a small bowl, whisk the egg, brown sugar, butter, and yogurt together until well mixed. Stir the liquid ingredients into the dry ingredients just until blended, about 20 strokes. Gently fold in the apples.

Spoon the batter evenly into the muffin cups. To make the topping, in a small bowl, stir together the brown sugar, flour, and melted butter until the mixture resembles moist crumbs. Spoon the mixture over the muffins and pat down slightly. Bake for 15 to 20 minutes, or until the muffins are lightly browned and a wooden skewer inserted into the center of a muffin comes out clean. Cool 1 minute; then remove from the muffin tins and transfer to a wire rack to cool or to a basket to serve warm.

MAKES 12 MUFFINS

Cranberry Banana Chunk Muffins

Use ripe but not overripe bananas in these muffins. They will add a moist bite, while the apples add a chewiness and the cranberries a tart burst of flavor.

1 cup all-purpose flour
1 cup whole wheat flour
4 teaspoons baking powder
½ cup sugar
¼ teaspoon salt
2 medium bananas, sliced

½ cup chopped dried apples
¼ cup dried cranberries
1 egg
4 tablespoons melted butter
1 cup milk
1 tablespoon vanilla

Preheat the oven to 425°F. Lightly grease or coat with nonstick spray 12 standard muffin cups, or line them with paper baking cups and spray lightly with nonstick spray.

In a large bowl, stir together the flours, baking powder, sugar, and salt. Add the bananas, apples, and cranberries. Mix lightly to coat all the pieces of fruit. In a small bowl, mix the egg, butter, milk, and vanilla.

Pour the liquid ingredients over the dry ingredients and mix gently until the dry ingredients are moistened. Do not overmix. Spoon the batter evenly into the prepared muffin cups. Bake for 18 to 20 minutes, or until a wooden skewer inserted in the center of a muffin comes out clean. Cool 1 minute; then remove from the muffin tin and transfer to a wire rack to cool or to a basket to serve warm.

MAKES 12 MUFFINS

Blueberry Oatmeal Muffins

When fresh blueberries are not in season, I prefer to use the dried berries. You can, however, use frozen berries, but they should be added in the frozen state or the muffins will discolor. If you use frozen berries, the entire mixture will be very cold and the muffins may take as much as 5 minutes longer to bake. These muffins taste wonderful and have a great texture, although they are somewhat flat on top rather than rounded.

1 cup fresh or ½ cup dried blueberries	**1 egg**
1½ cups all-purpose flour	**⅓ cup sugar**
½ cup quick-cooking rolled oats	**3 tablespoons melted butter**
1 tablespoon baking powder	**1 cup lemon or vanilla-flavored nonfat**
½ teaspoon salt	**yogurt**

Preheat the oven to 400°F. Lightly grease or coat with nonstick spray 12 standard muffin cups, or line with paper baking cups and spray lightly

In a small bowl, dust the berries with 1 tablespoon of the flour. In a large bowl, combine the remaining flour, rolled oats, baking powder, and salt until well mixed. In another small bowl, whisk the egg, sugar, butter, and yogurt together until well mixed. Stir the liquid ingredients into the dry ingredients just until blended, about 20 strokes. Gently fold in the blueberries.

Spoon the batter evenly into the muffin cups. Bake for 15 to 20 minutes, or until the muffins are lightly browned and a wooden skewer inserted into the center of a muffin comes out clean. Cool 1 minute; then remove from the muffin tin and transfer to a wire rack to cool or to a basket to serve warm.

MAKES 12 MUFFINS

Bran and Applesauce Muffins

Here's a "branny" muffin that's moist, yet chewy, and not too sweet. Applesauce works well to replace part of the oil in the original recipe. Whole wheat flour was just too crumbly, but when I replaced some of the white flour with oat flour, that added a nuttiness and the tenderness I was looking for.

2 cups bran breakfast cereal
1 cup milk
1 egg, lightly beaten
½ cup unsweetened applesauce
1 tablespoon corn or canola oil

1 cup all-purpose flour
¼ cup oat flour (see Note)
1 tablespoon baking powder
¼ teaspoon salt

Preheat the oven to 400°F. Lightly grease or coat with nonstick spray 12 standard muffin cups, or line with paper baking cups and spray lightly

In a large bowl, combine the cereal, milk, egg, applesauce, and oil. Stir well and set aside.

In another bowl, stir together the flours, baking powder, and salt. Stir the liquid ingredients into the dry ingredients just until the dry ingredients are moistened. Spoon the batter into the prepared muffin cups and bake for 18 to 20 minutes, or until a wooden skewer inserted into the center of a muffin comes out clean. Cool 1 minute; then remove from the muffin tin and transfer to a wire rack to cool or to a basket to serve warm.

MAKES 12 MUFFINS

Raisin Bran Muffins

To make raisin bran muffins, add 1 cup dark or golden raisins to the dry ingredients.

Note: To make oat flour, place quick-cooking or regular rolled oats into a food processor with the steel blade in place. Process until the oats are ground into flour.

Ginger Rhubarb Muffins
with Cinnamon Sugar

The sophisticated flavor of these muffins makes an interesting change of pace. Serve them hot!

2¼ cups all-purpose flour
2 teaspoons baking powder
1 teaspoon baking soda
½ teaspoon salt
2 tablespoons finely chopped
    crystallized ginger
¾ cup sugar
½ cup milk

½ cup vanilla nonfat yogurt
2 egg whites
1 cup finely chopped fresh rhubarb stalks
1 tablespoon vegetable oil

CINNAMON SUGAR
2 tablespoons sugar
1 teaspoon cinnamon

Preheat the oven to 400ºF. Lightly grease or coat with nonstick spray 12 standard muffin cups, or line with paper baking cups and spray lightly.

In a large bowl, stir the flour, baking powder, soda, salt, and ginger together.

In another bowl, whisk the sugar, milk, yogurt, egg whites, and rhubarb together. Pour the liquids over the dry ingredients and gently mix with a rubber spatula until almost all of the dry ingredients are moistened. Drizzle the oil over the top and very gently mix all of the ingredients. Fill each muffin cup about ¾ full with the batter. Bake for 15 to 17 minutes, or just until a wooden skewer inserted into the center of a muffin comes out clean.

Mix the sugar and cinnamon in a small bowl. Remove the hot muffins from the pan and immediately roll the top of each muffin in the cinnamon sugar mixture. Place in a basket and serve immediately.

MAKES 12 MUFFINS

Orange-glazed Pineapple Oatmeal Muffins

These muffins are almost indulgently full of flavor. They are great served with tea in the afternoon as well as for breakfast.

1 (8-ounce) can crushed pineapple, packed in natural juices
1 cup rolled oats, quick-cooking or old-fashioned
⅓ cup nonfat sour cream
4 tablespoons melted butter
⅓ cup brown sugar, packed
1 teaspoon grated orange zest
½ teaspoon ground ginger

1 egg, lightly beaten
1¼ cups all-purpose flour
1 teaspoon baking powder
½ teaspoon baking soda
1 teaspoon salt

ORANGE GLAZE
1 cup powdered sugar
1 to 2 tablespoons orange juice

Preheat the oven to 400°F. Lightly grease 12 standard muffin cups or coat with non-stick spray.

In a large mixing bowl, combine the pineapple, rolled oats, and sour cream and let stand 15 minutes. Stir in the butter, brown sugar, orange zest, ginger, and egg until blended. Sift the flour, baking powder, soda, and salt into the pineapple mixture. With a rubber spatula, mix just until the dry ingredients are moistened.

Spoon the batter into the muffin cups, dividing the batter equally. Bake for 15 to 17 minutes, or just until a wooden skewer inserted into the center of a muffin comes out clean.

While the muffins bake, mix the powdered sugar and orange juice to make a smooth, thin glaze. Drizzle the glaze over the hot muffins. Cool the muffins in the pan for 5 minutes; then remove and place in a basket and serve warm, or finish cooling on a wire rack.

MAKES 12 MUFFINS

Upside-down Cranberry Muffins

Spoon whole cranberry sauce into the bottom of the muffin cups before adding the muffin batter, bake, then invert the muffins and serve them hot! These muffins are perfect with any holiday meal.

6 tablespoons whole cranberry sauce
1 cup quick-cooking rolled oats
1 cup milk
3 tablespoons canola or corn oil
1 egg, lightly beaten

1 cup all-purpose flour
½ cup brown sugar, packed
2 teaspoons baking powder
¼ teaspoon salt
¼ teaspoon cinnamon

Preheat the oven to 400°F. Lightly grease or coat with nonstick spray 12 standard muffin cups, or line with paper baking cups and spray lightly. Spoon ½ tablespoon of the cranberry sauce into the bottom of each muffin cup.

In a large bowl, combine the oats, milk, oil, and egg and let the mixture stand for 5 minutes. In another bowl, stir the flour, brown sugar, baking powder, salt, and cinnamon together. Add the dry ingredients to the oat mixture and stir with a wooden spoon just until blended, about 20 strokes.

Spoon the batter into the muffin cups. Bake for 15 to 20 minutes, or until the muffins are lightly browned and a wooden skewer inserted into the center of a muffin comes out clean. Cool the muffins in the pan for 1 minute; then invert onto a serving tray and serve warm.

MAKES 12 MUFFINS

....

Breakfast Apple Muffins

....

Rolled oats ground into a flour make these muffins exceptionally tender and nutritious. Hazelnut oil is available in the gourmet section of many supermarkets, although melted butter adds a delicious flavor too.

2 cups uncooked quick-cooking
    rolled oats
½ cup all-purpose flour
2 tablespoons whole wheat flour
½ cup brown sugar, packed
2 teaspoons baking powder
½ teaspoon baking soda
½ teaspoon salt
1½ teaspoons cinnamon
¼ teaspoon ground nutmeg

¼ cup dried currants
1 cup nonfat buttermilk
3 egg whites
1 tablespoon hazelnut oil or melted
    butter
3 tablespoons corn oil
1 teaspoon vanilla
1 large Granny Smith apple, peeled, cored,
    and diced into ¼-inch cubes
1 tablespoon sugar

Preheat the oven to 400°F. Lightly grease 12 standard muffin cups, or coat with nonstick spray.

Measure the rolled oats into the container of a blender or into a food processor with the steel blade in place. Process or blend until the oats are finely ground.

In a large bowl, stir together the oat flour, all-purpose flour, whole wheat flour, brown sugar, baking powder, soda, salt, cinnamon, nutmeg, and currants. In a small bowl, mix the buttermilk, egg whites, hazelnut oil or butter, corn oil, and vanilla. Stir the liquid ingredients into the dry ingredients until almost blended, about 20 strokes. Gently stir in the apple until evenly mixed into the batter.

Spoon the batter into the muffin cups, dividing the batter evenly. Sprinkle the tops of the muffins with the 1 tablespoon sugar. Bake for 20 to 25 minutes, or until the muffins are lightly browned and a wooden skewer inserted in the center of a muffin comes out clean. Cool 1 minute; then remove from the muffin tin and transfer to a wire rack to cool or to a basket to serve warm.

MAKES 12 MUFFINS

Wild Rice and Blueberry Muffins

Wild rice adds a chewy texture to these muffins, but you should make sure the rice is very well cooked or it will be hard and crunchy. I store extra cooked wild rice in plastic bags in the freezer so that I can have it on hand to add to muffins, breads, and soups.

1½ cups all-purpose flour
½ cup sugar
3 teaspoons baking powder
1 teaspoon ground coriander seeds
½ teaspoon salt
1 cup cooked wild rice

1 cup fresh blueberries, dried blueberries, or raisins
4 tablespoons corn oil
1 egg, beaten
½ cup milk

Preheat the oven to 400°F. Lightly grease 12 regular-sized muffin cups, or coat with nonstick spray.

In a large bowl, mix the flour, sugar, baking powder, coriander, salt, wild rice, and blueberries or raisins. In a small bowl, beat the oil, egg, and milk together. Stir the liquid ingredients into the dry ingredients just until blended, about 20 strokes.

Spoon the batter into the muffin cups, dividing the batter evenly. Bake for 20 to 25 minutes, or until the muffins are lightly browned and a wooden skewer inserted in the center of a muffin comes out clean. Cool 1 minute; then remove from the muffin tin and transfer to a wire rack to cool or to a basket to serve warm.

MAKES 12 MUFFINS

Orange-glazed Whole Wheat Muffins

These flavorful and light muffins are wonderful hot out of the oven. But the orange glaze keeps them moist, so they are just as delicious the next day.

¾ cup whole wheat flour
½ cup sugar
1 cup all-purpose flour
½ teaspoon baking powder
½ teaspoon baking soda
¼ teaspoon salt
1 cup nonfat lemon yogurt
⅓ cup vegetable or corn oil

2 teaspoons grated orange zest
1 tablespoon lemon juice
1 egg, beaten
2 tablespoons orange marmalade

ORANGE GLAZE
3 tablespoons sugar
3 tablespoons orange juice

Preheat the oven to 400°F. Lightly grease 12 regular-sized muffin cups, or coat with nonstick spray.

In a large bowl, stir together the whole wheat flour and sugar. Add the all-purpose flour, baking powder, soda, and salt and mix well. In a small bowl, stir together the yogurt, oil, orange zest, lemon juice, and egg. Add the liquid ingredients to the dry ingredients and stir just until blended, about 20 strokes. Spoon the batter into the muffin cups, dividing the batter evenly. Make an indentation in the center of each cup of batter and spoon ½ teaspoon of the marmalade onto each muffin.

Bake for 18 to 20 minutes, or until golden brown or a wooden skewer inserted in a muffin just off center comes out clean.

To make the glaze, while the muffins bake, combine the sugar and orange juice in a small pan. Bring to a boil over medium heat. Stir until the sugar is dissolved. As soon as the muffins are done, brush the tops of the muffins with the glaze, brushing each muffin several times until all the glaze is used. Cool for 5 minutes; then remove from the muffin tin and transfer to a wire rack or to a basket to serve warm.

MAKES 12 MUFFINS

Seven-Grain Muffins

In my local whole foods cooperative, I buy a cereal composed of seven different cracked grains: wheat, oats, triticale, buckwheat, rye, corn, and millet. You can use any similarly textured multigrain cereal, from simple cracked wheat to various grain combinations of four to nine grains, to make these muffins. Cracked grains need to be softened, but not completely cooked, before using.

½ cup seven-grain cereal
¾ cup boiling water
2 cups all-purpose flour
2 teaspoons baking powder
1 teaspoon baking soda

1 teaspoon salt
¾ cup buttermilk
⅓ cup honey
1 egg, lightly beaten

Measure the seven-grain cereal into a small bowl and pour the boiling water over. Let it stand 10 minutes, or just until the cereal has softened. Drain off any excess water.

Preheat the oven to 400°F. Lightly grease 12 regular-sized muffin cups, or coat with nonstick spray.

In a large bowl, stir the flour, baking powder, soda, and salt together. Add the buttermilk, honey, and egg to the soaked cereal and stir to blend.

Add the liquid ingredients to the dry ingredients and stir just until combined, about 20 strokes. Spoon the batter into the muffin cups, dividing the batter evenly. Bake for 20 to 25 minutes, or until a wooden skewer inserted in the center of a muffin comes out clean. Cool 1 minute; then remove from the muffin tin and transfer to a wire rack to cool or to a basket to serve warm.

MAKES 12 MUFFINS

Apricot Honey Muffins

No fat, but the generous amounts of apricots and honey in these muffins provide lots of flavor and give these guilt-free treats a beautiful, warm color. And, in the quest to create incredibly tender muffins, the apricot-honey puree makes these winners. They are lovely for a summer breakfast.

2 cups all-purpose flour
¼ cup sugar
4 teaspoons baking powder
½ teaspoon salt
¼ teaspoon ground nutmeg

½ cup honey
1 cup milk
1 cup dried apricot puree (see Note)
2 egg whites, lightly beaten

Preheat the oven to 400°F. Lightly grease 12 regular-sized muffin cups, or coat with nonstick spray.

In a large bowl, stir together the flour, sugar, baking powder, salt, and nutmeg. In a small bowl, mix the honey, milk, apricot puree, and egg whites.

Stir the liquid ingredients into the dry ingredients just until blended, about 25 strokes.

Spoon the batter into the muffin cups, dividing the batter evenly among the cups. Bake for 20 to 25 minutes, or until the muffins are lightly browned and a wooden skewer inserted in the center of a muffin comes out clean. Cool 1 minute; then remove from the muffin tin and transfer to a wire rack to cool or to a basket to serve warm.

MAKES 12 MUFFINS

Note: To make the apricot puree, combine 1 cup dried apricots and ½ cup water in a saucepan; bring to a boil over medium-high heat. Reduce the heat and simmer for 8 minutes, or until most of the liquid has boiled away. Place in a blender or in a food processor and process until puréed. Cool.

Applesauce Blueberry Muffins

Using applesauce is a fantastic way to cut down on oils and fats in baked goods while keeping them moist. Here fats are completely eliminated because these muffins are also made with skim milk and egg whites only.

1½ cups all-purpose flour
½ cup plus 1 tablespoon wheat germ
¼ cup sugar
3 teaspoons baking powder
½ teaspoon salt
1 teaspoon cinnamon
1 cup fresh blueberries

½ cup light corn syrup
¾ cup skim milk
1 cup unsweetened applesauce
1 cup bran flakes, slightly crushed
2 egg whites, lightly beaten

Preheat the oven to 400°F. Lightly grease 12 regular-sized muffin cups, or coat with nonstick spray.

In a large mixing bowl, combine the flour, ½ cup wheat germ, sugar, baking powder, salt, cinnamon, and blueberries.

In a small bowl, mix the corn syrup, milk, applesauce, bran flakes, and egg whites. Stir the liquid ingredients into the dry ingredients just until the dry ingredients are moistened, about 20 strokes.

Spoon the batter into the muffin cups, dividing the batter evenly. Sprinkle the remaining tablespoon of wheat germ evenly over the muffins. Pat down gently onto the muffins. Bake for 20 to 25 minutes, or until the muffins are browned and a wooden skewer inserted in the center of a muffin comes out clean. Cool 1 minute; then remove from the muffin tin and transfer to a wire rack to cool or to a basket to serve warm.

MAKES 12 MUFFINS

Cinnamon Prune Muffins

Puréed prunes replace the fat in these rich, dark muffins that have a hint of maple flavor as well.

2 cups all-purpose flour
¼ cup sugar
3 teaspoons baking powder
½ teaspoon salt
1 teaspoon cinnamon
½ cup maple syrup
¾ cup milk

1 cup unsweetened prune puree (see Note)
2 egg whites, lightly beaten

WHEAT GERM TOPPING
1 tablespoon wheat germ
1 tablespoon brown sugar
½ teaspoon cinnamon

Preheat the oven to 400°F. Lightly grease 12 regular-sized muffin cups, or coat with nonstick spray.

In a large bowl, stir together the flour, sugar, baking powder, salt, and cinnamon. In a small bowl, mix the maple syrup, milk, prune puree, and egg whites. Stir the liquid ingredients into the dry ingredients just until blended, about 25 strokes.

Spoon the batter into the muffin cups, dividing it equally among the cups. For the topping, in a small bowl, mix the wheat germ, brown sugar, and cinnamon. Sprinkle the tops of the muffins with the wheat germ mixture. Bake for 20 to 25 minutes, or until the muffins are lightly browned and a wooden skewer inserted in the center of a muffin comes out clean. Cool 1 minute; then remove from the muffin tin and transfer to a wire rack to cool or to a basket to serve warm.

MAKES 12 MUFFINS

Note: To make the prune puree, combine 1 cup pitted prunes and ½ cup water in a saucepan. Bring to a boil over medium-high heat, reduce the heat, and simmer for 8 minutes (most of the liquid will boil away). Place the prunes in a blender or a food processor and process until puréed. Cool.

Pumpkin Bran Muffins

These spicy muffins taste like pumpkin pie, and even without added fat, they have a tender texture that can be attributed to the combination of puréed pumpkin and corn syrup. The tiny amount of fat in these muffins comes from the wheat germ.

1¾ cups all-purpose flour
¼ cup wheat germ
½ cup sugar
3 teaspoons baking powder
½ teaspoon salt
1½ teaspoons pumpkin pie spice

2 egg whites
1 cup fresh or canned puréed cooked pumpkin
1 cup shredded bran cereal
¾ cup milk
½ cup dark corn syrup

Preheat the oven to 400°F. Lightly grease 12 regular-sized muffin cups, or coat with nonstick spray.

In a large bowl, mix together the flour, wheat germ, sugar, baking powder, salt, and pumpkin pie spice. In a small bowl, mix together the egg whites, pumpkin, bran cereal, milk, and corn syrup. Add the liquid ingredients to the dry ingredients and stir just until the dry ingredients are moistened, about 20 strokes.

Spoon the batter into the muffin cups, dividing the batter evenly. Bake for 20 to 25 minutes, or until the muffins feel firm and a wooden skewer inserted in the center of a muffin comes out clean. Cool 1 minute; then remove from the muffin tin and transfer to a wire rack to cool or to a basket to serve warm.

MAKES 12 MUFFINS

Spiced Bran Muffins

Corn syrup and applesauce add not only great taste and a nice browning quality to these muffins, but a smooth texture as well.

2 cups all-purpose flour
⅓ cup sugar
3 teaspoons baking powder
½ teaspoon salt
1 teaspoon cinnamon
¼ teaspoon ground nutmeg

⅛ teaspoon ground cloves
2 egg whites, lightly beaten
1 cup unsweetened applesauce
1 cup bran flakes, slightly crushed
¾ cup milk
½ cup light corn syrup

Preheat the oven to 400°F. Lightly grease 12 regular-sized muffin cups, or coat with nonstick spray.

In a large bowl, mix together the flour, sugar, baking powder, salt, cinnamon, nutmeg, and cloves.

In a small bowl, mix together the egg whites, applesauce, bran flakes, milk, and corn syrup. Add the liquid ingredients to the dry ingredients and stir until mixed, about 25 strokes.

Spoon the batter into the muffin cups, dividing the batter evenly. Bake for 20 to 25 minutes, or until the muffins are browned and a wooden skewer inserted in the center of a muffin comes out clean. Cool 1 minute; then remove from the muffin tin and transfer to a wire rack to cool or to a basket to serve warm.

MAKES 12 MUFFINS

English Muffin Muffins

This muffin should eliminate any baker's fear of baking with yeast. Fast-rising yeast makes these light and delicious muffins as easy as any quick bread. There's no special handling of the yeast because it is measured into the flour mixture just like the other dry ingredients. After the muffin dough is mixed and spooned into the muffin pans, the muffins are left to rise at room temperature for about 30 minutes.

Yeast-raised muffins are tender without added fat. They're irresistible fresh from the oven spread with cream cheese and homemade jam.

2½ cups all-purpose flour
1 package (3 teaspoons) quick-rising yeast

1 tablespoon sugar
1 teaspoon salt
1½ cups very warm milk (about 135°F)

Lightly grease 12 regular-sized muffin cups, or coat with nonstick spray.

In a large mixing bowl, stir together the flour, yeast, sugar, and salt. Add the milk and beat with a wooden spoon until the mixture is smooth and elastic, about 3 minutes.

Spoon the mixture into the muffin cups, dividing it equally. Let the dough rest uncovered for 30 minutes, or until it fills the muffin cups.

Preheat the oven to 400°F.

Bake for 20 minutes, or until a wooden skewer inserted in the center of a muffin comes out clean. Cool 1 minute; then remove from the muffin tin and transfer to a wire rack to cool or to a basket to serve warm.

MAKES 12 MUFFINS

Herbed English Muffin Muffins

Add 1 tablespoon mixed Italian herbs to the dry ingredients before adding the milk.

Sun-dried Tomato and Black Olive English Muffin Muffins

These ingredients will add a little fat to the basic recipe, but not much. Add ½ cup chopped well-drained oil-packed sun-dried tomatoes and 1 cup chopped black olives to the dry ingredients before adding the milk.

Wheated English Muffin Muffins

Replace 1 cup of the all-purpose flour with whole wheat flour.

Three-Grain Honey and Fruit Muffins

Healthy tasting, these are ideal for serving with a chunky vegetable soup. Honey brings out the whole-grain flavors, and dried fruits provide a sweetness and chewy texture.

1 cup whole wheat flour
½ cup all-purpose flour
½ cup unsifted dark stone-ground
    rye flour
½ cup old-fashioned rolled oats
3 teaspoons baking powder
½ teaspoon baking soda
½ teaspoon salt

2 cups nonfat buttermilk, or 2 cups water
    mixed with ½ cup nonfat buttermilk
    powder
2 egg whites, lightly beaten
½ cup honey
1 cup chopped mixed dried fruits, chopped
    dates, or raisins

Preheat the oven to 400°F. Lightly grease 12 regular-sized muffin cups, or coat with nonstick spray.

In a large mixing bowl, stir together the whole wheat flour, all-purpose flour, rye flour, rolled oats, baking powder, soda, and salt. In a medium bowl, mix the buttermilk, egg whites, and honey. Stir the buttermilk mixture into the dry ingredients until the flour mixture is almost moistened. Stir in the fruit just until combined.

Spoon the batter into the muffin cups, dividing the batter evenly. Bake for 20 to 25 minutes, or until a wooden skewer inserted in the center of a muffin comes out clean. Cool 1 minute; then remove from the muffin tin and transfer to a wire rack to cool or to a basket to serve warm.

MAKES 12 MUFFINS

Honey Wheat Muffins

A good, basic whole-grain muffin, these have a not-too-sweet, healthy taste and are excellent served with a fruit salad or with an omelet for breakfast or brunch.

¾ cup unbleached all-purpose flour
¾ cup whole wheat flour
2 teaspoons baking powder
½ teaspoon salt

½ cup honey
½ cup milk
¼ cup melted butter or margarine
1 egg, lightly beaten

Preheat the oven to 400°F. Lightly grease 12 regular-sized muffin cups, or coat with nonstick spray.

In a large mixing bowl, combine the all-purpose flour, whole wheat flour, baking powder, and salt. In a small bowl, mix together the honey, milk, butter, and egg. Pour the liquid ingredients over the dry ingredients, and with spatula fold together until the dry ingredients are just moistened. Spoon the mixture into the muffin cups, dividing the batter evenly. Bake for 15 to 25 minutes or until golden. Serve hot with butter.

MAKES 12 MUFFINS

Blueberry Wheat Muffins

Bursting with fresh blueberries and with a rich grainy taste, these muffins are great with any meal of the day. For an unusual shape, bake these in small individual pie tins.

¾ cup unbleached flour
¾ cup whole wheat flour
1 tablespoon baking powder
½ teaspoon salt
½ cup light or dark brown sugar,
    well-packed

1½ to 2 cups fresh blueberries, or frozen
    unsugared blueberries
½ cup milk
½ cup melted butter or margarine
1 egg, lightly beaten

Preheat the oven to 400°F. Lightly grease 12 regular-sized muffin cups or one 9-inch round pan, or coat with nonstick spray.

In a large mixing bowl, combine the all-purpose flour, whole wheat flour, baking powder, salt, and brown sugar. Add the blueberries and stir just until they are coated, being careful not to break them. If you are using frozen blueberries, do not thaw them completely before adding them to the dry ingredients. In a small bowl, mix together the milk, butter, and egg. Pour the liquid ingredients over the dry ingredients and carefully fold together until dry ingredients are just moistened. Spoon batter into muffin cups. Bake for 15 to 25 minutes or until golden. Remove from muffin tin and cool on rack.

MAKES 12 MUFFINS OR 1 COFFEE CAKE

Honey Fruit Nut Muffins

Grainy and wonderful, these muffins have the flavor and perfume of honey. For a special treat, roll these muffins in melted butter, then in cinnamon sugar while they are still hot.

2 cups whole wheat flour
½ cup chopped dates or dark raisins
½ cup chopped walnuts or pecans
2 tablespoons light or dark brown sugar
1 tablespoon baking powder
½ teaspoon salt

⅔ cup milk
⅓ cup honey
⅓ cup melted butter or vegetable oil
2 eggs, beaten
Melted butter (optional)
Cinnamon sugar (optional)

Preheat the oven to 400°F. Lightly grease 12 regular-sized muffin cups, or coat with nonstick spray.

Combine the flour, dates, nuts, brown sugar, baking powder, and salt in a large bowl. In another bowl, combine the milk, honey, butter, and eggs. Pour the liquid ingredients over the dry ingredients and stir just until the dry ingredients are moistened. Fill prepared muffin cups ⅔ full. Bake for 15 to 20 minutes. If desired, roll hot muffins first in melted butter, then in cinnamon sugar, and serve immediately.

MAKES 12 MUFFINS

Honey Bran Muffins

Fragrant with honey, these muffins are excellent served with butter and orange marmalade for breakfast, brunch, or lunch.

1½ cups 100% bran cereal
1¼ cups milk
1 egg, beaten
⅓ cup melted butter
½ cup honey

1¼ cups unbleached all-purpose flour
1 tablespoon baking powder
½ teaspoon salt
1 cup chopped dates or dark raisins
¼ cup toasted wheat germ

Preheat the oven to 400ºF. Lightly grease 12 regular-sized muffin cups, or coat with nonstick spray.

In a large mixing bowl, mix the bran cereal and milk; let stand 5 minutes. Stir in the egg, butter, and honey. Combine the flour, baking powder, salt, and dates or raisins. Sprinkle the flour mixture over the bran mixture and fold together just until flour is moistened. Spoon batter into muffin cups. Bake for 15 to 20 minutes or until golden. Remove from muffin tin and cool on wire rack.

MAKES 12 MUFFINS

Raisin Rye Muffins

The molasses and other flavorings give these muffins a color and taste similar to Swedish rye bread.

1 cup light rye flour
1 cup unbleached all-purpose flour
1 teaspoon baking powder
1 teaspoon baking soda
½ cup dark or light raisins
1 tablespoon grated orange rind
1 teaspoon caraway seeds

1 teaspoon fennel seeds
½ teaspoon salt
⅔ cup buttermilk
⅓ cup dark molasses
⅓ cup melted butter or vegetable oil
2 eggs, beaten

Preheat the oven to 400ºF. Lightly grease 12 regular-sized muffin cups, or coat with nonstick spray.

In a large mixing bowl, combine rye flour, all-purpose flour, baking powder, soda, raisins, orange rind, caraway seeds, fennel seeds, and salt. In another bowl, combine the buttermilk, molasses, butter, and eggs. Pour the liquid ingredients over the dry ingredients and stir just until the dry ingredients are moistened. Fill prepared muffin cups ⅔ full. Bake for 15 to 20 minutes or until muffins are golden and done in the center. Serve warm with butter.

MAKES 12 MUFFINS

Refrigerator Three-Grain Muffins

Keep a batch of this muffin dough on hand to bake in short order. In fact, you can bake up just 1 or 2 muffins at a time in the microwave oven if you choose. Simply double-line a Pyrex custard cup with cupcake papers, fill about ½ full with the muffin batter, and microwave on high for about 30 seconds for each muffin; 6 muffins will take about 2½ minutes. Refrigerated, this dough will keep up to 4 weeks.

2 cups boiling water
6 cups 100% bran cereal
1 cup shortening
1 cup dark or light brown sugar
1 cup sugar
1 cup honey
4 eggs
4 cups buttermilk

1 cup dark or light rye flour
1½ cups rolled oats, quick or old-fashioned
1 cup whole wheat flour
2 cups unbleached all-purpose flour
5 teaspoons baking soda
2 teaspoons salt

In a large bowl, pour boiling water over 2 cups bran cereal. Cool. In another mixing bowl, blend the shortening, sugars, and honey. Add eggs, buttermilk, rye flour, rolled oats, whole wheat flour, all-purpose flour, soda, and salt; mix well. Stir in soaked bran cereal and remaining dry cereal. Store in covered container in refrigerator and bake as needed. To bake, fill well-greased muffin cups ⅔ full. Preheat oven to 400°F. Bake for 15 to 20 minutes.

MAKES 5 TO 6 DOZEN MUFFINS

Three-Grain Nut Muffins

After filling greased muffin cups with muffin batter, spoon 1 tablespoon chopped walnuts over the top of each muffin.

Three-Grain Spice Muffins

After filling greased muffin cups with muffin batter, sprinkle tops of muffins with cinnamon sugar.

Three-Grain Date Nut Muffins

After filling greased muffin cups with muffin batter, press chopped dates and nuts into center of each muffin with a spoon.

Oat Cranberry Muffins with Cinnamon Crust

Cinnamon and oatmeal give character to the "Dutchy crust" topping on these muffins. If you do not have fresh or frozen cranberries, either leave out the fruit or substitute blueberries, fresh pitted cherries, or fresh chopped apple.

¾ cup whole wheat flour
¾ cup unbleached all-purpose flour
½ cup rolled oats, quick or old-fashioned
2 teaspoons baking powder
1 teaspoon baking soda
½ cup dark or light brown sugar, well-packed
1 cup fresh or frozen whole cranberries
½ cup buttermilk

2 eggs
½ cup melted butter or margarine

TOPPING
¼ cup softened butter or margarine
¼ cup dark or light brown sugar, well-packed
¼ cup rolled oats, quick or old-fashioned
¼ cup unbleached all-purpose flour
1 teaspoon cinnamon

Preheat the oven to 400°F. Lightly grease 12 regular-sized muffin cups, or coat with nonstick spray.

In a large mixing bowl, combine the whole wheat flour, all-purpose flour, rolled oats, baking powder, soda, and brown sugar. Add the cranberries and stir until coated. In a small bowl, beat together the buttermilk, eggs, and butter. Pour over dry ingredients and fold together just until moistened. In a small bowl, make the topping by combining the softened butter, brown sugar, rolled oats, flour, and cinnamon, stirring until mixture is crumbly. Spoon batter into muffin cups, filling each ⅔ full. Top with the crumbly mixture. Bake for 15 to 25 minutes or until golden. Remove from pans and cool on a wire rack.

MAKES 12 MUFFINS

Plum Biscuits

Reminiscent of the flavors of Czech plum dumplings, these sugary topped plum-filled biscuits are great for breakfast or brunch. They are also lovely for a late-afternoon snack with a cup of hot tea.

2 cups all-purpose flour
1 tablespoon baking powder
¼ cup sugar
⅛ teaspoon salt
½ teaspoon grated lemon zest
¼ cup butter, chilled and cut into pieces
1 egg, beaten
½ cup whipping cream

TOPPING
12 fresh Italian prune plums, halved and
   pitted
4 tablespoons butter, at room
   temperature
6 tablespoons sugar

Preheat the oven to 400°F. Lightly grease a baking sheet or cover with parchment paper.

In a large bowl or in a food processor, combine the flour, baking powder, sugar, salt, and lemon zest. Process or cut in the butter until the mixture resembles coarse meal. Turn into a mixing bowl if using a food processor. In a small bowl, beat the egg and cream together. Add to the flour mixture and stir with a fork until the dough holds together in a ball. Turn out onto a lightly floured surface and knead once or twice to compact the ball.

Roll out to 1-inch thickness. Using a 2¾-inch biscuit cutter, cut out rounds. Place on the prepared pan. Press a plum half into the center of each round. Then dot each with ½ teaspoon butter and sprinkle with 1 teaspoon sugar.

Bake for 20 to 25 minutes, until golden. Slide the parchment onto the countertop to cool or transfer the biscuits onto a wire rack to cool slightly. Serve warm.

MAKES 24 BISCUITS

....

Mom's Biscuits

....

When I was growing up, biscuit-baking day was always perfumed by the aroma of a coffee syrup boiling on the woodstove. The biscuits got brushed with the syrup just as they came out of the oven. To make the lightest yeast dough, Mom always advocated keeping the dough as soft as possible—that is, avoiding the addition of too much flour.

2 packages (5½ teaspoons) active
    dry yeast
¼ cup water (105°F to 115°F)
2 cups rich milk, scalded and cooled to
    lukewarm
½ cup sugar
½ cup melted butter
3 slightly beaten eggs
1 teaspoon salt
5 to 5½ cups all-purpose flour

FILLING
½ cup softened butter
1 cup white or brown sugar, packed
1 tablespoon cinnamon

GLAZE
1 cup strong coffee
1 cup sugar

In a large mixing bowl, dissolve the yeast in the water. Add the milk and stir until blended. Let stand 5 minutes.

Stir in the sugar, butter, eggs, and salt. Beat in half the flour until the batter is smooth and satiny. Let stand 15 minutes. Slowly beat in enough flour to make a stiff dough.

Turn dough out onto a floured surface. Cover with a bowl and let it stand again for 15 minutes. Knead for 10 minutes until the dough is smooth and satiny, being stingy with the addition of the flour so as not to add too much. If the dough gets sticky, let it sit and "relax" a few minutes. Then go back to kneading it.

Wash the mixing bowl, oil it, and add dough to the bowl, turning to oil the top of the dough. Cover and let rise in a warm place until doubled.

On a lightly oiled work surface, roll out about half the dough at a time to make a square about 20 inches on each side, sprinkling just lightly with flour, if necessary. Spread with softened butter to the edges. Mix the sugar and cinnamon and sprinkle over the butter. Roll up tightly jelly-roll fashion. Cut slices and place in buttered muffin tins, or close together in a buttered 13 × 9-inch baking pan, or slightly separated on buttered baking sheets. Repeat procedure until all the dough is shaped into rolls.

Let rise until doubled. Preheat the oven to 375°F. Bake for 15 minutes or until golden. While rolls bake, bring the coffee and sugar to a boil; boil 2 to 3 minutes.

Brush hot rolls with the coffee glaze. Cool.

MAKES 36 BISCUITS

Old Virginia Cheddar Biscuits

For well over three centuries, Virginia has been famous for its good food and hospitality. The taverns of Williamsburg, like the taverns of London, played an important part in town life during the late 1600s. Councilors and burgesses, ship captains and lawyers, merchants and planters met within tavern doors to transact business and gossip over a bottle of wine, a bowl of punch, or a tankard of ale. Biscuits made rich with cheddar cheese were offered because they were easier to make than the laborious beaten biscuits. These are an excellent accompaniment to cocktails or a simple green salad. They keep well and taste best served cold.

1 cup all-purpose flour	**⅓ cup firm butter**
¼ teaspoon salt	**1 cup shredded cheddar cheese**

Preheat the oven to 350°F. In a medium-sized bowl, combine the flour and salt. Using a pastry blender or 2 knives, cut in the butter until mixture resembles coarse crumbs. Blend in cheese. Mix until the dough holds together in a ball. On a lightly floured surface, roll out the dough to about ½-inch thick. Cut with the tiniest biscuit cutter you have, even as small as 1 inch. Prick tops with a fork. Place on an ungreased baking sheet. Bake for 12 to 15 minutes or until biscuits are a rich cheddar color but not browned. Cool and store in an airtight container.

MAKES ABOUT 36 BISCUITS

Beaten Biscuits

The job of "beating the biscuits" is much simpler for today's baker than it was in the past. I give three methods of mixing here: the food processor, heavy-duty mixer, and the old-fashioned hand method.

Beaten Biscuits make great bases for canapés. The cup-like halves will hold tiny bits of creamed and salad-style fillings.

2 cups all-purpose flour
½ teaspoon salt
3 tablespoons butter or shortening

1 egg
½ cup cold milk

Preheat the oven to 350°F.

To mix in a food processor: Fit food processor with the steel blade. Add flour, salt, and butter to the work bowl. Process until the butter is worked into the dry ingredients. In a small bowl, mix the egg and milk. Pour the liquid mixture through the feed tube with the processor on until a ball of dough forms that spins around the work bowl. Process 3 minutes longer.

To mix using a heavy-duty mixer: Combine the flour, salt, and butter in the mixing bowl. Attach the dough paddle (not dough hook) to the mixer. Turn on the mixer and mix until the butter is blended into the dry ingredients. Add the egg and milk and turn on the mixer. Mix for 25 minutes or until dough blisters and is very satiny.

To mix by hand: In a large bowl, combine the flour and salt. Using a pastry blender or 2 knives, cut in the butter until completely blended. In a small bowl, mix the egg and milk. Stir into the flour mixture to make a stiff dough. Put the dough on a block or countertop. Beat with a blunt wooden mallet until the dough blisters; this takes about 25 minutes. Fold the edges of dough toward the center as you beat it.

To roll, cut out, and bake: On a lightly oiled surface, roll out the dough to a 14-inch square. Fold the dough in half and press layers together. Roll out again to the same size to smooth out the edges. Cut into 1½-inch rounds. Place on ungreased baking sheets. Pierce each biscuit once with a fork. Bake for 25 minutes or until puffed and lightly browned. Remove from the oven and split the biscuits. If centers are soft, return to the oven 3 to 4 minutes longer.

MAKES ABOUT 48 SPLIT BISCUITS

Old-fashioned Buttermilk Biscuits

Southerners often serve buttermilk biscuits with sausage and grits for breakfast or with fried chicken for any meal.

2 cups all-purpose flour
½ teaspoon salt
2 teaspoons baking powder
½ teaspoon baking soda

⅓ cup butter or shortening
½ to ⅓ cup buttermilk

Preheat the oven to 450°F. Combine the flour, salt, baking powder, and soda in a medium-sized bowl. Using a pastry blender or 2 knives, cut in the butter until the mixture resembles coarse crumbs. Add the buttermilk. Stir just until moistened; do not overmix. Turn out the batter onto a floured surface; knead very lightly, just until dough is smooth. Roll out to ½-inch thick. Cut into 2-inch rounds. Place on ungreased baking sheets. Bake for 12 to 15 minutes or until golden. Serve hot.

MAKES 24 BISCUITS

Southern-style Biscuits

Use lard. Cut biscuits into 3-inch rounds. Place on ungreased baking sheets ½ inch apart. Dust tops of the biscuits with flour. Bake as above.

Calico Biscuits

Add ½ cup finely chopped green bell pepper, 3 tablespoons finely chopped drained pimentos, and 2 tablespoons minced fresh onion to flour mixture before adding buttermilk. Bake as above.

Ranch-style Biscuits

Divide dough into 4 parts. Pat into circles about ¾-inch thick. Bake as above. Makes 4 large biscuits.

Whole Wheat Biscuits

Substitute whole wheat flour for all-purpose flour. Bake as above.

Baking Powder Biscuits

Use 3 teaspoons baking powder and omit baking soda. Replace buttermilk with fresh milk. Bake as above.

Cornmeal Biscuits

Add ½ cup cornmeal and 3 tablespoons sugar to flour mixture. Bake as above.

Casserole Biscuits

You can keep this biscuit dough refrigerated in a casserole for one week.

¼ cup warm water (110°F)
2 packages (5½ teaspoons) active
   dry yeast
5 cups self-rising flour

⅓ cup sugar
1 teaspoon baking soda
1 cup shortening
2 cups buttermilk

Pour warm water into a small bowl; stir in the yeast until dissolved. Let stand until foamy, about 5 minutes. In a large bowl, combine the flour, sugar, and soda. Using a pastry cutter or 2 knives, cut in the shortening until mixture resembles coarse crumbs. Stir in the yeast mixture and buttermilk; mix well. Turn into a medium casserole. Cover and refrigerate at least 2 hours before using. Remove desired amount of dough from casserole. On a lightly floured surface, roll out dough ½-inch thick; cut into 2-inch rounds, squares, crescents, or triangles. Place biscuits on an unbuttered or parchment-lined baking sheet. Let rise in a warm place until doubled, about 2 hours. Preheat the oven to 450ºF. Bake for 10 minutes or until golden.

MAKES ABOUT 48 BISCUITS

Orange Date Nut Scones

Springtime and scones seem to go together, especially these orange-perfumed scones that are speckled with dates and nuts.

2 cups all-purpose flour	**½ cup chopped dates**
1 cup uncooked rolled oats	**½ cup chopped walnuts or pecans**
½ cup sugar	**2 eggs, beaten**
4 teaspoons baking powder	**¼ to ⅓ cup milk**
¼ teaspoon salt	**½ cup melted butter**
2 teaspoons grated orange zest	

Preheat the oven to 400ºF. Cover a large baking sheet with parchment paper or coat with nonstick spray.

In a large mixing bowl, combine the flour, oats, sugar, baking powder, salt, orange zest, dates, and nuts. In another bowl, stir together the eggs, ¼ cup of the milk, and butter. With a fork, stir the liquids into the dry ingredients just until blended. Add the remaining milk, if necessary, to make a dough that holds together. Divide the dough into 2 parts. Shape each part into a ball. Place well apart on the baking sheet and flatten each to make 8-inch rounds. With a sharp knife, cut each round into 6 wedges, leaving the wedges in place.

Bake for 10 to 13 minutes or until golden brown. Serve warm with butter and orange marmalade, if desired.

MAKES 12 SCONES

Note on the Preparation and Baking of Scones: For tender scones, many of the same rules apply as for other quick breads:

1. Mix the dry ingredients with the liquids just until the dry ingredients are moistened. Overmixing results in a less tender texture.

2. Scones should not be overbaked, or they will be dry. Check them about 5 minutes before the suggested baking time is up (ovens vary, and the scones may be done sooner than the recipe states).

3. Baked scones can be frozen for serving later. Wrap them airtight and freeze as soon as possible after cooling. They will freeze well for up to 2 months. To thaw, remove from the freezer and allow them to thaw, still wrapped; then reheat in a low oven (300°F) for about 5 minutes until heated through. Or unwrap the scones, place on a baking sheet, and simultaneously thaw and reheat at 300°F for 10 to 15 minutes.

Currant Scones with Orange Marmalade Butter

Quick to make, these scones have the texture of baking powder biscuits and the slight sweetness of a coffee cake.

2 cups all-purpose flour
1 tablespoon baking powder
¼ cup sugar
½ teaspoon salt
½ cup butter, chilled and cut into pieces
⅓ cup currants
1 egg, beaten
⅓ cup milk

FOR THE TOP
Milk for brushing
1 teaspoon sugar

ORANGE MARMALADE BUTTER
4 tablespoons butter, at room temperature
4 tablespoons orange marmalade

Preheat the oven to 400°F. Cover a baking sheet with parchment paper or coat lightly with nonstick spray

In a large mixing bowl, combine the flour, baking powder, sugar, and salt. Cut in the butter until the mixture resembles coarse crumbs. Stir in the currants. In a small bowl, combine the egg and milk; stir into the flour mixture with a fork, just until the dough gathers easily into a ball. Turn the dough out onto the baking sheet and pat into an 8-inch circle.

With a sharp knife, cut the dough into 8 wedges, leaving the wedges in place. Brush the top with milk and sprinkle with sugar.

Bake for 12 to 15 minutes, until light brown.

While the scones bake, make the orange marmalade butter. In a small bowl, beat the butter until light and fluffy; then gradually beat in the orange marmalade.

Serve the scones warm with the orange marmalade butter.

MAKES 8 SCONES

Raisin Walnut Scones

These scones are especially good served with whipped cream cheese blended with shredded smoked cheddar cheese.

3 cups all-purpose flour	**1 cup raisins**
1 tablespoon baking powder	**½ cup chopped walnuts**
½ teaspoon cinnamon	**3 eggs**
½ cup sugar	**½ to ⅔ cup plain yogurt or buttermilk**
1 cup butter, chilled and cut into pieces	**1 tablespoon sugar, for sprinkling**

Preheat the oven to 400°F. Lightly grease a large baking sheet or cover with parchment paper.

Combine the flour, baking powder, cinnamon, and sugar in a food processor or a large bowl. Add the butter and process or cut in until the butter is in pea-size pieces. Turn the mixture into a bowl, if using the food processor, and mix in the raisins and walnuts.

In a small bowl, mix the eggs and ½ cup of the yogurt or buttermilk. Add to the dry ingredients and blend with a fork just until a dough forms (add a bit more yogurt or buttermilk if needed). Shape the dough into a smooth ball. Dust lightly with flour if sticky. Place on the baking sheet and flatten to a 7- to 8-inch circle. With a sharp knife, score into 12 wedges; leave the wedges in place. Sprinkle the top with sugar.

Bake for 15 to 20 minutes, until light brown. Cool on the baking sheet on a wire rack. To serve, break into wedges. Serve warm with butter or cream cheese.

MAKES 12 SCONES

Pecan Pineapple Scones

The most notable difference between scones and baking powder biscuits is that scones use eggs. Basic scones are such a quick and easy bread, perfect for company breakfast or brunch. Vary the flavor by using dates, chopped dried apple, pears, or prunes for the raisins and pineapple. Or eliminate all the fruits and nuts and serve the scones with your favorite fruit jam or jelly and Devonshire cream (available in gourmet stores or high-quality supermarkets).

3 cups all-purpose flour
3 tablespoons sugar
2 tablespoons grated orange zest
4 teaspoons baking powder
½ teaspoon salt
½ cup butter, chilled and cut into pieces
3 eggs, beaten
½ cup milk

½ cup raisins
½ cup chopped pecans
½ cup chopped dried or candied pineapple (see Note)

TOPPING
2 teaspoons water
1 tablespoon sugar

Preheat the oven to 450°F. Lightly grease a large baking sheet or cover with parchment paper. Dust with flour.

In a large bowl or a food processor, mix the flour, sugar, orange zest, baking powder, and salt. Process or cut in the butter until the mixture resembles coarse crumbs. In a small bowl, mix together the eggs and milk. Add to the flour mixture and mix just until blended; don't overmix.

Fold in the raisins, pecans, and pineapple.

Turn the dough out onto the prepared baking sheet. Dust your hands with flour and pat the dough into an 8-inch round. With a straight-edged knife, cut the dough into 8 wedges, leaving the wedges in place. Brush the top with water and sprinkle with the sugar.

Bake for 15 to 18 minutes, until golden. Slide the parchment paper onto the countertop to cool or transfer to a wire rack. Serve warm, in wedges.

MAKES 8 SCONES

Note: I buy my dried pineapple at the local whole foods cooperative store. It has no extra sugar added, and the flavor is sweet and intense. Commercially packaged candied pineapple works fine too.

Berry Nut Scones

Dried fruit scones make a wonderful last-minute gift, especially if you can deliver them soon after they're baked. Pack them in a pretty basket and tuck in a jar of homemade jam. The hint of cardamom brings out the flavor of the fruits.

3 cups all-purpose flour
1 tablespoon baking powder
1 teaspoon freshly ground cardamom
¾ cup sugar
½ cup dried blueberries, strawberries, cherries, or raisins

½ cup chopped almonds
1 cup butter, chilled and cut into pieces
3 eggs
½ cup lemon yogurt or buttermilk
1 tablespoon sugar

Preheat the oven to 400ºF. Lightly grease a large baking sheet or cover with parchment paper.

Combine the flour, baking powder, cardamom, ¾ cup sugar, fruit, and almonds in a food processor or a large bowl. Cut in the butter until it is in pea-size pieces. If using a food processor, turn the mixture into a large bowl.

Mix the eggs and yogurt or buttermilk in a small bowl. Add to the dry ingredients and blend quickly just until a dough forms (add a bit more yogurt if needed). With a ½-cup-size ice cream scoop or measuring cup, scoop the dough onto the prepared baking sheet, placing the mounds about 3 inches apart. Sprinkle the tops with the 1 tablespoon sugar.

Bake for 10 to 15 minutes until light brown. Slide the parchment paper onto the countertop to cool or transfer to a wire rack. Serve warm.

MAKES 12 SCONES

Almond Cardamom Scones

Aromatic with cardamom and crunchy with almonds, these scones are perfect for any holiday.

3 cups all-purpose flour
1 tablespoon baking powder

1 teaspoon freshly ground cardamom
½ cup sugar

1 cup chopped almonds

1 cup butter, chilled and cut into pieces

3 eggs

½ to ⅔ cup plain yogurt or buttermilk

1 tablespoon sugar

Preheat the oven to 400°F. Lightly grease a large baking sheet or cover with parchment paper.

Combine the flour, baking powder, cardamom, ½ cup sugar, and almonds in a food processor or large bowl. Add the butter and cut in until the butter is in pea-size pieces. If using a food processor, turn the mixture into a large bowl.

Mix the eggs and ½ cup of the yogurt in a small bowl. Add to the dry ingredients and blend quickly, just until a dough forms (add a bit more yogurt or buttermilk if needed). Using a ½-cup-size ice cream scoop or measuring cup, scoop the dough and place the mounds on the prepared baking sheet about 3 inches apart. Sprinkle the tops with the 1 tablespoon sugar.

Bake for 10 to 15 minutes, until light brown. Slide the parchment paper onto the countertop to cool or transfer to a wire rack or directly into a serving basket. Serve warm.

MAKES 12 SCONES

....

Scottish Buttermilk Scones

....

Unlike baking powder biscuits, these scones are relatively low in fat, yet light and fluffy. Serve them anytime you would serve biscuits, with cream cheese and fresh berry jam.

2 cups all-purpose flour

½ teaspoon baking soda

1 teaspoon cream of tartar

½ teaspoon salt

2 tablespoons butter, chilled and cut into small pieces

1 egg, lightly beaten

½ to ¾ cup low-fat buttermilk

Preheat the oven to 425°F. Cover a baking sheet with parchment paper or coat with nonstick spray.

Mix the flour with the soda, cream of tartar, and salt in a large mixing bowl. Blend in the butter until completely incorporated into the dry ingredients.

Stir in the egg and then just enough buttermilk to make the dough hold together in a ball. Turn the dough out onto a lightly floured surface and knead just a few seconds until smooth. Divide the dough into 12 equal pieces. Place them on the baking sheet and flatten with your knuckles or the tips of your fingers to form a roughly round shape. Pierce all over with a fork. Bake for 8 to 10 minutes, or until very lightly browned.

MAKES 12 SCONES

Cream Scones

Try these for breakfast with butter and jam.

1 cup flour	2 tablespoons butter
½ teaspoons baking powder	1 egg, beaten
1 tablespoon sugar	2½ tablespoons heavy cream
¼ teaspoon salt	2 teaspoons sugar

Preheat the oven to 400°F. Cover a baking sheet with parchment paper or coat with nonstick spray.

Combine the flour, baking powder, sugar, and salt. With a fork, cut in the butter until the mixture resembles fine crumbs. Stir in the egg and cream to make a stiff dough. Turn out onto a slightly floured surface and knead lightly until dough sticks together. Pat into a 6-inch circle about 1 inch thick. With a straight-edged knife, cut the dough into 4 parts, making 4 wedge-shaped pieces. Place them on the baking sheet and sprinkle with the sugar. Bake for 15 minutes or until golden. Serve immediately.

MAKES 4 SCONES

Scots Wheat Crumpets

Unlike English crumpets, these contain no yeast and are more like crêpes. They can be spread with butter and jam, then rolled up before serving.

2 eggs, separated	2 tablespoons sugar
2 cups whole wheat flour	2 tablespoons melted butter
¼ teaspoon salt	2 cups milk

In a large bowl, beat the egg yolks; then blend in the flour, salt, sugar, butter, and milk to make a smooth batter the consistency of thin cream. Whisk egg whites until they hold soft peaks. Fold into the batter. Heat a 10- or 12-inch frying pan or crêpe pan and coat with a light film of oil. Drop in 2 tablespoons of the batter and spread around the pan with a spatula to make a thin cake. Cook until browned on one side; then turn over to cook the other side. As the crumpets are cooked, stack them. When they are cool, spread them with butter and honey or jam and roll up.

MAKES ABOUT 16 CRUMPETS

6

Smoothies,
Jams,
and
Preserves

My Favorite Breakfast Smoothie

Depending on the season and what I've squirreled away in the freezer, a smoothie for breakfast can be delicious and different every day. Of course, if you use all frozen ingredients, you may need to add enough liquid to allow the blades of the blender to do their work. There is enough sugar in natural fruits that you do not need to add more. Here's my basic plan:

½ large or 1 small banana, preferably frozen, cut up

½ cup blueberries, strawberries, or blackberries, fresh or frozen

½ medium-sized apple, pear (including peel), or fresh or frozen peach, or other fruit to equal about ½ cup

½ cup plain or flavored yogurt, regular, Greek, low fat or full fat

Pinch of freshly ground cardamom or cinnamon (optional)

¼ cup orange juice, apple juice, milk, or water

Put all ingredients into a blender and whirl until smooth and thick. If this turns out to be too thick for you, add more juice, milk, or water. Serve with a straw if desired.

MAKES 2 SERVINGS, ABOUT 1 CUP EACH

Rhubarb Marmalade

Rhubarb is an Asian native that was introduced to Europe in the fourteenth century and no doubt was packed along with the baggage of the early settlers. There is hardly a climate in our country where rhubarb does not thrive. It is one of the first of the springtime harvests. The first thing I do is to make a rhubarb pie. But when the harvest is abundant—and it usually is—we follow with stewed rhubarb served over rice pudding, and a variety of other rhubarb desserts. The straggler stems go into a rhubarb marmalade spiked with a bit of fresh ginger.

2 pounds sliced rhubarb (about 8 cups)
¼ cup fresh orange juice
¼ cup fresh lemon juice
2 tablespoons coarsely chopped fresh gingerroot
2¼ cups sugar

1 tablespoon grated orange peel
2 teaspoons grated lemon peel
2 oranges, peeled, seeded, and sectioned
1 lemon, peeled, seeded, and sectioned
1½ cups walnut halves

In a large enameled or stainless-steel pot, combine rhubarb, orange juice, lemon juice, and ginger. Bring to a boil. Cover. Reduce heat and simmer 30 minutes or until rhubarb is soft. Stir in sugar. Bring to a boil. Boil rapidly for 5 minutes, stirring constantly. Add peel and orange and lemon sections. Return to a boil; then remove from heat. Add walnuts. Pour into 6 hot sterilized 1-pint jars. Cap with sterilized lids and rings. Place filled capped jars on a rack in a large canning kettle. Add boiling water until jars are covered with 2 inches of water. Simmer for 15 minutes. Remove from the water and cool on racks away from drafts. Label before storing.

MAKES 6 (1-PINT) JARS

Fat-free Fresh Berry Jam

When I have just a small amount of berries—like the wild strawberries we pick in the meadow near our house, or a small carton of blackberries from the grocery store—I like to make this quick fresh-tasting jam. Because this makes just a cup of jam and we use it right away, I don't seal it as I do when making large amounts of preserves. It's irresistible served when the jam is still a little warm from cooking.

1 cup fresh strawberries or other berries
¾ cup sugar

1 teaspoon lemon juice

To cook in a microwave, combine the berries, sugar, and lemon juice in a glass bowl. Mash the berries into the sugar and stir until the sugar is dissolved. Cook in the microwave, uncovered, at high power for 5 minutes. Stir and scrape down the sides of the bowl. Microwave for 1 to 3 minutes longer, or until thickened (mixture should reach 218°F on an instant-reading thermometer).

For stove-top cooking, combine the berries, sugar, and lemon juice in a non-aluminum saucepan. Cook over medium-high heat, stirring constantly, until the mixture comes to a boil. Boil for 5 to 8 minutes, until thickened.

Pour the jam into a serving dish.

MAKES ABOUT 1 CUP

Quick No-fat Apple and Apricot Preserves

Here's another delectable spread that you can make in just minutes, using the microwave or a saucepan, whichever is most convenient.

1 cup chopped fresh apricots	**1 cup sugar**
1 large Granny Smith apple, peeled, cored,	**½ cup water**
and chopped	**1 3-inch cinnamon stick**

Combine all of the ingredients in a 1-quart glass bowl, for the microwave, or in a 2-quart saucepan, for the stove top. Microwave the mixture in the glass bowl for 10 minutes, at high power, stirring once or twice while cooking. Or, heat the mixture in the saucepan to boiling and cook, stirring frequently, for about 10 minutes, or until the mixture is reduced to 2 cups.

Cool; then turn the mixture into a serving dish or a jar. Serve at room temperature. Store, tightly covered, in the refrigerator for up to 6 weeks.

MAKES 2 CUPS

Fat-free Jalapeño Orange Preserves

I like to keep jars of these preserves on hand to serve with light cream cheese and muffins or crackers for a quick snack. It makes a great gift too, packed with some ready-baked Cornmeal Pineapple Muffins (see page 161) in a pretty basket. Don't try to double or halve this recipe: the cooking times given are just right for these ingredient amounts. On properly sealed canning jars, the jar lids should pop inward, rather than remain convex. You can keep unsealed preserves refrigerated for up to 6 months.

¾ cup finely chopped green bell pepper

¼ cup finely chopped, seeded, and stemmed jalapeño peppers

1 dried ancho chili pepper, seeded and cut into ¼-inch dice

2 tablespoons grated orange zest

6 cups sugar

1½ cups white vinegar

1 bottle (6 ounces) liquid pectin

Place six 8-ounce canning jars, lids, and rings into a large pot. Add water to cover the jars by 2 inches; heat to boiling and boil the jars and lids for 20 minutes. Reduce the heat to simmering while preparing the preserves.

In a 4-quart saucepan, combine the green pepper, jalapeño peppers, ancho pepper, orange zest, sugar, and vinegar. Heat to boiling. Boil for 1 minute, stirring to prevent the mixture from boiling over. Remove from the heat.

Add the pectin and stir to mix well. Let the preserves stand for 5 minutes. Skim off the white film that forms on top.

With a pair of tongs, remove the jars from the simmering water. Pour the preserves into the hot sterilized jars, dividing them equally.

With a damp cloth, wipe the rims of the jars to remove any preserves. Remove the jar lids and rings from the simmering water and place them on top of the jars, fastening them securely. Cool on a rack. As the preserves cool, the lids will invert when they seal. Refrigerate any jars that did not seal, and use within 6 months.

MAKES SIX 8-OUNCE JARS

Fat-free Spicy Pumpkin Butter

I like to spread whole-grain muffins, like cracked wheat and rye, or whole wheat muffins with nonfat or low-fat cream cheese, then top them off with pumpkin butter; the combination tastes like pumpkin pie.

1 cup fresh or canned puréed cooked pumpkin

1 cup sugar

1 teaspoon ground cinnamon

¼ teaspoon ground nutmeg

¼ teaspoon ground ginger

⅛ teaspoon ground cloves

2 tablespoons lemon juice

Stir the pumpkin, sugar, cinnamon, nutmeg, ginger, cloves, and lemon juice together in a glass bowl for the microwave or in a nonreactive saucepan for the stove top. Cook the mixture in the glass bowl in the microwave at high power for 5 minutes, stirring twice. Or, in the saucepan over medium-high heat, stir the mixture until it comes to a boil; then boil 5 minutes, stirring constantly. Cool; then turn the pumpkin butter into a serving dish and serve immediately with fresh, hot muffins. Store, refrigerated, for 4 to 6 weeks.

MAKES ABOUT 1¼ CUPS

Fat-free Three-minute Blueberry Jam

With just a cup of berries, a bit of sugar, and 3 minutes' cooking time in the microwave, you can serve fresh blueberry jam with your favorite breakfast muffin.

1 cup fresh or frozen and thawed unsweetened blueberries

½ cup sugar
1 tablespoon lemon juice

To make in a microwave, in a 1-quart glass bowl, combine the berries, sugar, and lemon juice. Stir to coat the berries with the sugar. Microwave at high power for 3 minutes, stirring halfway through the cooking time.

To cook on the stove top, combine the ingredients in a 1-quart saucepan. Heat to boiling and boil for 3 minutes, stirring often.

Pour into a serving dish, or cool and store, covered, in the refrigerator for 4 to 6 weeks.

MAKES 1 CUP

Low-fat Yogurt Cheese Spread

Rich and creamy yogurt cheese is an ideal substitute for cream cheese or sour cream in spreads for both sweet and savory muffins.

You can make your own yogurt cheese by draining the whey from low-fat yogurt through a filter. I have a special reusable plastic filter, available in specialty cookware shops and some cookware catalogs, that works very well. You can also use several thicknesses of cheesecloth or a coffee filter to drain the yogurt. The process usually takes 12 to 24 hours.

There are several flavor variations possible, and you might invent your own.

1 cup low-fat or fruit-flavored plain yogurt   **Flavoring of choice**

Line a strainer with 4 thicknesses of dampened, clean cheesecloth or with a coffee filter. Spoon the yogurt into the lined strainer. Place over a bowl and cover with plastic wrap. Refrigerate for 12 to 24 hours. Discard the drained liquid.

Turn the yogurt cheese into a bowl and stir in the desired flavoring ingredients. Serve as a spread for sweet or savory muffins. The spread will keep, covered, in the refrigerator for 3 days.

MAKES ABOUT ½ CUP

Savory Vegetable Spread

Stir 2 tablespoons finely shredded carrots, 2 tablespoons finely chopped radishes, 1 tablespoon chopped green onions, ⅛ teaspoon salt, and 1 small, mashed garlic clove into the yogurt cheese.

Peppered Chive and Dill Spread

Stir 1 tablespoon finely chopped chives, 1 teaspoon chopped fresh dill, ½ teaspoon coarsely ground black pepper, and ⅛ teaspoon salt into the yogurt cheese.

Herb Cheese

Stir 4 to 6 tablespoons finely chopped fresh herbs, such as parsley, cilantro, savory, dill, marjoram leaves, chervil, or chives, or a combination of two or more, and salt and pepper to taste into the yogurt cheese.

Turkish Apricot Butter

Turkish apricots are small whole, pitted dried apricots. Quickly cooked and puréed, this spread works deliciously with any breakfast or snack muffin.

1 cup (about 30) packed dried Turkish apricots
1 cup water

½ cup sugar
1 teaspoon butter

Combine the apricots, water, and sugar in a 1-quart glass bowl, for microwaving, or in a 1-quart saucepan, for stove-top cooking. Microwave the mixture for 10 minutes, stirring once halfway through the cooking. Or heat the mixture on the stove to boiling and cook, stirring, for 10 minutes.

Turn the cooked mixture into a food processor or blender and process until smooth. Add the butter while the motor is going.

Pour the mixture into a serving dish or cool and pour into a jar. Store, covered, for up to 5 months in the refrigerator.

MAKES 1¼ CUPS

Index

Beatrice Ojakangas is the author of thirty cookbooks, including *Scandinavian Cooking, Great Old-Fashioned American Recipes,* and the award-winning *Great Scandinavian Baking Book,* all published by the University of Minnesota Press. Her first book, *The Finnish Cookbook,* has been in print since 1964. She has also written a memoir, *Homemade: Finnish Rye, Feed Sack Fashion, and Other Simple Ingredients from My Life in Food* (Minnesota, 2016).

She began her writing career as a food editor for *Sunset Magazine* and has contributed to many national magazines, including *Bon Appétit, Gourmet, Family Circle, Redbook, Cooking Light, Southern Living,* and *Ladies' Home Journal.* She has been a columnist for the *Minneapolis–St. Paul Star Tribune* and the *Duluth News Tribune.* A frequent television personality, she starred in a five-part television series on holiday baking for the Food Network, *The Baker's Dozen.*

In 2005, she was selected to the James Beard Cookbook Hall of Fame. She and her husband live in Duluth, Minnesota.